D0765696

# PSYCHOANALYSIS

# PSYCHO-ANALYSIS

TOWARD

THE

SECOND

CENTURY

EDITED BY
ARNOLD M. COOPER, M.D.
OTTO F. KERNBERG, M.D.
ETHEL SPECTOR PERSON, M.D.

YALE UNIVERSITY PRESS
NEW HAVEN AND LONDON

Published with assistance from the foundation established in memory of
Amasa Stone Mather of the Class of 1907, Yale College.

Set in Garamond type by The Composing Room of Michigan, Inc., Printed in
the United States of America by Vail-Ballou Press, Binghamton, New York.

*Library of Congress Cataloging-in-Publication Data*

Psychoanalysis : toward the second century / edited by Arnold M.
Cooper, Otto F. Kernberg, Ethel Spector Person.

    p.  cm.

  Bibliography: p.

  Includes index.

  ISBN 0–300–04558–1 (alk. paper)

  1. Psychoanalysis.  2. Psychoanalysis—History—20th century.  I. Cooper,
Arnold M.  II. Kernberg, Otto F., 1928– .  III. Person, Ethel Spector.

RC506.P774  1989

150.19′5—dc20                         89–14711

                                        CIP

The paper in this book meets the guidelines for permanence and durability
of the Committee on Production Guidelines for Book Longevity of the
Council on Library Resources.

10 9 8 7 6 5 4 3 2 1

# ■
# ■
# CONTENTS

**v**

## 3. THE EGO AND THE SELF

## 4. PSYCHOANALYSIS, PSYCHOLOGY, AND NEUROBIOLOGY

# PREFACE

■
■

T his volume is a celebration of both the beginning of the second century of psychoanalysis and the fortieth anniversary of the Columbia University Psychoanalytic Center. Such birthdays are occasions for joy and satisfaction and opportunities for the assessment of our present status and likely future directions. The Columbia Psychoanalytic Center was founded in 1944–45 by Drs. Sándor Radó, David M. Levy, and George E. Daniels, joined shortly thereafter by Dr. Abram Kardiner. These pioneers were dedicated to a vision of the continuing flowering of psychoanalysis in an open community where intellect and creativity would hold sway in the struggle among ideas, and where disputes might ultimately be influenced, if not settled, by clinical research data. The founders were convinced that the centuries-old university tradition offered the best guarantee of continued academic freedom; thus Columbia became the first psychoanalytic institute to be an integral part of a great university. Further, they were firm in their view that psychodynamics was a basic science of psychiatry—the physiology of the discipline—and that psychoanalysis would best flourish in continuing discourse with other disciplines in neuroscience and social science. They believed, as did Freud, that psychoanalysis was not only a treatment but a powerful research tool that would have an impact on vital areas of cultural, social, and intellectual life. The university community seemed likely to provide the best opportunity for these mutual influences. They were certain that psychoanalysis was an open-ended system of unlimited potential.

It is a measure of how much psychoanalysis has changed that the bitter battles of only a few decades ago today seem historically interesting, often with still productive areas of theoretical or clinical exploration, but surely not topics for acrimonious dispute. When Radó and Kardiner and their colleagues proposed that the libido instinctual theory and its energic point of view was outmoded and had in fact been superseded by Freud's later work on psychic structure and the nature of anxiety, the establishment of the time did not respond to this suggestion lightly. Similarly, when Kardiner demonstrated the powerful role played by culture in psychic development and the need to include a detailed account of cultural directives when trying to understand drive derivatives, he was labeled a culturalist, implying that he had abandoned the psychoanalytic perspective of intrapsychic mental functions. His contemporaries seemed unable to understand that he was describing another source of internalized mental functions and opening up new possibilities for psychoanalytic exploration of the mind as an open rather than a closed system. Again, both Radó and Kardiner insisted that psychological life would have to be understood in terms of the agency of a person with wishes, needs, and desires, not in terms of drives and their vicissitudes or in terms of structures. Their suggestion was surely unwelcome at the time.

In each of these instances, what was then considered the subversive point of view was an effort to open psychoanalysis to newer perspectives in science, newer knowledge of biology and development, and a broadened view of the mission of psychoanalysis in society. Today, as psychoanalysis enters its second century, the verdict of psychoanalytic history is clearer. The libido economic point of view is no longer the core explanatory mode in psychoanalytic discourse. The relative flexibility and astonishing inborn psychological capacities of the infant and the developmental significance of his early environment of attachment are better understood and have led to stimulating new possibilities in analytic thinking about early development. Psychoanalysis is engaged in a continuing effort to find appropriate ways to speak of the person and of the self as agent without losing the advantages of being able to understand structured unconscious patterns of thought and feeling. The psychoanalytic study of groups and societies has only just begun.

During the first forty years, under a succession of wise directors and facilitating chairmen of the Department of Psychiatry, the Columbia University Center for Psychoanalytic Training and Research has provided an extraordinary nurturing environment for psychoanalysis. The Center has graduated almost three hundred psychoanalysts who are today practicing in all parts of the country, making major contributions to psychoanalytic literature. Many have served or are serving as chairmen of departments of psychiatry, and one was the chief of the National Institute of Mental Health. The Center has a faculty of over 170, many internationally prominent, an association of 240 members, and, most important of all, a thriving student body. Psychoanalysts with a considerable range of theoretical views work side by side, influencing each other and developing their psychoanalytic concepts without pressure to maintain a preconceived idea of analytic truth. We have been far from immune to the demands of the analytic climate outside Columbia, sometimes battling successfully for our position, sometimes overreacting to minor issues, and at other times excessively passive on important questions. We have also at times flirted with creating our own dogma. Although our research achievement is significant, we have failed to establish an ongoing program of research and research training. But we have come through these four decades with a solid psychoanalytic and scientific identity of our own, centered on the idea of free psychoanalytic inquiry. Our fortieth birthday was an occasion for joy, a more youthful marker for an educational institution than for an individual. We are pleased to present this volume as a token of our progress.

The editors wish to acknowledge the contributions of other members of the Program Committee for the symposium from which this book was drawn: Richard G. Druss, Frederick M. Lane, Helen C. Meyers, and Robert Michels. In addition, we want to thank the members of the Arrangement Committee of that symposium: Gerald I. Fogel (chairman), Bruce Ballard, Estelle P. Bender, David V. Forrest, Muriel G. Morris, Philip Muskin, David D. Olds, Lawrence Shaderowfsky, and John J. Weber. Joan Jackson, the administrator of the Columbia Center, and Doris Parker, its librarian, have collated materials, typed manuscripts, and done all the essential coordination in bringing together this volume. We are, of course, grateful to our contributors, who have been generous of their time and effort, and to our editor Gladys Topkis for her patience, good humor, and editorial tact in shaping this manuscript.

Arnold M. Cooper, M.D.

Otto F. Kernberg, M.D.

Ethel S. Person, M.D.

# Introduction

*Arnold M. Cooper, M.D.,*
*Otto F. Kernberg, M.D., and*
*Ethel Spector Person, M.D.*

This volume is an expanded and edited version of the papers presented at the symposium celebrating the fortieth anniversary of the Columbia University Center for Psychoanalytic Training and Research on April 26–27, 1985. A group of major psychoanalytic contributors participated at that time in a two-day meeting entitled "Psychoanalysis: The Second Century." The title of this volume is intended to indicate not only that psychoanalysis is one hundred years old but that it is now in a period of rapid development, with the prospect of far-reaching changes in our theory and technique. It is a truism that during its first hundred years, the revolutionary spirit of psychoanalysis profoundly changed the intellectual and cultural life of at least Western man, creating both obvious and subtle changes in our views of ourselves and our relationships to each other, our children, and our society. It is equally true that during this century, while psychoanalysis was changing the world, psychoanalysis was itself changing, from a relatively simple positivist model of mental mechanisms to a brilliantly complex synchronic system of models more attuned to our current thinking in science and humanities.

Psychoanalysis began with the feverish, almost unparalleled explosion of Freud's creativity between roughly 1885 and 1905. In that time he produced *Studies on Hysteria, The Interpretation of Dreams, The Study of the Dora Case,* and *Three Essays on Sexuality.* By 1915 Freud had outlined most of the major theoretical and technical propositions that have characterized psychoanalysis to this day. He did not stop there, of course, and in his later works he saw new landscapes and new ways of understanding the now familiar terrain of his earlier discoveries. In 1929 he introduced the structural model of ego, id, and superego, a large advance from the topographic scheme of conscious and unconscious. With *Inhibitions, Symptoms and Anxiety* (1926 [1925]), Freud introduced a radical shift in his view of the origins of anxiety, describing it as the ego's response to the perception of danger and the signal for the use of defense mechanisms rather than the result of dammed-up libidinal energy, as he had previously described it. With this change, adaptation—the ways in which the individual copes with the internal and external environment—assumed new importance. As Anna Freud elaborated in *The Ego and Mechanisms of Defense* (1966 [1937]), analysis increasingly became ego analysis rather than id analysis, as before. In *Beyond the Pleasure Principle* (1920) Freud gave full importance to the role of aggression in mental life. In *Analysis Terminable and Interminable* (1937), he foreshadowed the current interest in narrative and hermeneutics as a core of analytic theory. One could go on listing the changes of viewpoint and the suggestions for new developments that characterize Freud's work. One consequence of the breadth of his vision was the set of contradictions and inconsistencies among views and theories that he put forward at different points in his work. Many psychoanalysts, including the founders of the Columbia Center, have written of the discrepancy between the incredibly rich and informative modernist view of the world presented in Freud's clinical formulations, despite his reluctance to give full attention to preoedipal and object-relational aspects of psychic life, on the one hand, and, on the other, the relative conservatism of aspects of his scientific worldview, shaped as it was during the late nineteenth century and exemplified in his formulations of the drives and the energic point of view. These contradictions are apparent in his late paper, *Analysis Terminable and Interminable* (1937). Freud left to his inheritors—the current generation of analysts—the tasks of expanding, reformulating, and working out the inconsistencies of his ideas and developing newer ideas out of our own data and intellectual climate. Many of our enduring psychoanalytic disputes have been part of our continuing efforts to understand and expand the legacy Freud left us. Since Freud's death there have been advances in ego psychology, object-relations theory, self psychology, and interpersonal psychology, to mention a few of the many currents in contemporary psychoanalysis. But these views have yet to be integrated into a single overarching analytic theory.

Following Freud's death, two efforts sharply opposed to each other became apparent. One was the attempt to codify and solidify a version of "classical" or "orthodox" psychoanalysis, intended to do homage to Freud. Although some observers have felt that this attempt is, in fact, at odds with Freud's clinical and scientific intent, it has nonetheless been productive in increasing our knowledge. The other approach was to confront some of the more glaring contradictions and problematics in Freud's work and to look for ways to continue Freud's legacy of discovery without being bound to parts of the theory that clearly were not integral to the psychoanalytic core. Now, half a century after Freud's death, the willingness to depart from ideas that Freud himself was unwilling to relinquish has produced a large yield of new clinical and theoretical ideas. It has also become apparent that although the core of psychoanalytic research and advance remains the clinical situation, psychoanalytic thought can be immensely enriched through the ideas and discoveries of infant research, ethology, cognitive psychology, narrative studies, and neurobiology. At the very least, findings in these areas place constraints upon theories that are available to psychoanalysis. For example, we would be loath to hold a theory of development that contradicts solid findings in infant studies. Some analysts have suggested that psychoanalysis should abandon all pretense to science, give up its effort to retain the footing in biology that Freud maintained so tenaciously, and accept its place as one of the interpretive or hermeneutic disciplines, interested only in meanings. It will be apparent from this volume that most of the contributors retain the conviction that psychoanalysis is a scientific system, even though much of its theory is not subject to simple verification, nor its data subject to experimental intervention.

The four areas selected for discussion, "Culture and Psyche," "Drives and Desires," "The Ego and the Self," and "Psychoanalysis, Psychology, and Neurobiology," are at the heart of the most interesting areas of psychoanalytic theory and techniques and clinical investigation today. Each of these domains has been and is a field of controversy among opposing points of view, but, more important, each area demonstrates the effort to open psychoanalysis to newer perspectives in science, newer knowledge of biology and development, and a broadened view of the mission of psychoanalysis in society. In each of these topics we can also find the meeting place of psychoanalytic points of view that historically have competed for primacy. These, then, are the appropriate topics for the beginning of the second century of psychoanalysis, and how the disputes and investigations of these areas are developed and resolved will shape psychoanalysis for decades to come. Not coincidentally, these were also the intellectual issues around which the Columbia Center was founded in 1945.

The section on "Culture and Psyche" addresses the intertwining of cultural and psychological imperatives. Early on, analysts were loath to emphasize the effects of culture, fearing that a "mere" cultural perspective might promote the erroneous belief that behavior (and motives, intentions, and wishes) was learned or simply mirrored cultural imperatives, thus giving away the hard-won insights that focused on the unconscious and on drives. The task of integrating the culturist perspective awaited the development of a more complex psychoanalytic theory, one that had a language for psychic representation and could address the question of how the external world becomes internalized. Such an approach investigates questions of the limits of malleability of the human mind, the universality of certain traits or conflicts, and the inherent resistance of the individual core to compliance with cultural directives. But additionally it focuses on variability, the "construction" of such things as masculinity and femininity, and the need to acquiesce. And, of course, the culturist perspective also explores large issues of transference, the need for individuals to belong to groups, espouse causes, and find leaders, thus continuing the work of Freud in *Group Psychology and the Analysis of the Ego* (1921).

The section on "Drives and Desires" explores the nature of motivation and the sources of human action in the light of the vast new knowledge that we have acquired concerning the early years of life and the relationship of psychoanalytic theory to biological science and to hermeneutics. Freud's motivational system, based on two core biological drives of libido and aggression and a hedonic compass of pleasure and unpleasure, grand and beautiful in conception, has been extraordinarily durable and useful. There has, however, been an increasing strain on that system as new knowledge has accumulated from several sources. The energic concepts important to Freud have seemed far less relevant for contemporary psychoanalysts. Psychoanalysts have begun to give increasing weight to the role of safety and security needs, their accompanying affects, and the psychic activities generated by these needs. Developmental researchers have pointed to the multiple sources of activation of the infant organism, stressing the extraordinary complexity of "wired-in" motivational systems. Ethological evidence has led psychoanalysts to reassess the role of object-attachment in primary motivational systems. Others have emphasized the centrality of the human need for order and comprehension—for narrative coherence, as it is often phrased—as a major motivation. The ego ideal has also been proposed as a major motivational system. With these multiple views of the nature of motivation, a comprehensive theory of motivation is more difficult to construct. Some would maintain Freud's drive theory with modifications, while others would abandon that theory in favor of new constructions. Clearly, an adequate understanding of motivation is an urgent task for analytic theory.

The section on "The Ego and the Self" takes up the problem of psychological agency and the ways we conceptualize and understand person and mind. In recent years, growing interest in issues of narcissism, as narcissistic personality disorders seemed to assume a new importance in analytic practice, has given rise to a major effort to improve our understanding of both the underlying concepts and the clinical manifestations of self development and self disorder. For English-speaking analysts there have been questions concerning the translation of *ich* in the *Standard Edition* and suggestions that the use of the term *ego* has given a pseudoscientific cast to Freud's much more direct intention to speak of the "I" and the "self." The formulations of Jacobson, Kernberg, and Kohut on the development of the self have led all psychoanalysts to rethink their views on narcissism and the self. Earlier, Radó and Kardiner had attempted to focus on the "action-self" as the core of mind and development. In this section the authors explore the structural conception of mind and the nature of self-development and self-awareness, and discuss the models of the mind that are most likely to serve us well in the future.

In addition, we include a small section on psychoanalysis and its relationship to other disciplines. While it is not comprehensive, this addresses the question of the borders between psychoanalysis and some of its contiguous fields.

This volume is an attempt to look ahead to our psychoanalytic future. In effect, we are asking, in the light of the experience and researches of the past decades, where are we heading? The title reveals our *un*cautious optimism. Obviously, we think not only that there will be a second century of psychoanalysis but that the second century will be as productive and as unpredictable as the first one. None of the papers in this volume attempts to predict the future, but the authors do try to indicate the lines of cleavage, the cracks in the structure that are likely to lead to new ideas and new advances. The chapters also outline the state of the art in current psychoanalytic thought and point toward the new directions of our science and profession. It is our hope that this book will encourage the rising generation of psychoanalysts to pursue their studies and researches with the enthusiasm and vigor that will help psychoanalysis to continue to fulfill its promise for the relief of suffering and the understanding of man.

■ ■ ■
**PART 1**        **CULTURE AND PSYCHE**

# Introduction
*Lionel Ovesey, M.D.*

t is extremely fitting that the opening section of this book should be
entitled "Culture and Psyche." The Center for Psychoanalytic Training
and Research, from its inception, has had a special interest in the relationship between the individual and his society. In fact, that is how it all
began. Historically, the roots of the interest go back to the early 1930s, well
before the Center was established, when the four founders, Drs. Sándor Radó,
Abram Kardiner, David Levy, and George Daniels, banded together in opposition to the libido theory.

In their opinion, the libido theory had outlived its usefulness because it did
not sufficiently take into account the role of society in human behavior. It was
a rigid framework that ultimately traced behavior to inherent instinctual
drives with fixed courses of development. The founders, in contrast, believed
that the bulk of human behavior was adaptive and learned. The libido theory,
in their view, was a case of the instinctual tail wagging the cultural dog.

In order to redress this imbalance and expand the social dimension, the
founders proposed that the libido theory be abandoned. They favored an ego
psychology that focused on the adaptive functions of the ego as it interacted
with the social environment. This was the origin of the term "the adaptational
frame of reference" with which the Center has always been associated.

In pursuing their own work, the founders demonstrated that the new frame
of reference, in contrast to the libido theory, more consistently provided
logical psychodynamic explanations that fitted the clinical data. In addition,

the adaptational framework opened up new avenues for fruitful research, whereas the libidinal framework, being a closed system, frequently sealed them off.

One can imagine the uproar their proposal created. It was met by a stone wall of opposition from an overwhelming majority of the faculty of the New York Psychoanalytic Institute and its affiliate organization, the New York Psychoanalytic Society. The battle was joined. There was no retreat. Each side held fast to its point of view. The situation remained static until the big breakthrough in 1943, when the four dissidents were invited by Columbia to establish the Psychoanalytic Center. This, however, hardly ended the battle. Now they had an institute to defend.

I first learned about the Center in 1943 through an advertisement in the *Journal of the American Medical Association* announcing its formation. At the time, I was a flight surgeon on an island in the Central Pacific. After the war, I applied and was accepted for the second class, which began in November 1945. I was a total innocent. I knew nothing about the four founders, let alone about their battles with the psychoanalytic establishment. As a Californian who, prior to my war experiences, had planned to become an internist, I presented a clean slate. The most pertinent quality I brought to the state of siege was a proclivity for rebellion.

It was not long, therefore, before I was involved in what the students called "the battle of the frames of reference." One needed a suit of armor or an impervious sense of conviction, preferably both. In the course of the struggle, some of the students went over to the other side. Some stayed, but without either commitment or conviction. Some became adherents. I was one of this last group.

What about the four men who brought all this to pass? What were they like? Keeping in mind that each of us recounts history in terms of personal bias, I feel their union was incredibly strong, despite their diverse personalities: Radó, a public man, a flamboyant mover and shaker; Kardiner, an intense investigator and quintessential teacher; Levy, a calm scholar and quiet ground-breaker; Daniels, a superbly skilled organizer and intuitive diplomat. What was it that held four such disparate men together? In a sentence: a refusal to accept the ordained and the courage to ask new questions and press for new answers.

Faint heart has never won anything significant in the sciences—or in anything else for that matter. And faint heart was the last thing the founders could be accused of. They rose to the occasion and fought every inch of the way for their views. They believed in change, not for its own sake, but to enhance our understanding of the human psyche. Their belief in the adaptational theory unlocked many doors and opened up a free exchange of ideas. In the end, the founders achieved their goal. The libido theory is no longer the sacred cow of psychoanalysis and the adaptational view, at first so violently opposed, is now part of the mainstream of psychoanalytic thought. By bringing about this radical change, the four founders of the Columbia Center played a seminal role in shaping psychoanalysis as we know it today.

In looking back, it is hard to believe the tumult of those early years. The status quo was challenged. Confrontation and debate flourished. I would not have missed it for the world. Long live the rebels. They are the stuff from which dreams are realized.

**One**
■ ■

**The Temptations
of Conventionality**
Otto F. Kernberg, M.D.

y objective in this chapter is to explore, from a psychoanalytic
viewpoint, the nature of the appeal of mass culture, particularly as
it is communicated by the mass media. My focus is on the relation
between the structural characteristics of mass culture and the latent expectations and dispositions of those to whom it is directed. I shall be examining the
regressive effects of group processes on the recipients of mass culture, and
the striking correspondence between the conventional aspects of mass
culture and the psychological characteristics of the latency years. This study
is intended as a psychoanalytic contribution to the exploration of the interface of individual and group psychology.

## SOME CHARACTERISTICS OF MASS CULTURE

I would like to begin with Freud's definition of mass psychology, because it
contains ideas that are relevant to my thesis. Freud, in defining mass psychology (a concept lost in the problematic *Standard Edition* translation of *mass*
and *crowd* into *group*), proposed (1921) "to isolate as the subject of inquiry
the influencing of an individual by a large number of people simultaneously,

An earlier version of this chapter was presented at the fortieth anniversary celebration of the
Columbia University Center for Psychoanalytic Training and Research, "Psychoanalysis: The
Second Century," New York City, April 27, 1985. The present version was presented at the thirty-
fifth International Psychoanalytical Congress in Montreal, Canada, July 26–31, 1987.

people with whom he is connected by something, though otherwise they may in many respects be strangers to him. Mass psychology is therefore concerned with the individual man as a member of a race, of a nation, of a caste, of a profession, of an institution, or as a component part of a crowd of people who have been organized into a mass at some practical time for some definite purpose" (p. 70). In this quotation I have changed *group* back to the original *mass* in order to keep close to Freud's original thinking.

I am defining *mass culture* as those forms of cultural expression aimed to appeal to individuals under conditions that activate or utilize their being influenced by real or fantasied masses, that is, under conditions when mass psychology is operating upon them. I am concerned less with the question of the "operators"—who or what manipulates mass culture (a question dealt with in great detail by Horkheimer and Adorno 1971; Bourdieu 1979; and Brantlinger 1983, among others)—than with exploring from a psycho-analytic perspective some common characteristics of mass culture and the basis of its appeal.

My definition of mass culture dovetails with its traditional definition in the American and European sociological literature dealing with this subject in the 1940s and 1950s (Rosenberg and White 1957; Brantlinger 1983), when mass culture referred to industrialized, mass-produced products intended for mass consumption (Howe 1948; MacDonald 1953; Rosenberg 1957). Previous discussions of mass culture focused around such questions as whether it is a product of contemporary, industrialized society that "packages" pseudoculture to satisfy economic needs of the producers, cheapening the taste of the consumer in the process, or whether it is an instrument for social control, which "packages" gratifying, nondisturbing entertainment in order to implant the dominant ideology of the society. Or whether mass culture is the consequence of the ascendancy of the poorly educated and nondiscrimi-nating masses, who by their sheer number and economic power dilute both high culture and traditional folk art. Or whether mass culture reflects the changing sociological characteristics of modern urban society, which fosters "other-directedness" rather than "inner-directedness" (Riesman 1950), or—in a more recent version, the characteristics of a "culture of narcissism" (Lasch 1978).

My focus is primarily on entertainment offered by the press, radio, cinema, and television, the content of which is intended for the broadest segments of the population. While entertainment is not the only form of mass culture, it is universally recognized as its dominant form (Rosenberg and White 1957; Horkheimer and Adorno 1971). Entertainment reveals most clearly the psy-chological characteristics of all mass culture.

The aspect of simultaneity of communication is important. I am referring here to both actual and fantasied simultaneity: Freud's earlier quoted statement underlines simultaneity as a key condition of mass psychology. While a gathering of people as passive spectators in a theater or cinema places the individual in an actual temporary crowd, entertainment from the press, radio, and television provides simultaneity without such actual contact. These latter media create by implication an invisible crowd in the fantasies of each of the isolated spectators sitting in their respective homes. The canned laughter of situation comedies not only punctuates the jokes, it provides an illusory crowd of spectators that contributes to an illusory sense of community (Moscovici, 1981). This quality receives emphasis when one watches television in a foreign country in a foreign language one understands, an experience that may induce, at first, a strange sense of loneliness, as if one were an intruder into a community to which one does not belong.

Reading the news or watching it on television also creates the illusion of being a member of a crowd focusing on the communication from a central figure who communicates what is important and what one should think about it. This brings us to another aspect of mass culture: pleasure to be had from passively receiving what is exciting and important without having intellectual demands made on the recipient. Newspapers have to be read "fresh": they lose their appeal once the implicit mass of fellow readers has finished with them. And although they inform rather than entertain, any intellectual demand they make on the reader reduces their appeal. An authority addressing a multitude of passive, implicitly equal, though uninformed readers heightens the mass appeal of the communication.

In soap operas, situation comedies, films geared for adolescents or "family entertainment," war movies, thrillers, and soft porn (the explicitness of pornography tolerated by any community is relatively unimportant—the characteristics remain the same) the people presented are typically oversimplified: all good or all bad, bereft of internal complexities, totally involved in their immediate reality, with obvious motivations in their interpersonal behavior. The spectator, with the familiarity that comes with exposure, can predict their next moves. In fact, watching the developments among people on the screen whom one seems to know completely, whose motives and moves one can predict, conveys a feeling of pleasure and power, of superiority and amusement; here we find a narcissistic dimension of self-aggrandizement in the viewer.

Drama is introduced when good people face danger from obvious evil, criminality, violence, or dishonesty in one or more characters. The viewer's reaction thus includes a paranoid dimension as he involves his emotions in the content. Villains eventually develop in one of two directions: they either become understandable in their motivation and repent, or else, incurably evil, they are finally punished, leaving the spectator feeling morally satisfied.

The unhappiness of the characters is given dramatic but not disturbing forms: joy, sorrow, rage, and fear are all portrayed as dramatic yet reassuring. Expression dominates over content, and sentimentality over sentiments. Sentimentality is often conveyed by means of an implicit or explicit nostalgia for the past, for familiar forms of happiness, with a particular emphasis on universally shared symbols of innocence, cuteness, naive trust, and appeal for tenderness that is associated with the security of early childhood or a happy, safe, contented old age. Nostalgia, the bittersweet longing for a lost and/or longed-for state of happiness, reunion, or fulfillment, evokes an idealized object of desire while implicitly confirming the possibility of its recovery.

In war films, although some of the heroes must die, a sufficient number of centrally important ones survive so that the spectator can feel happily identified with a survivor. The enemy is always evil, except when an actual historical shift has resulted in a former enemy country becoming a friendly one. Then there are wise and knowledgeable members of the enemy camp who agree that war is basically bad and would like to replace it by universal love and friendship. In the German film *Das Boot,* for example, a huge success in many countries, the audience's identification with a Nazi submarine crew is facilitated by the submarine commander's obvious loathing of the Nazi leadership.

Thrillers and films dealing with psychopathic killers are of particular interest for the study of mass culture in that the excitement of danger, the horror of the victims, the excitement of the persecution of the criminal, and the implicit identification with the hero who finally destroys him obviously gratify aggressive impulses in the reader or viewer. The barely disguised gratification in fantasy of aggressive impulses as part of mass culture is central in its appeal. The same is true of war movies but usually without the intense excitement of the identification with a particular hunter. If violence can be enjoyed vicariously but fully under these circumstances, the same is only partially true for sexual impulses.

The dissociation of erotism from tenderness is sharp and consistent in mass culture and is another of its central characteristics. Very little direct reference is made to the erotic aspects of love. Explicit sex, if depicted, is typically between individuals who have no emotional relation or is an expression of aggression, such as rape or a group-tolerated sexually rebellious activity against conventional mores. The protagonist may indulge in sexual behavior with other characters but not with the one with whom he or she has a romantic link. Or the actual sexual aspects of the relation between two tender lovers are presented in a veiled and romanticized style. In *The Breakfast Club,* for example, a film popular with the adolescent audience at which it was aimed, details are limited to crude sexual encounters: when two of the young protagonists fall in love, the sexual details of their relation are totally eliminated.

This basic characteristic has not been at all affected by the apparent relaxation of censorship that has permitted more direct expression of sexuality in film. By the same token, pornographic films are usually empty descriptions of mechanical sex between persons having an almost robotlike quality. The most striking dissociation of erotism from tenderness is in connection with polymorphous perverse sexuality; this aspect of sexuality is almost entirely restricted to pornography and is totally absent in mass entertainment, even in the exceptional instances wherein the protagonists are shown in bed together.

When the cinematic and television entertainment I am describing deals with so-called philosophical questions, the ideas offered are trivial, clichés predominate, banality is the order of the day, and originality is conspicuously absent. The complexities of life and of people are denied. Conventional assumptions predominate over individual thinking. There is love and compassion for the underdog, consolation for the person who loses a competition, and pride and applause for the one who triumphs after a long and difficult effort. Justice always prevails. The world is a safe and simple place.

Similar characteristics are found in the communication of news. The detailed communication of criminal developments in the last twenty-four hours as a main staple of news in the mass media obviously gratifies the excitement with dissociated aggression and violence, including the horror of sex crimes. The subtly self-righteous, moralistic tone of oversimplified reports on world affairs is less self-evident. News is presented with an implicit division of the world into good and bad people, countries, and events and with a latent assumption that the commentator and his mass audience are morally superior.

There is, in addition, one aspect of news presentation that is of particular interest: within the general flatness of the information conveyed, we find a tendency to shift between the trivial—for example, a slightly ironic description of something that is strange, incomprehensible, amusing, and entertaining, perhaps a comedy of errors in a distant village—and the dangerous, that is, the report of something close to home that runs counter to the value system we all share and that would require urgent corrective action—for example, local criminal activities.

Here we find again the stimulation of two dimensions in the receiver: narcissistic (catering to our amused superiority) and paranoid (justified suspicion, indignation, and revenge). What evokes fear, suspicion, and indignation, on the one hand, and what seems trivial, entertaining, and reassuring, on the other, vary quickly. The application of a simplistic morality to political and social matters and the philosophy of the situation comedy take the form of clichés. Such clichés state, for example, that if people of goodwill get together, the problem will be solved, or that there is a right and a wrong view about some matter that will become obvious with further study.

If we shift from the content communicated in mass culture to the forms of artistic expression through which it is conveyed, a number of related phenomena can be detected. There is a characteristic style in the presentation of programs. Decor, background, objects of art are usually mass-produced articles that appeal to conventional tastes. Popular decors, a preference for bright colors to indicate dramatic atmospheres or a uniformly dull brown for homely places, sentimentality in displayed art and particularly in background music again illustrate the dominance of sentimentality over sentiment and the prevalence of symbols evocative of carefree happiness, innocence, and childhood. Paintings are of sentimental landscapes or tragicomic clowns, or they are trivialized imitations of recent dominant artistic expressions. The illustrations on mass-produced Christmas cards are a typical expression of this style.

Taken together, the characteristics I have enumerated also define kitsch: they are appealing, comfortable, reassuring, sentimental, and overloaded expressions of a culturally dominant style that is charged with conventional symbols of wealth, happiness, romanticism, and childhood (Greenberg 1946; Adorno 1954; Moles 1971; Deschner 1980; Friedlander 1984).

## A PSYCHOANALYTIC HYPOTHESIS: THE CORRESPONDENCE BETWEEN MASS CULTURE AND THE INTERNAL WORLD OF THE LATENCY CHILD

From a psychoanalytic viewpoint, the picture of mass culture that emerges is of a world that bears a striking resemblance to the internal world of the latency-age child. Within the psychoanalytic theory of child development, latency refers to the developmental period that begins with the consolidation of the oedipal superego and ends with the psychodynamic reorganization at the initiation of puberty. It roughly corresponds to the child of elementary school age. In what follows, I shall outline characteristics of latency that are replicated in the dominant features of mass culture.

A first major aspect of the latency child is the strictness, rigidity, and overdependence on simplified conventional notions of morality of his or her superego. The child's system of morality affirms the trusted parental authority and is characterized by an unambiguous separation of good from bad (deeds as well as people), transformation of sadism into superego-integrated righteous indignation, enjoyment of morally justified aggression, adaptation to a peer group that provides the first experience of firm, simple, stable, group norms, including norms of acceptable entertainment, and the unequivocal dissociation of (depreciated) anal sexuality, on the one hand, from tender love (for the oedipal parents), on the other. It is the morality of a well-loved yet misbehaving child's reconciliation with his or her temporarily angry parents before falling asleep. In general terms, we have a morality of brief, time-limited sequences of misbehavior, guilt, punishment, and/or forgiveness. The child is "in the know," however, regarding genital sexuality and its eventual, though distant, feasibility in the future.

At the same time, the latency child also harbors fantasies of independence and power, the illusion of being independent from parents. He or she becomes interested in adventure stories with heroes and ideals that provide identification models for the future and also gratify the urge to control the instinctual world through real and fantasied control of the social environment. The child is finding substitute gratifications for aggressive and sexual assertion. Watching adult life in reality and through cultural products is a new achievement. Illusions of independence and power are gratified by watching, with a sense of superiority, the predictable lives of the "funny" grownups, while fantasies of narcissistic reconfirmation are simultaneously enacted through identification with superheroes, who destroy dangerous monsters— all this within the stability of a warm and cozy home. Berman's (1987) analysis of the psychology of James Bond and its correspondence to the author Ian Fleming's latency conflicts provides an in-depth illustration of this psychoanalytic approach to the structure of commercial thrillers. To be entertained by striking images, to be excited by violence without being threatened by it, and to feel thrilled by sexual excitement without being threatened by the potential contacts between erotism and love are characteristic of the latency child's internal world.

These characteristics stem from both ego and superego: from narcissistic, erotic, and aggressive impulses framed in a latency child's perspective of ego-syntonic fantasies and wishes and from the child's unconscious morality, which respects oedipal prohibitions and dissociates sex from tenderness. In fact, the latency child as spectator of mass entertainment is probably the prototype of the totally gratified consumer of mass culture.

Here he or she is watching the presentation of entertainment in harmony with the superego, loved by parents, unconsciously accepting the oedipal prohibitions while indulging in fantasy in the total gratification of dependency needs and enjoying an illusional sense of equality, regardless of sex and age, with his fellow consumers. The child's oral-dependent needs are gratified directly, and other sexual and aggressive needs are gratified by projection onto the spectacle and the socially encouraged identification with the actors. His or her psychological needs correspond to the characteristics of mass entertainment itself, the perfectly harmonious quality of mass culture already described.

For the latency child, exciting stories or adventures that fit the general characteristics outlined above are not merely entertainment. They are socially sanctioned, culturally transmitted confirmations and expansions of his or her universe. These experiences are major events that reconfirm superego structure, provide cognitive learning experiences, and consolidate ego skills and controls over drive derivatives (Sarnoff 1976; Shapiro and Perry 1976). Social conventions expand the field of intrafamiliar conventions and facilitate the child's integration into the broader world of peers and school. For an adult, rigid adherence to social and cultural conventions that constitute the normal world of latency reflects conventionality. Insofar as adults are total consumers of mass culture, they become conventional. The question arises, why is conventionality—the excessive adaptation to social, cultural, and aesthetic norms—so central an aspect of mass culture and so attractive to its consumers?

If my description is accurate and my correlation valid, how can we explain the consistent presence of latency-age superego and ego features in mass culture? Why does mass culture gratify most adults, as it clearly does? Earlier psychoanalytic approaches to mass culture have focused on its conventional aspects and on personality characteristics fostering conventionality (Adorno et al. 1950). What required explaining were the conventional aspect of mass psychology and the exploitation and/or induction of that conventional mass psychology by the "ruling classes" through mass production of consumer goods. Before discussing the relation between mass culture's conventionality and latency-child psychology, let us briefly review these theories.

## EARLIER PSYCHOANALYTIC THEORIES OF CONVENTIONALITY

Adorno et al. (1950) considered conventionality a significant part of the authoritarian personality, which reflects an individual's disposition to excessive adherence to middle-class values, a consequence of instability of his own value system. It is the rigidity with which individuals adhere to conventional values and with which they respond to external social pressure that characterizes conventionality. Kitsch, as many authors have pointed out, has a typically middle-class nature, and even kitsch in the hands of the culturally disadvantaged conveys an idealized and sentimentalized version of middle-class values (Adorno 1954). This is also true for the "high-class kitsch" geared to the luxury trade (Greenberg 1946). The underlying theory assumed that individuals with authoritarian personalities are overly sensitive to external reinforcement of their internal, excessively strict superego demands and that conventionality is related to excessive submission to authority as well as to an identification with "authoritarian" aggression (aggression carried out by an authority in unfair ways and with excessive or "nonfunctional" uses of power and rationalized by that authority in the very process of the implied abuse of power). According to Adorno, the authoritarian personality represents a prototype of identification with the aggressor, first in the genesis of a sadistic, strict superego, and then in identifying with its own sadistic superego. While I agree with Adorno's linkage of conventionality and overidentification with a sadistic, infantile superego, he misses the contributions to conventionality of regressive group pressures—the mass-psychology aspect of conventionality.

Adorno et al.'s efforts continue those of Wilhelm Reich (1935) to integrate psychoanalytic thinking with Marxist theory and to explain the repressive nature of sexuality, both in Western society and in Soviet Russia. Generalizing from his understanding of German fascism, Reich proposed that the capitalist system had transformed the personality structure of all individuals in that capitalist society by exerting authoritarian power through the paternalistic family. Whereas Freud thought that the repression of sexuality was the price paid for cultural evolution, Reich thought that the repression of sexuality and of genital sexuality in particular represented the effects of a pathological superego, which in turn resulted from the social structure of capitalism. He traced a socially generalized submission to conventional mores to the same cause: conventionality was based on excessive repression of genital sexuality.

In contrast to Reich, Marcuse (1955) felt that the capitalist system repressed, not genital sexuality but pregenital polymorphous infantile sexuality. Marcuse thought this repression aimed at restricting sexual functions to the genital zone so that man's unsatisfied broader eroticism could be utilized in the service of social production. Marcuse suggested that it was the surplus repression of pregenital sexuality—a socially unnecessary repression—that constituted the main problem with the capitalist system.

In fact, however, Marcuse was faced with an increasing tolerance of sexuality in the Western world, particularly in the United States. He therefore coined the term *repressive desublimation* to refer to what he called a pseudosexual freedom, which engaged the individual in capitalist society in consuming unnecessary goods and distracted him from the basically repressive conditions of his existence. Marcuse asserted that by presenting sex as a capitalist lure for consumption, by eroticizing advertising and creating artificial consumer needs and demands, mass culture exerts a social and economic pressure through repression and advertising toward mindless conventional consumption.

Horkheimer and Adorno eloquently articulate a similar view in their *Dialectic of Enlightenment* (1971), where what they consider to be the degradation of culture in the hands of the modern entertainment industry is presented as a typical example of the attempt to destroy the individual's capacity to reason independently and to make independent value judgments. Culture produced for and oriented to the masses, they suggest, reflects how capitalist society both commercializes art and uses this commercialization to reduce the consumer's capacity to resist mass-produced, degraded art, objects, and entertainment.

The question of excessive conformity with the established social order has engaged many Marxist and neo-Marxist theoreticians in western Europe ever since the early 1930s and has been a major focus of the Frankfurt school, of which Adorno, Horkheimer, Marcuse, and Habermas are leading theoreticians. The ascent of fascism in western Europe and the autocratic and totalitarian evolution of Soviet Russia caused these theoreticians to ask to what extent the proletariat was developing a "false consciousness." The working class, and, in fact, all social classes, seemed to become easy prey to the ways of thinking dictated by dominant authoritarian regimes of the extreme right and left. Western European Marxists experienced the need to develop a theory of common belief systems induced by any ruling class to assure its hegemony over society.

Gramsci (1959) was the first to define *hegemony* as a system of power (in this case, of the capitalist class) to obtain a degree of consent from the masses via cultural institutions and the development of a corresponding ideology. Several other Marxist writers developed this line of reasoning over the years, and Althusser (1976) utilized Freud's concept of the unconscious to construct a new theory of ideology. Ideology, for Althusser, was an unconsciously determined system of illusory representations of reality. This system derived from the internalization of the dominant illusion a social class harbored about the conditions of its own existence, achieved by means of the internalization of the "paternal law" as part of the internalization of the oedipal superego.

In a related theoretical development, Habermas (1971, 1973) analyzed the origins of ideology as motivated false consciousness of social classes; he proposed to resolve this false consciousness with a "critical theory" that would provide self-reflective enlightenment together with social emancipation. Habermas drew a parallel between the analysis of ideologies and the psychoanalytic situation, in which the patient also starts his treatment with a "false consciousness" and is helped by the analyst, by means of self-reflection and honest interaction with the analyst, to gain an enlightenment aimed at freeing the patient from repression and neurosis.

While these Marxist and neo-Marxist writers, in part using psychoanalytic concepts, have focused on the characteristics of conventionality and (rightly, I believe) the superego-mediated receptivity of individuals to the conventional aspects of mass culture, their linkage of class-determined ideology to the characteristics of mass culture is questionable. After first critically analyzing mass culture of capitalism, they were forced to diagnose similar trends in the communist cultures as well and to introduce the concept of false consciousness (no longer attributed exclusively to the capitalist system). They missed, however, the historical continuity of conventionality and particularly of kitsch and the surprising universality of the appeal of mass culture across radically different cultures, for example, the remarkable appeal of western mass culture to the youth and young adults in Russia, China, India, and South America.

Marxist and neo-Marxist writers also have failed to analyze the common structural properties of mass culture reflecting totally opposite ideologies. Thus, for example, soap operas in East Berlin have the same characteristics of mass culture as those on Western television. There are different villains, corresponding to standard, conventional categories of "good" and "bad" people in the communist world. The structure of mass culture, the structure of its conventionality, is missed when the focus is exclusively on the motivation of the producers.

A more recent psychoanalytic approach to mass culture focuses on the absence—in contrast to hypertrophy—of normal superego functions. Mitscherlich (1963) pointed to the cultural consequences of the father's absence as a principle of organization at the social and familial level. He described the rejection of the father in contemporary society as part of the rejection of traditional cultural values and the replacement of such values with overdependence on immediate social influences. He pointed to the intoxicating effects of mass production, with its promise of immediate gratification of needs, and a consequent fostering of a psychology of demand for immediate gratification and a lack of sense of individual responsibility. Mitscherlich described the new "mass person" as a classless individual and stressed the combination of the real absence of the father in the contemporary family as a consequence of the organization of work, and the loss of individual functions of the father in large institutions. The primary absence of the father, whose work functions are now incomprehensible, is worsened by the secondary absence of the father in massive group experiences. These massive group experiences are effects of the immediate gratification of mass consumption and of the breakdown of taboos in society at large that leads to a loss of the capacity for full sexual gratification because of the concomitant dissociation of "immediate" sexual gratification from its linkage with emotional intimacy. Anonymous work, Mitscherlich stated, is complemented by anonymous mass entertainment that permits the projection of internal aggression onto external mass events.

In this country, Lasch (1977, 1978) independently concluded that the breakdown of the family as a moral guidance system, the avoidance of conflicts by compromising, and the accentuation of instinctual gratification corrode the development of mature superego functions in the child. In short, for Mitscherlich and Lasch the failure of normal superego development, not the development of an excessively harsh superego, characterizes the superego pathology that facilitates the submission to mass culture.

For the psychoanalyst interested in the study of conventionality, the individual differences in adherence to conventional values seem to be as important as the social determinants. André Green (1969) suggests that a relation exists between the developmental level of idealization and the type of ideological commitment one makes. These levels of idealization range from earliest narcissistic omnipotence through the intermediary stages of idealization of parental objects to the final consolidation of the ego ideal. The nature or quality of the commitment to ideologies, Green suggests, is determined by the extent to which the ideologies reflect the projection of an omnipotent self or the externalization of a mature ego ideal.

In an earlier work (1982), I suggested, in agreement with Green, that the incapacity to commit oneself to value systems beyond self-serving needs usually indicates severe narcissistic pathology. Commitment to an ideology that includes sadistic demands for perfection and tolerates primitive aggression or value judgments of a conventional naïveté indicates an immature ego ideal and lack of integration of a mature superego. To identify with a messianic ideology and accept social clichés and trivialities is commensurate with narcissistic and borderline pathology. In contrast, an identification with more differentiated, open-ended, nontotalistic ideologies that respect individual differences, autonomy, and privacy, and that tolerate sexuality while rejecting collusion with the expression of primitive aggression reflects characteristics of the value systems of the mature ego ideal. An ideology that respects individual differences and the complexity of human relations and that leaves room for a mature attitude toward sexuality appeals to those with a more evolved ego ideal.

In short, Adorno's, Green's, and my own work agree that ego and superego aspects of the personality predispose an individual to depend excessively on conventional values and attitudes. To say that the specific content of what is conventional is influenced by social, political, and economic factors is reasonable enough, but the universality of the structure of conventionality in mass culture and of its appeal to the masses still requires an explanation.

## NEW PERSPECTIVES: PSYCHOANALYTIC THEORY OF LARGE GROUP PROCESSES

Given that some individuals are more prone than others to adopt conventional values, and given that powerful social and economic factors influence the characteristics of mass culture—including the culturally and historically determined predominance of a certain artistic style or "language"—we are still left with the puzzling question: what is responsible for the ease with which adults accept cultural artifacts, entertainment, and news, all of which have qualities characteristic of the emotional developmental level of a latency-age child? I believe that a specific regression is involved in this process, a regression linked to the activation of group processes in the transmission of mass culture. In what follows, I shall spell out these processes in some detail.

Freud (1921) first described the regression in superego functions in certain mass gatherings. He suggested that the projection of the ego ideal onto the idealized leader eliminates individual moral constraints as well as the higher functions of self-criticism and responsibility that are mediated by the superego. The mutual identifications of the members of the mob give them a sense of unity, belonging and power, all of which protect them against losing their sense of identity but which are accompanied by severe reduction in ego functioning. As a result, primitive, ordinarily unconscious needs take over, and the mob functions under the sway of the drives, affects, excitement, and rage stimulated and directed by the leader.

Freud's theory is complemented by Bion's (1961) observations regarding the small group. Bion analyzed the primitivization of ego functions in small, unstructured groups in terms of the activation of three constellations of regressive group functioning: the "basic assumptions" groups of "pairing," "fight-flight," and "dependency." I have elsewhere (1980a) summarized Bion's contributions to the psychology of small groups and shall limit myself here to mentioning the findings relevant to this discussion. The dependency group seeks an all-giving, self-sufficient leader who will "feed" it; it shows concomitantly narcissistic features in its expectations of passive gratification from its leader. The "flight-fight" group has a markedly paranoid atmosphere and tends to select a leader with paranoid features.

This primitivization of group processes under conditions of unstructured small-group functioning becomes more dramatic in the case of unstructured large groups. Turquet (1975) described prevalent anxieties in large groups and characteristic defenses against such anxieties. These anxieties include individual members' sense of total loss of identity in large group situations and an accompanying dramatic decrease in their capacity to evaluate realistically the effects of what any particular individual says and does within such a group setting. Even projective mechanisms fail, because it is impossible to evaluate realistically the behavior of anyone else, and projections are therefore multiple and unstable. Turquet also described fears of aggression, or loss of control, and of violent behavior that might emerge at any time in the large group. These fears are the counterpart to provocative behaviors among the individuals of the group, behaviors expressed randomly in part and mostly directed at the leader. The unstructured large group basically has strong paranoid qualities.

According to Turquet, only "commonsense" trivialities permit a temporary unification of the large group and the emergence of a leader whose soothing banalities are eagerly accepted by most group members in an effort to calm the group; those who try to stand up to this banal, cliché-ridden atmosphere and maintain some semblance of individuality are most attacked. It is as if the members of the large group envied people who maintain their sanity and individuality. At the same time, efforts at homogenization are prevalent, and any simplistic generalization or "ideology" that permeates the group may easily be picked up and transformed into an experience of absolute truth. In contrast to the simple rationalization of the violence that permeates the mob, however, a vulgar or "commonsense" philosophy in the large group functions as a calming, reassuring doctrine that reduces all thinking to obvious clichés. Such calming trivial ideology may both protect the large group from aggression and also subtly express aggression in the form of envy of thinking, of individuality, and of rationality. Individuals with marked narcissistic features may provide the soothing leadership the unstructured large group desires in order to escape from its paranoid atmosphere and may give the large group a narcissistic quality of self-satisfaction.

Under these conditions, superego functions are projected on the group at large in a way that shows characteristics of a simplistic, conventional, black-and-white morality (Kernberg 1980a, 1980c). In light of the present analysis, I propose that an individual's temporary loss of identity in the large group carries with it the temporary loss of the higher level of autonomous, abstract, and individualized superego functions as well. A regression to the latency child superego occurs, which is projected onto the group at large.

Anzieu (1984), building upon Bion's and Turquet's work, studied the nature of evolving common illusions in groups and described some common features of the ad hoc ideologies that emerge under regressive conditions in both small and large groups. He suggested that, under conditions of regression in the unstructured group, the relationship of individuals to the group as a whole acquires characteristics of fusion of their individual instinctual needs with a fantastic conception of the group as a primitive ego ideal equated to an all-gratifying primary object: the mother of the earliest stages of development. The psychology of the group at that point, according to Anzieu, reflects the shared illusion that the group is constituted of individuals who are all equals (thus denying sexual differences and castration anxiety), that the group is self-engendered—that is, a powerful mob in itself—and that by itself the group might solve all narcissistic lesions (the group as an idealized "breast-mother").

Chasseguet-Smirgel (1984), expanding on Anzieu's observations, suggested that, under such conditions, groups both small and large tend to select leaders that represent not the paternal aspects of the prohibitive superego but a pseudopaternal "promoter of illusions," who provides the group with an ideology that confirms the narcissistic aspirations of fusion of the individual with the group as a primitive ego ideal, the all-powerful and all-gratifying preoedipal mother.

The psychoanalytic studies of group processes thus point to mechanisms of immediate regression of individuals in mobs and unstructured large and small groups and explain why groups are characterized by superego regression, narcissistic orientation, paranoid developments, and a general pressure toward conformity. But not all regressive group formation occurs under conditions of purposefully designed unstructuredness (such as in group-dynamics groups or group-relations conferences), or at the involuntary breakdown of a group's ordinary work structure (such as in organizations in crisis, under conditions of failure or when task leaders are unavailable), or with spontaneous crowd formations. There also exists regressive group formation prompted by the sheer pleasure of the regressive experience of being part of a group process, the pleasure of the regressive fusion with others derived from the generalized identification processes in a crowd. I am referring here to what Canetti (1978) has called the "feast crowd." His description of feast crowds captures my meaning well enough for me to quote him:

> There is abundance in a limited space, and everyone near can partake of it. There is more of everything than everyone together can consume and, in order to consume it, more and more people come streaming in. As long as there is anything there they partake of it, and it looks as though there would be no end to it. There's an abundance of women for the men, and an abundance of men for the women. Nothing and no-one threatens and there is nothing to flee from; for the time being, life and pleasure are secure. Many prohibitions and distinctions are waived, and unaccustomed advances are not only permitted but smiled on. For the individual the atmosphere is one of loosening, not discharge. There is no common identical goal which people have to try and attain together. The feast *is* the goal and they are there. (P. 62)

Here the socially sanctioned gratification of instinctual needs and their legitimate fulfillment, well deserved and without threats from malevolent authorities, brings us back to the psychological conditions of the latency child.

In light of the preceding considerations, the striking correspondence between latency psychology and mass culture may now be reformulated. The appeal of mass culture consists in the facilitation of a group regression induced by mass entertainment that is structured to appeal to the level of latency: reality and fantasy are clearly differentiated; instinctual wishes that can be gratified directly are differentiated from those that can be gratified only in fantasy or by proxy. The oedipal prohibitions are in place, reflected by the dissociation of emotional commitment from genital erotism; genital strivings, except for direct gratification of voyeuristic needs, are gratified only by proxy; and preoedipal polymorphous perverse sexuality is either suppressed or tolerated only in highly mechanical, depersonalized, or ritualistic fashion. Within the regressed group atmosphere of mass culture, superego functioning regresses to a latency level and weakens because personal responsibility is suspended or diluted when superego functions are projected onto the group (the implicit group sanctioning of the spectacle in which the individual participates as a group member: Freud's basic mechanism of the projection of the ego ideal in mass psychology). Individual thinking, decision-making, value judgments, and discriminating functions are markedly reduced, as are higher levels of superego and ego functioning. The social sanctioning of mass culture and the corresponding group regression reflecting mass psychology represent the combined approval from parental authority and peer groups that provides security to the latency child; conventionality of values and interests confirms these sanctions and approval and assures personal safety and security. Kitsch, with its idealized and sentimentalized activation of nostalgia, gratifies dependency longings, while the identification with the actors or the heroes confirms autonomy and power by proxy. Dependence and independence, instinctual gratification, autonomy, moral justification, and longings for peace with oneself are thus assured in an illusion that, because socially shared, seems convincingly real.

## MASS ENTERTAINMENT, GROUP REGRESSION, AND THE CORRESPONDING LEADERSHIP

We now have the elements for a developmental schema of regression in groups, with particular reference to mass culture and the nature of the leadership enacted by the anchor person, host, commentator, or columnist. I shall describe two levels of regression: the first, a milder one typical of mass entertainment, and the second, more severe.

The first level of regression, the mildest and most prevalent, occurs when people gather temporarily in crowds at celebrations and the theater; it also occurs in invisible temporary crowds formed by the simultaneous exposure to mass media (newspapers, radio, and particularly television), where individuals are actually isolated in their homes.

At this level, the threat of losing personal identity in an unstructured large group (Turquet 1975) is compensated by the common purpose shared with others. Unconscious identification with the other members of the crowd not only compensates for the temporary loss of personal identity but imparts a sense of power, importance, and security. As long as everybody else is there, the individual is doing the right thing (Canetti 1978). Because superego functions are projected onto the large group under conditions of group regression, and because of the need to counteract the uncertainty that emerges initially in all regressive group processes, the individual becomes markedly dependent on his fantasies regarding everybody else's opinion about the quality of what is presented.

When large-group leadership emerges under such circumstances, there is heightened respect for the person in authority and an increased willingness to accept his or her judgment, which is customarily expressed in simple generalizations. A benign father figure, or even a firm but fair one, will strengthen the suggestive effects of conventional truth, and mild swings into either a paranoid or a narcissistic direction on the part of such a leader will intensify the experience of group cohesion, power, and elation (Kernberg 1980a). The self-indulgent, self-satisfied, flattering attitude of the narcissistic personage will produce a sense of sentimental and gratified well-being, while the mildly persecutory attitude of the leader who attacks something that flies in the face of conventional standards will arouse a righteous indignation in the group members, which, in identification with the leader, strengthens the members' self-esteem as well.

At this first level of regression in group processes a projection of the oedipal superego occurs, but the individuals still preserve an integrated self-concept and the related, integrated, realistic object representations that jointly constitute ego identity. The preservation of ego identity is assured by a partial or time-limited activation of group processes in the context of social conditions or structures that maintain ordinary status and roles in the individual's life outside the group experience.

In contrast, at the second, deeper level of regression, the integrated concept of the self and of others is threatened by the loss of ordinary role and status conditions and by the simultaneous presence of many persons in reality that reproduce the multiplicity of internalized part-object relations at a primitive level of ego development. This second level of regression occurs in large unstructured groups, such as emerge during a power vacuum in a previously well-organized social structure: for example under conditions of breakdown of ordinary structure in large organizations, or in the temporary formations of mobs under conditions of social tension and unrest. Suspension of ordinary social roles, the presence of multiple individuals in a totally unstructured relationship, and inability to escape from such a frightening social condition may be observed in the small- and large-group situations studied by Bion, Turquet, and Anzieu. But a similar regression also occurs in ordinary social organizations when the work structure breaks down, when a failure of functional leadership produces immediate regression in all task systems, and under social conditions where social upheaval, external threats, disorganization of ordinary protective social structures, or extreme social isolation on the part of a social subgroup produce the conditions described by the authors mentioned (Kernberg 1980b).

Here, projection of the integrated oedipal superego fails due to the lack of an integrated social structure or the loss of functional leadership on which to project. Regression into the preoedipal precursors of the superego and efforts to project them massively parallel the regression into preoedipal constituents of ego formation. The regressive dependency and fight-flight groups described by Bion (1961) overshadow by far the pairing group and the remnants of oedipal sexuality. Now the search is for the primitive ego-ideal leader who reflects preoedipal parental images of a totally giving and gratifying kind—in the last resort, the pseudopaternal "promoter of illusions" who represents the all-powerful and all-gratifying preoedipal mother described by Anzieu and Chasseguet-Smirgel.

The mass rally of the Nazi party at Nuremberg depicted in the classical propaganda film *The Triumph of the Will* dramatically illustrates these characteristics of group regression. Under such conditions, the group illusion of total gratification (by the primary object, represented by the leader) can be enacted as long as the minimal latency age requirements for the earliest social group formation are met. The latency child's outlook on life and morality thus provides the unconscious preconditions for an almost hypomanic, thoughtless, and irresponsible merger with the mass gathering.

Or else, under conditions of social upheaval, turmoil, or stress and in the presence of a powerful paranoid leadership, the group may shift to the opposite extreme of endorsing of a primitive, powerful, and sadistic leader who assures the group that, by identifying collectively with the threatening primitive aggression he incorporates, members will be safe from persecution.

In other words, at this second level of regression, group processes activate the search for primitive narcissistic or paranoid leaders, depending on the extent to which external circumstances impose actual threats or frustration upon the group, thus reinforcing the real threat of violence and the need to defend against it by projecting it outward and fighting malignant external forces. Under conditions in which such social threats are relatively absent, and with the possibility of realistic gratification of primitive needs within a tolerant and flexible social environment, primitive narcissistic leadership may prevail. In any case, the swing of the pendulum in both group emotions and leadership to either a paranoid or a narcissistic polarity is extreme. One solution to a group's uncertain oscillation between narcissistic and paranoid orientations may be the combination of primitive leadership of an extremely narcissistic and paranoid kind that, in condensing primitive narcissism and aggression, reproduces the psychopathology of what I have called "malignant narcissism" (1984).

When narcissistic group formation prevails, diffuse polymorphous erotism may be idealized and sadistic aspects of sexual interactions denied and projected; with paranoid group formations, sadistic sexual behavior may become ego-syntonic and rationalized, as occurred, for example, in Jim Jones's religious cult. In large group formations and political masses, violent destructiveness and murder may result.

What is the relationship between the first and second level of regression? In the large group, narcissistic regression and leadership definitely defend the group against a basic paranoid disposition. Is mass culture and mass entertainment an innocent protection against potentially more severe regression in group formation? Or is there a continuum of group regression that makes mass culture a dangerous springboard for potential further regression? The potential relationship between the regressive group processes involved in "innocent" mass culture, on the one hand, and in severely regressive, paranoid mass movements, on the other—a relationship reflected in the communality of many of their underlying processes—raises the question of whether mass media serve the potentially dangerous and protective functions.

Horkheimer and Adorno ( 1971 ) and Anders ( 1956, 1980 ) have suggested that mass culture is a malignant process leading to infantilism and control of the masses by capitalist or communist ruling circles. On the other hand, Brantlinger ( 1983 ) considers mass culture a small price to pay for the gratification of regressive group processes at a relatively innocuous level—a small price in return for the availability of information, artistic communication, and entertainment for large segments of the population. Moscovici ( 1981 ), paraphrasing Engels, states that "communication is the Valium of the people." The narcissistic world of the soap opera and the paranoid scenario of the ordinary thriller may be considered regressions in the service of the ego that are a far cry from the second level—severely narcissistic and paranoid regressions in group processes and leadership under turbulent social and political circumstances.

It seems likely that the level of group regression codetermines, together with the degree of individual psychopathology, the level of regression of an individual's commitment to any group-sponsored ideology. The mildly regressive group ideology fostered by ordinary mass media supports the most trivial and conventional manifestation of any ideology, such as, for example, conventional lip service to Marxism in Communist societies or to Catholicism in Latin American countries. These same ideologies, at a less conventional and trivial level, as part of highly-differentiated value systems of autonomous individuals, may be expressed in deep and complex personal ideological commitments that have a quality of independence, ethical depth, and firmness of conviction while still open to specific individual circumstances. At the other extreme, these same ideologies may regress into primitive, sadistic, and psychopathic forms, such as the blending of terrorism and ordinary criminality in some Marxist groups in Western Europe and the Middle East, or the terrorist groups linked to fundamentalist Islamic regimes. The transformation of mass communication and entertainment into the propaganda machinery of totalitarian regimes illustrates the dangerous nature of the potential for group regression thus activated (Welch 1983).

Perhaps the greatest danger to the democratic political process of a pluralistic society is the effect of mass media on the political process itself. The understanding of mass psychology may be an important contribution psychoanalysis can make regarding a development that may endanger intelligent participation in the political process. We do not yet know to what extent, in the long run, higher education itself might protect individuals against regressive group processes or to what extent the triviality of mass culture and mass entertainment may simply illustrate a constant historical dialectic between the individual and the masses, gratifying regressive needs in socially adaptive ways and replacing historically earlier forms of ritualized social regression. Even if mass entertainment is exploited by economic and political interests, its effectiveness requires further exploration of the psychological needs it gratifies.

At this moment it seems reasonable to conclude that the regression induced by and reflected in mass culture and mass entertainment actualizes tendencies of value systems and morality of latency years triggered by large group processes, as applied to the invisible group activated by mass media. These latency characteristics include the participants' projection of the unconscious superego structure of the postoedipal period onto the illusional group, the reassurance of personal identity within this group by embracing conventionality, the dissociation of sex and tenderness, and preoedipal (narcissistic and paranoid) gratification at a mostly sublimatory level. The danger of more severely regressive large-group processes consists in the immediate activation of primitive object relations, projection of preoedipal superego precursors onto potential leaders, and the corresponding activation of primitive narcissistic and/or paranoid tendencies in leadership that may lead to direct enactment of violence, primitive equalization, and totalitarian control. Conventionality may be the price of social stability, but it may indicate the ever-present danger of more severe group regression. There are societies that, by consciously manipulating the mass psychology activated by mass culture, may expand the domain of conventional thinking—or reduce that of individual judgment. For the individual, conventionality is a function of his or her personality and of the activation of regressive mass psychology. Most persons submerge themselves temporarily in the conventionality of mass culture for recreational purposes; for some, conventionality becomes a permanent prison.

## References

Adorno, T. 1954. Television and the patterns of mass culture. In *Mass culture*, ed. B. Rosenberg and D. M. White, 474–88. New York: Free Press, 1957.

Adorno, T., et al. 1950. *The authoritarian personality.* New York: Harper.

Althusser, L. 1976. *Positions.* Paris: Editions Sociales.

Anders, G. 1956. *Die Antiquiertheit des Menschen,* vol. 1. Munich: Verlag C. H. Beck.

———. 1980. *Die Antiquiertheit des Menschen,* vol. 2. Munich: Verlag C. H. Beck.

Anzieu, D. 1984. *The group and the unconscious.* London: Routledge and Kegan Paul.

Berman, L. E. 1987. Psychoanalytic comments on James Bond and Ian Fleming. Unpublished manuscript.

Bion, W. R. 1961. *Experiences in groups.* New York: Basic Books.

Bourdieu, P. 1979. *La distinction: Critique social du jugement.* Paris: Les Editions de Minuit.

Brantlinger, P. 1983. *Bread and circuses.* Ithaca: Cornell Univ. Press.

Canetti, E. 1978. *Crowds and power.* New York: Seabury Press.

Chasseguet-Smirgel, J. 1984. *The ego ideal.* New York: Norton.

Deschner, K. 1980. *Kitsch, Konvention und Kunst.* Frankfurt: Ullstein.

Freud, S. 1921. Group psychology and the analysis of the ego. *Standard Edition,* 18.

Friedlander, S. 1984. *Reflections of Nazism.* New York: Harper.

Gramsci, A. 1959. *The modern prince and other writings.* New York: International Publishing.

Green, A. 1969. *Sexualite et ideologie chez Marx et Freud.* Paris: Etudes Freudiens 1-2:187–217.

Greenberg, C. 1946. Avant-garde and kitsch. In *Mass culture,* ed. B. Rosenberg and D. M. White, 98–110. New York: Free Press. 1957.

Habermas, J. 1971. *Knowledge and human interests.* Boston: Beacon Press.

———. 1973. *Theory and practice.* Boston: Beacon Press.

Horkheimer, M., and Adorno, T. 1971. *Dialektik der Aufklarung.* Frankfurt: Bucher des Wissens.

Howe, I. 1948. Notes on mass culture. In *Mass culture,* ed. B. Rosenberg and D. M. White, 496–503. New York: Free Press. 1957.

Kernberg, O. 1980a. Regression in groups. In *Internal world and external reality.* 211–34. New York: Aronson.

———. 1980b. Organizational regression. In *Internal world and external reality.* 235–52. New York: Aronson.

———. 1980c. The couple and the group. In *Internal world and external reality.* 307–31. New York: Aronson.

———. 1982. Identity, alienation, and ideology in adolescent group processes. Presented at Annual Meeting of American Society for Adolescent Psychiatry in Toronto, Canada, May 16, 1982. In *Unconscious fantasy, myth, and reality,* ed. H. P. Blum. 381–99. Madison, Conn.: International Universities Press, 1988.

———. 1984. Paranoid regression and malignant narcissism. In *Severe personality disorders: Psychotherapeutic strategies.* 290–311. New Haven: Yale Univ. Press.

Lasch, C. 1977. *Haven in a heartless world.* New York: Basic Books.

———. 1978. *The culture of narcissism.* New York: Norton.

MacDonald, D. 1953. A theory of mass culture. In *Mass culture,* ed. B. Rosenberg and D. M. White, 59–73. New York: Free Press. 1957.

Marcuse, H. 1955. *Eros and civilization: A philosophical inquiry into Freud.* Boston: Beacon Press.

Mitscherlich, A. 1963. *Auf dem Weg Zur vaterlosen Gesellschaft: Ideen Zur Sozial-Psychologie.* Munich: R. Piper.

Moles, A. 1971. *Le kitsch: L'art du bonheur.* Paris: Maison Mame.

Moscovici, S. 1981. *L'age des foules.* Paris: Librairie Artheme Fayard.

Reich, W. 1935. *The sexual revolution: Toward a self-governing character structure.* New York: Noonday Press. 1962.

Riesman, D. 1950. *The lonely crowd: A study of the changing American character.* New Haven: Yale Univ. Press.

Rosenberg, B. 1957. Mass culture in America. In *Mass culture,* ed. B. Rosenberg and D. M. White, 3–12. New York: Free Press. 1957.

Rosenberg, B., and White, D. M., eds. 1957. *Mass culture.* New York: Free Press.

Sarnoff, C. 1976. *Latency.* New York: Aronson.

Shapiro, T., and Perry, R. 1976. Latency revisited: The age 7 plus or minus 1. In *Psychoanalytic Study of the Child* 31:79–105.

Turquet, P. 1975. Threats to identity in the large group. In *The large group: Dynamics and therapy,* ed. L. Kreeger, 87–144. London: Constable.

Welch, D. 1983. *Propaganda and the German cinema: 1933–1945.* New York: Oxford Univ. Press.

**Two**
■ ■

■
■
■
**Psychoanalytic Biography and Its Problems: The Case of Wilhelm Reich**
*Steven Marcus*

To speak of Freud's influence on the life of Western culture has by now become something of a quasi-comical exercise. There is something slightly laughable in sitting down to make up a list of intellectual pursuits or cultural categories on which his work has had perceptible bearings. There is, however, one area or activity that has been so momentously affected by Freud's discoveries that it still merits discussion—I am thinking about the writing of biographies. Between the characteristic nineteenth-century notion of biography and the notion that is current today there stand differences that are revolutionary in both magnitude and quality. Nineteenth-century biographies were typically of "great men"—much less frequently of great women; they were meant to be exemplary, monumental, inspirational, elevating, and instructive. Biographers were as a rule highly selective in the material they included and discreditable events, opinions, or circumstances were by and large freely overlooked or censored.

Almost all of that has now changed. Biography today seeks to discover, disclose, and illuminate rather than to instruct. Its notions of causal circumstances are normatively sought in the experiences visited upon the biographical subject in childhood and early family life rather than in internal moral resources, strength of inborn will, or accidents of fortune in later life. It does not disregard native creative gifts, but it endeavors to analyze how those gifts were shaped and sometimes deformed by experiences of early life that remained largely unconscious in the grown person and his creative or active

**35**

undertakings in the world. And it hunts out, I think it fair to say, quirks, neuroses, thwartings, and internal forces that act to limit or defeat achievement as much as it seeks to enlighten us on the counterpart forces that make for actual and actualized achievement. And, as in psychoanalysis itself, it tends to draw no theoretical or moral limit on what is relevant or permissible material: no secret embarrassment, no shameful memory or episode is to be ruled out if it is pertinent to the central project of understanding how a significant life came about. That central project today regularly overrides such previous considerations as privacy, modesty, propriety, and a reticence to tarnish or detract from the idealized image of a person of great distinction or creative power.

If this is relatively true of biography in general, then it is true in an even more salient way of that new and growing subgenre of biography, the psychoanalytic biographies of psychoanalysts themselves. And it is so by reason of several considerations. In the first place, the changes in the nature of biography that psychoanalytic theory and practice induced were bound to strike most deeply upon psychoanalysts themselves, since they were the original analysts and architects of these new conceptions of what the deep shapes and structures of human lives were typically like, and the theorists and explicators of how they came into being. In addition, they were among the earliest persons of interest and distinction to have had their own lives gone over and reconstructed by these new analytic-biographical methods. Second, the earliest generations of psychoanalysts tended more rather than less to be distinctively odd birds themselves. In general they had strikingly marked and strong characters, flamboyant neuroses, and eccentric but acute intelligences; they were capable of behavior both inside and outside the clinical-analytical situation that would today be regarded as scandalous and entirely unallowable within the confines of the analytic profession. Freud himself, genius though he was, does not fall entirely outside this description. He made the rules, but he also felt free to break them. By and large, however, there was enough Victorian probity and rectitude in his character—not to speak of his fundamental sanity—to preserve him from many of the excesses of his earliest generations of adherents.

Third, and a matter of greater interest and importance, there is the presence in all such biographies of the transference, a phenomenon largely discovered and wholly named by Freud as a result of his clinical experiences, both successful and aborted. Some transferencelike attributes are to be found in almost all biographies, usually in the form of the biographer's positive identification with and idealization of his biographical subject—rarely but occasionally with a negative valence, as, say, in Lytton Strachey's *Eminent*

*Victorians.* In psychoanalysis the experience of the transference constitutes the dynamic center and ongoing structure of the analytic transaction—and the analysis itself, as is well known, consists in some considerable measure in working over the transference. However, there is much more to it than this. The earliest psychoanalysts made their transferences onto Freud. And even when their analysts were not Freud, they tended to internalize his figure as some kind of ego-ideal. This doubled circumstance holds true, I believe, of psychoanalysts today as well. It holds, in addition, for the biographers of psychoanalysts too, all of whom tend to establish transferencelike relations with both their subjects and Freud. Furthermore, it is by no means evident or certain that the transference—along with all its distortions, idealizations, and radical antagonisms—can ever be entirely neutralized or analyzed away. It can be sustained in consciousness, but it may not be possible, once it has been established, to do away with it altogether. That, I believe, is the major point of François Roustang's otherwise largely incomprehensible recent book, *Dire Mastery: Discipleship from Freud to Lacan.* Roustang is a Lacanian who has lost his illusions about Lacan but at the same time cannot get rid of him—or the unreadable prose he has inherited from him. He calls the transference an "infernal machine" and tries to demonstrate how destructive and indissoluble it can be. At best one can acknowledge its lasting presence and try to be as aware of its workings as possible. An analogous set of circumstances, it seems to me, applies to the problems entailed in writing psychoanalytic biographies of psychoanalysts.

Fourth, and last, the heirs, estates, and executors of the documentary and biographical material left behind by the most important figures in the discipline have, to say the least, been irregular and inconsistent in their policies and dealings with the legacies entrusted to them. In particular, conditions of access to the various archives have varied widely, and there is evidence in some quarters of dishonesty, double-dealing, and unscrupulous behavior. All this, one need hardly say, is not quite in keeping with the spirit of the profession itself, in which truth-telling is accorded the highest of moral and intellectual values.

Myron Sharaf's commendable recent biography of Wilhelm Reich, *Fury on Earth,* illustrates the varieties of oddness, difficulty, and general unpleasantness amid much murky weather that I have been ascribing to this new subgenre of the biographical art. Sharaf, who is himself a psychotherapist, is aware of many of the problematicalities that I have just touched upon; hence the first two chapters of his book are called "The Viewpoint of the Observer" and serve to introduce us both to the conditions under which he wrote this book and to his relations with Reich. Sharaf pursued his project entirely without access to the mass of archival documents left behind by Reich. In his will, Reich stipulated that all his unpublished papers were to be "put away and stored for 50 years to secure their safety from destruction and falsification by anyone interested in the falsification and destruction of historical truth." Mary Boyd Higgins, who is the trustee of his estate, has pursued a strict or narrow interpretation of this clause, and so Sharaf has not been able to consult any of the unpublished material, including some of his own notes and papers, written while he was working with Reich but which Reich sequestered from him on the grounds that they properly belonged to Reich himself. Sharaf wants the reader to know that in his view Reich was a "great man," someone who has "disturbed the sleep of the world more fundamentally even than Freud or Marx." And he has reached these conclusions, in part, from his "ten years of association with Reich as student, patient, and assistant, and from the kind of transference I had toward him."

But Sharaf's connection with Reich goes back much farther than those ten years of actual association. Its prehistory began in 1931, when Sharaf was five and his mother suffered a psychotic breakdown that caused her to be hospitalized for two years. She never fully recovered from her psychosis, and she passed on to her young son a number of obsessions—she called them her "dreams"—that she had cooked up during her madness. The first of these was that apocalyptic destruction of the present order of society was imminent, and that out of the ashes of ruination there would arise a new world that was "economically Communist and psychologically 'free.'" In addition to this, she had determined that the secret to immortal life was to be found in the "scientific study of the orgasm." More specifically it would be discovered in an "experiment" in which "a chemical in the blood" would be "isolated" during "the acme of orgastic experience." She communicated these visions to her worshipful and distressed young son. *The Function of the Orgasm* was first published in English in 1942. Shortly thereafter she obtained a copy of it, met Reich personally, and gave the book to her son, who was then seventeen, believing apparently that "it provided the ultimate confirmation of her dream." Sharaf read the work and had a religious experience: he found in Reich a "mentor" as well as a combined parent who represented "the synthesis between my mother's penchant for the new and daring and my father's feeling for reality and genuine experience." He thereupon decided to devote his own life to Reich and his work. He first visited Reich in Forest Hills in 1944, just before Sharaf was drafted into the army. He visited him again in 1946 at Rangeley, Maine, where Reich spent his summers, and then after his discharge from the army, he enrolled at Harvard with the idea of working for Reich dominating his whole existence. He learned German in order to read

Reich in the original; Reich's picture hung on his wall; he had an orgone "box," or "accumulator," as it was properly called, in his room; and he had a close friend and fellow student with whom he mutually practiced amateur Reichian therapy. In 1947, his mother visited him in his Cambridge room and casually disclosed to him that she and his close friend were having an affair.

Sharaf rather understandably felt betrayed by this turn of events and fled to Reich. He met a young woman who had been in therapy with Reich and soon married her. The marriage was immediately miserable, but Sharaf hung on— he is nothing if not tenacious. Reich then asked him to translate a manuscript of his, and in the summer of 1948 Sharaf began to work regularly with Reich at Orgonon, his "research center" in Maine. It was only a matter of time before Reich accepted him for therapy, and Sharaf under Reich's physical manipulation of his naked body soon began to feel the "orgonotic streamings" that Reich had discovered, written about, and declared existed everywhere in the cosmos. As a therapist, Reich was no longer interested in working with psychological problems—and it is probably equally fair to say that he was no longer interested in people, except insofar as they served his purposes. The great man was a tyrant, contemptuous of people in general, even of his most loyal disciples, from whom he asked for "considerable financial help." Sometimes at night he and Sharaf would work together in the laboratory, with Reich wearing "a revolver strapped to his waist. The combination of the gun and a bandana tied around his neck made him look like a guerilla chieftain." If there seems to be something slightly odd about any of this, it's nothing to what is yet to come.

Sharaf's relation to Reich became in due time troubled; Reich raged away at him, but the young man always returned for more. He began to keep systematic, quasi-Boswellian notes about Reich and the goings-on at Orgonon, and Reich began to refer to him as the "historian" of orgonomy, "a role," Sharaf writes, "that fitted my own conception of myself." Unlike Dr. Johnson, however, Reich insisted that Sharaf hand over all his writing to him, and Sharaf meekly complied—these notes, I have already remarked, remain part of the sealed archives. Sharaf also began to work toward his doctorate at Harvard, and in the summer of 1954, while he was working at Orgonon, Reich began an affair with Sharaf's wife, doing to him again what his mother had done to him earlier. Reich also decided that the marriage was no good and should come to an end, which it eventually did. Nevertheless, Sharaf continued to be a faithful adherent. By 1956 things had gotten into such a stew for him that he was unable to go on with his doctoral dissertation. Sharaf then made the prudent decision to enter psychoanalysis, from which he learned "a great deal about my neurotic bondage to Reich." Perhaps he did not learn quite enough, for he continued to be loyal to him unto Reich's death and after, and since, he writes, he "intended to make use of the analysis to fulfill my aim of understanding him and our relationship." In the event, he became a therapist himself, and now finally he has fulfilled his obligation to Reich by writing the extremely, and most unlikely, readable and interesting biography that I am referring to. This is a fairly hair-raising way to begin a biography, but Reich's life itself is by and large a series of hair-raising events and episodes.

Wilhelm Reich was born in 1897 in Galicia, then part of the Austro-Hungarian Empire. His father was a well-to-do Jewish cattle farmer, a man of dominating temperament, prone to violence and outbursts of jealous rage at his wife. When Reich was about twelve he discovered that his mother was having an affair with a young tutor who lived with the family. He observed this affair voyeuristically, with both horror and sexual excitement; finally he managed to inform his father of what was taking place. The father confronted the mother as the "whore" he had always accused her of being, and she then drank enough household cleanser to kill herself in the most painful way. The tutor was of course banished; the father never recovered from the event and a few years later also did himself in, or tried to: he stood for hours in cold weather in a pond, "ostensibly fishing" but trying to contract pneumonia, which he did. He rapidly developed tuberculosis and died in 1914. One can only imagine what in the way of unbearable guilt, torment, and anguish the young Reich endured. He too was never to recover from these horrible experiences and indeed in later life tended to repeat these primary crises in varied forms. His chief defense—as well as his partial repetition of the traumas—was the tendency to blame everyone else in quarrels, disagreements, and fracases that were largely conflicts of Reich's own creation. There was also born in him at this time a "sense of a mission," a need to live "a heroic life," which, Sharaf speculates, would bring him some surcease from the unconscious guilt that he was always to feel and would work to repair "the conditions that had produced the early tragedies."

After a stint in the army during World War I, Reich entered the University of Vienna. He had become a social radical and was prepared to become a sexual radical too. In March 1919, he wrote in his diary, "I have become convinced that sexuality is the center around which revolves the whole of social life as well as the inner life of the individual." This is at once much simpler than Freud but a good preparation for the experience of Freud as well. That experience came almost at once; Reich was immediately hooked, found in Freud the surrogate for the parents (especially the father) that he had lost, and entered upon a period of discipleship. Freud took quickly to this bright and vigorous young man, and by the end of 1920, while he was still in medical school, Reich was already a practicing analyst. He also had two brief periods of analytic therapy at about this time, one with Isidor Sadger and one with Paul Federn, both of whom eventually came to detest Reich with exceptional intensity.

Some of Reich's early work retains an interest today both in itself and as part of the history of psychoanalytic theory and clinical practice. He was one of the first psychoanalysts to become involved extensively in the treatment of people who were suffering from what was then called "impulsive character"—today the relevant terminology would be "character disorder" or "borderline personality." These patients were not afflicted so much by specific neurotic symptoms as by entire styles of life that were "chaotically disorganized." Reich's own early history had certainly prepared him to understand such people. He also learned to direct attention to what he came to call "character analysis"—namely, analysis of the entire array of defenses that patients erect and that Reich characteristically termed "character armor." He was, in addition, among the first psychoanalysts to see that in such patients pieces of neurotic behavior are not treated as entities that are alien to the ego—as hysterical or obsessional symptoms are—but are instead regarded as an integral part of the self, as ego-syntonic. He tried to devise ways of dealing with these problems, and some of them were of considerable interest. For example, Reich was among the early analysts to begin to try to pay systematic attention to the nonverbal behavior of patients and to use such behavior as analytic material. He also directed very close attention to the latent negative transference in his patients and made every effort to elicit it and make it overt.

He made as well what he regarded as his first fundamental discovery: the phenomenon of "orgastic potency," which was for him the cornerstone for all his later work and his standard for human health. Reich was something of a Freudian fundamentalist; he believed that neuroses entailed literal, perhaps measurable, blockages of libidinal energies, and that the primary aim of psychotherapy ought to be to find ways and means of discharging these electrophysiological currents through the convulsive experience of the orgasm. To this end, Reich began to work directly with his patients' genital sensations; in due course this directness, ever increasing, began to trouble his fellow analysts. There is no question that Reich is the key figure in the modern cult of the orgasm that has, so to speak, plagued Western middle-class culture for some decades now. And there is no question either that he rather simplemindedly equated sexual potency and responsiveness with psychic health in general. He was nothing if not utopian.

But these early achievements went along with the circumstance that from the beginning he kept getting into hot water with his colleagues. First there was his personal behavior among them; with the exception of Freud, Reich could not resist the impulse to dominate, lead, compel, and command everyone else in all situations. Second, Reich's own free—if not promiscuous—sexual life (he was always something of a womanizer), conducted openly, added fuel to the fire he was building. Then there was the manner in which he put forward his ideas among his analytic peers: Helena Deutsch, recalling the 1920s, writes with distaste about Reich's "aggressiveness" and "fanaticism" in advancing his ideas on sexuality. That is to say, he had no conception of how to behave collegially. Freud himself rather dryly recognized that there were problems brewing around Reich. In 1928, he wrote to Lou Andreas-Salomé that "we have here a Dr. Reich, a worthy but impetuous young man, passionately devoted to his hobby horse, who now salutes in the genital orgasm the antidote to every neurosis." Freud insisted on the irreducible importance of pregenital components of the sexual drive. And when, at an evening meeting held at Freud's house in 1928 or 1929, Reich held forth his views on orgastic potency, "Freud replied that 'complete orgasm' was not the answer. There were still pregenital drives that could not be satisfied even with orgasm. 'There is no single cause for the neuroses' was his verdict." Freud was right in his diagnosis of Reich's essentially reductionist and simplifying view of matters of exceptional complexity. But when Reich persisted in arguing for his theoretical view, Freud is reported to have replied sharply, "He who wants to have the floor again and again shows that he wants to be right at any price," suggesting that he understood more about Reich than that his thesis alone was inadequate.

In addition to this, Reich had some years earlier fallen in love with and subsequently married a female patient of his. Although Annie Reich was later analyzed by both Hermann Nunberg and Anna Freud and became in her own turn a respected member of the analytic community, there seems no doubt that Reich was at least in part impelled to this behavior precisely because it was tabooed. And it served to intensify the growing disapproval in which he was held by that community. This circumstance of deepening estrangement was not helped when, in about 1927, he sought a personal analysis from Freud and was refused. It was clearly becoming very difficult for Reich to remain one of the "good sons" that Freud needed to have around him, although it is also clear that part of him, during this period, tried to fulfill itself in that role. Things were not helped either by Reich's increasingly open social radicalism and his participation in the activities of the local Communist party. Just as he sought rapid and radical character change in his own kind of psychotherapy, so also he believed that strong action on the political left would bring about analogous rapid, revolutionary liberation for the "oppressed masses" in society at large. He also, openly and publicly, took extremely advanced positions for the time on abortion, contraception, and adolescent genital sexuality. It was at this moment that he came up with the crack-brained idea that there was nothing harmful in children watching their parents in sexual intercourse. In other words, Reich had made himself into a typical sexual-social modernist of the post–World War I period—but his doing so pushed him further toward the periphery of the psychoanalytic movement, which deliberately maintained a generally low and conservative profile on such inflammatory matters of social behavior and morality.

It was from about this time—circa 1927—that colleagues have retrospectively identified perceptible changes in Reich's behavior: his fierce adherence to his theories and convictions was expressed with increasing belligerence, and a number of his associates believed they could see "paranoid trends" emerging in his conduct. Whether this was the creative disorder of the intellectual adolescence that Reich permanently inhabited, or whether it was the overt development of a deep pathology, Sharaf is unable to say, but he has provided the reader with enough material to make up his or her own mind on such questions. In 1930, with matters rapidly coming to a crisis in the German-speaking world, Reich moved from Vienna to Berlin. He joined the Communist party there, tried to save the world through his personal campaign of sexual-political education and liberation of the working class, and continued to alienate almost everyone. By 1934, with Hitler in power, Reich found himself in exile in Scandinavia. His love affair with the Communist party was over; he had been expelled from the official psychoanalytic institutions and organizations; and his marriage had dissolved. He had broken with almost everyone and everything, including two young daughters. Reich believed that he was utterly right in what he had done: he had preserved "the integrity of his life and work," he later remarked to Sharaf, and besides, it was everyone else's fault anyway.

In Scandinavia from 1934 to 1939 (mostly in Norway), Reich pursued his own increasingly divergent way. He began to make experiments designed to discover the biological, physiological, and electrical foundations of the libido. In 1936 he claimed to have discovered the "bions," vesicles that, he declared, "represented transitional stages between nonliving and living substance." He was in fact looking for the secret of life itself. In this ambitious undertaking he was surrounded and abetted by a specific group of people.

Most of the people who helped Reich were in therapy with him and, often, in a kind of "training analysis" to learn his techniques. With justification, Otto

Fenichel has criticised Reich for abusing the transference situation—the patient's dependence upon and devotion to his therapist—by getting such people to help him through working or giving money or both. The fact that many were also students, eager for his stamp of approval, for referrals from him, heightened this situation.

Under these circumstances it is not altogether surprising that a number of his coworkers were also able to see the blue or blue-gray bions that Reich claimed became visible when he turned out the lights in his specially prepared laboratory.

A "kind of training analysis" is a kind way of putting it. Reich had passed from working analytically on the rigidities of "character armor" to working physically on the rigidities of "muscular armor." He no longer thought of himself as a psychoanalyst. Nudity, touching, the physical manipulation of the various segments of the musculature in order to facilitate "the dissolution of characterological and muscular rigidities," the eliciting of strong emotions and energy "streamings," the emphasis upon respiration, the effort to breathe more freely by means of released "blocked feeling, through the expression of rage or sorrow" now came to be the central focus of Reich's therapy—a kind of psychiatric chiropraxis, which Reich himself now termed "character-analytic vegetotherapy." It is not difficult to make out the ancestral connections between these innovations and such latter-day developments as primal scream therapy, Gestalt therapy, bioenergetics, and encounter groups. By the mid-1930s, Reich had become totally immersed in his own unique world—a world that, experientially, could be represented in condensed form by the "end phase" of therapy, a "world of intense sensation, of soft movements culminating in convulsions of the body (the orgasm reflex.)" He no longer had any friends, only students, helpers, and disciples. There were few limits that he placed on his own behavior: he did not hesitate to tyrannize over his patients and to take out his unending rage upon them; and in at least one "well-documented" episode he did not scruple to have sexual relations with them either. And he continued with his momentous laboratory researches into the secrets of the universe.

By this time things were getting sticky for Reich in Norway: his activities were subject to public criticism in the daily press, and he was forced to look for a new place of exile. He was extricated from his difficulties by Theodore P. Wolfe, a young American psychiatrist who had come to Norway to seek therapy and training from Reich, became an unwavering disciple, and, on his return to America, pulled strings in the State Department to obtain a visa so that Reich could immigrate. In August 1939, Reich arrived in New York and soon found a house in the unlikely region of Forest Hills—although when you come to think of it any place that he might settle down in would perforce become unlikely by virtue of his mere presence there. He needed patients, associates, money. To this end he secured a teaching position at the New School for Social Research. The course he offered was called "Biological Aspects of Character Formation," and he used it as a recruiting ground for patients and followers. His character continued to undergo change: in America he became more distant and aloof from those who surrounded him; to his intellectual delusions he now added a touch of personal grandiosity. Thus he was prepared for the epiphany that appeared to him at Mooselookmeguntic Lake, near Rangeley, Maine, in the summer of 1940. There, looking out over the lake, at night and during the day, he observed flickerings and other phenomena of light and suddenly realized that he was seeing "an energy outside the body, outside matter itself." It was the fundamental energy of the cosmos that he had discovered, and he thereupon called it "orgone energy." Just as he had seen spontaneous movement in the "total bodily convulsions of the orgasm" and in the "expansion and contraction of the bions," so now he saw it all around him in the "pulsation and movement of atmospheric orgone energy." This energy he believed to be the "same as the energy in the organism," in the body, and so it was the universal energy as well. It was visible everywhere and existed in everything; he had discovered the fundamental secret of nature.

How had it come about that no one had ever seen this energy before? Sharaf offers this quite accurate, if not succinct, summary of Reich's ruminations on this question. (Reich himself was utterly incapable of succinctness.)

> Unable to penetrate to the primordial, cosmic energy, man . . . erected two systems of thought, mysticism and mechanism, which were essentially built around the concepts of "God" and "ether," respectively. God was behind all subjective, spiritual, qualitative phenomena; the ether behind all material, physical processes. Without intending to . . . he had hit upon both the God and ether problem when he discovered the cosmic orgone energy. Orgone energy, like God and ether, was everywhere and permeated everything. It was behind both the physical processes in nature and the perceptual processes in the human organism. But whereas hitherto man had mechanically split up the cosmic energy into spiritual "God" and physical "ether" and then was unable to reach either, functional thinking discovered the cosmic orgone energy and was able to handle the concepts *practically*. And the same factor that throughout the centuries had prevented the discovery of orgone energy, of orgastic potency, of "what it is like to be a child"—man's armoring—now was at the basis of the tremendous fear and hatred of orgonomy.

With his delusionary system now in full bloom, Reich set about to observe the orgone energy closely, to gather, measure, and put it to use. He began, therefore, to build the orgone accumulator, in which the orgones would, naturally, accumulate and reach higher-than-normal intensities.

Early in 1941, Reich began to treat patients suffering from cancer with the orgone accumulator. He saw fifteen cases in all and claimed that the use of the accumulator caused cancerous tumors to disappear. He had now, he believed, discovered a widespread "biopathy" that might result in a cancer but could make its appearance equally as "an angina pectoris, an asthma, a cardiovascular hypertension, an epilepsy, a catatonic or paranoid schizophrenia, an anxiety neurosis, a multiple sclerosis . . . chronic alcoholism," and so on into the pathogenic night. What he saw in all these afflictions was what he had been seeing all his life, *"the pestilence of the sexual disturbances. "Cancer,"* he declared, *"is living putrefaction of the tissues due to the pleasure starvation of the organism,"* as in their own ways are all the other ailments included in his encyclopedic "biopathy." The orgone accumulator was intended to serve—if not save—mankind by acting as a preventive measure or device against the development of such malignant conditions.

In the meantime, Reich continued with his orgone therapy, and Sharaf has both the honesty and the courage (as well as the knowledge) to observe that Reich "never made clear publicly, though he sometimes did privately, that very few patients actually achieved orgastic potency." His degree of therapeutic success seems to have been even dimmer than that achieved by orthodox psychoanalysis, if such a thought is permissible. It is perhaps worthwhile, in this connection of unacknowledged failure, to note another involutional change in Reich's character that became visible at about this time (the mid-to-late 1940s). The former communist and social revolutionary had turned against the "masses," and in *Listen, Little Man* (1948), he wrote a jeremiad against the "average man," and in a tone, though not a style, that reminds one of D. H. Lawrence at his most shrill, he accused the "little man" of not being able to give, of only being able to hold back and take, and of causing the whole world to suffer from what he called "the emotional plague." He also had begun—again, like the later Lawrence—to identify himself with Jesus Christ.

In 1950 Reich pulled up stakes in Forest Hills and moved permanently to Rangeley, Maine, where he established his own little kingdom of 280 acres that he named Orgonon. During his early years in America he had many patients but few colleagues, apart from the always devoted Wolfe. After World War II, however, Reich began to gather about him more colleagues from the medical and psychiatric worlds, as well as from elsewhere. Sharaf gives a full account of all of them and then wonders in a revealing statement why the work of all these people has come to almost nothing. "It says something," he writes, "about the lack of creativity or the blocks to independent productivity among the physicians who studied with Reich that only a few of them were able to write about and teach orgonomy after Reich's death." The only possibility that Sharaf leaves unnoticed is that this nullity may have something to do with the hopeless vacuity of the larger theory itself, if not of each of its specific components. It is further worth noting that Sharaf is unable to recognize this possibility. This period after World War II was also the time of Reich's widest vogue in the intellectual and cultural worlds. William Steig, best known for his cartoons for the *New Yorker,* was a patient and generous supporter. Paul Goodman and Saul Bellow had been in therapy with students of Reich. Isaac Rosenfeld and Norman Mailer were also touched rather strongly by what they found in Reich's writings, principally, of course, in *The Function of the Orgasm.* and here and there one ran into other people who were in Reichian therapy. If I may introduce a personal recollection, I remember from the 1950s a conversation with a professional acquaintance of mine who, I thought, got particular pleasure in telling me detailed stories about his sex life. He was currently having an affair with a woman he had known long ago in high school and had recently met again. She wanted to be a musician and was working as a waitress to support herself. She was also in therapy with a Reichian. She lived in a small apartment in Washington Heights, and my acquaintance described it as being furnished with only three objects of significance: a bed, an orgone box, and a piano. Their relation apparently consisted in moving serially among these objects throughout the night. My interlocutor had sat in the orgone box but had no report on how or whether it affected him. It was all rather serious, slightly furtive, and a bit absurd at the same time; it still seems to me an anecdote that preserves or illustrates something of the atmosphere of the period following the war. For all his notoriety in the literary culture, however, Reich was never able to build up much of a following or create an organization in any sense of the word. He was much too authoritarian, labile, demanding, and emotionally uncontrolled to be the leader of a real group of colleagues and coworkers, to be primus inter pares among them.

Nevertheless, even as patients and followers came and went, Reich found plenty to keep himself busy. The exploding of the atomic bombs and the subsequent development of nuclear science had set off a great wave of inner agitation in him. He was determined to find some way of enlisting orgone energy to counteract or neutralize atomic energy, nuclear radiation, and the virulent fallout from the bombs. To this end he began to conduct experiments at Orgonon with radioactive material and orgone energy. The results, he reported, were catastrophic. When orgone energy came into contact with nuclear radiation, the orgone was altered by it and turned into DOR (Deadly Orgone) or Oranur. Mice died, the experimenters all got sick in one way or another, and the experiments had to be terminated. It was the discovery, Reich believed, of a planetary crisis: an entirely benign cosmic and orga-nismic energy could be transformed into something lethal. It was most strik-ing, he observed in a remark of whose meaning, I believe, he was only partly conscious, "that a healthy person, when fighting evil, might himself change and develop the same characteristics he was fighting against."

Shortly thereafter, Reich became concerned with another new develop-ment. The atmosphere itself was changing. He saw "stillness" and "bleak-ness" fall over the once sparkling Maine landscape. In particular, he noted the increased presence of "DOR-clouds," black and bleak, even in the midst of sunshine. It was all very much like John Ruskin, who in 1884 delivered his great lecture, "The Storm Cloud of the Nineteenth Century," a set of salient observations on changes in the atmospheric conditions of Britain and Europe brought about by industrialization; an analogous set of speculations upon how these outer changes were expressions of general inward spiritual deteri-oration, corruption, and deadening in modern society; and a third series of remarks that are distinct intimations of the psychosis that was soon to over-take him. Reich's DOR-clouds also look forward to what was to become a wide public concern with atmospheric pollution and smog. But for Reich himself the clouds were made up of Deadly Orgone, and so he set about to do something about the matter. He invented a machine that he called a "cloud-buster," which, he claimed, could either concentrate or disperse atmospher-ic energy. The machine consisted of pipes and cables, and he asserted that he could either make rain with it or disperse the deadly clouds. So in addition to everything else, Reich became a rainmaker, shaman, and witch doctor. Yet, Sharaf remarks, this last major "intellectual" preoccupation of Reich's life—his concern with orgone energy, DOR, and cloud-busting—only fulfills "the symphonic structure of his work." This had "as its basic themes the liberation of life energy in man and the harnessing of atmospheric orgone energy to help man." Indeed.

At the same time, this new phase of interest was marked, as usual, with "a burst of destructive rage in Reich's personal life." Reich still identified with his violent bully of a father; as Sharaf remarks, half-truthfully, half-wishfully, "Reich remained locked in repetitions of his past, even as he transcended them in his ever grander work." This alleged work was never brought to fruition because it was about to be stopped. And here, in the last years of his life, a very sad and rather disgraceful drama began to be played out. It seems to have actually begun when, in May 1947, the *New Republic* ran an article that attacked Reich in general and insinuated that he was both a swindler and a megalomaniac. This article quickly came into the hands of the Food and Drug Administration, which began to focus its attention on what soon became known as the "Reich problem." By the early 1950s, the FDA, aided and abetted by the official American organizations of both psychiatrists and psychoanalysts, was ready to move against Reich. It all makes for fairly painful reading. Here was this aging and essentially harmless loony being treated by official establishment institutions as if he were some kind of public menace (in the early 1950s orgone accumulators probably caused less harm and suffering than the measures that were then in accepted use for treating cancer). As the FDA agents began to descend on Orgonon, Reich responded by turning up the gas under the pressure cooker of his own psychosis. The agents themselves he called, among other things, "Higs," an acronym for "Hoodlums in government." He developed an elaborate array of fantasies; among them were the conviction that President Eisenhower was a secret friend of his; that the U.S. Air Force was sending planes over Maine to protect Reich; that flying saucers, powered by orgone energy and piloted by cosmic orgone engineers, were also about to make friendly contact with him and help his cause. (It was at about this time that Reich confided to Ilse Ollendorf Reich, who was then his wife, that he was the offspring of his mother and a man from outer space.)

The blow finally fell in February 1954 when, at the request of the FDA, the United States attorney for the state of Maine filed a complaint for an injunction against Reich and all his work. Reich responded by refusing to appear in court. Instead he sent the court a written document entitled "Response." That document contained such lulus as the following:

> To appear in court as a *defendant* in matters of basic natural research would in itself appear, to say the least, extraordinary. It would require disclosure of evidence in support of the position of the discovery of the Life Energy. Such disclosure, however, would involve untold complications and *possibly national disaster.*

Undeterred by this incontestable lunacy, the court and the FDA pushed ahead, and an injunction was issued: all orgone accumulators and all of Reich's in-stock soft-cover publications were ordered to be destroyed; his hardcover books were ordered withheld from further distribution. Officials of the American Psychiatric Association and the American Psychoanalytic Association wrote letters of commendation to the FDA for its "effective action" against

Reich. But the government was not done with him yet. Because he had failed to appear in court, Reich was now going to be tried for contempt. Reich decided to become his own lawyer and was tried in federal court in Portland for four days in May 1956. (The faithful Sharaf was there for three of the four days, taking notes all the time.) He was of course convicted and sentenced to two years' imprisonment.

Quite evidently almost entirely gone by now, Reich was only confirmed by all these measures in his belief in a worldwide "Red-Fascist" conspiracy that was acting against him. He appealed his conviction, but to no avail. The Portland *Evening Express* for March 11. 1957, reported Reich's words in court as follows:

> He pleaded against being imprisoned, saying that if the sentence were carried out, it inevitably would deprive the U.S. and the world at large of his equations on space and negative gravity.
>
> These equations he said . . . are carried only in my head, known to no one on this planet. This knowledge will go down with me, maybe for millennia, should mankind survive the present planetary DOR emergency.
>
> It would mean certain death in prison of a scientific pioneer at the hands of psychopathic persons who acted in the service of treason against mankind in a severe planetary emergency.

On March 12, Reich entered prison. It was a shameful business, as was the earlier destruction of all the orgone accumulators the FDA could find and the burning of tons of Reich's publications. On the morning of November 3, 1957, Reich was found dead in his prison cell. He had died of a heart attack during his sleep. Three parts crazy as he was, he had during these last bitter years behaved with greater dignity and decency than those who were opposed to him.

Sharaf has contrived to tell this long and complicated story with great clarity, honesty, tact, and sympathy despite the formidable difficulties that such an undertaking entailed, not the least of which, as I have said, consists of his own profound involvement in it. It is this involvement, and what it suggests, that is the matter of our final consideration. To begin with, Sharaf does not have a particularly high opinion of Reich as a therapist, and for very good reasons. Reich's own self-knowledge and self-control were clearly inadequate to create a sustained therapeutic situation. In addition, he tended always to be more interested in his own work and career than he was in the well-being of his patients or followers. Moreover, although Sharaf acknowledges the interest in Reich's early work on character analysis and defenses and although he is aware that the orthodox psychoanalytic community has long since made such contributions part of its own teachings, he tends to see these as relatively minor achievements. Sharaf remains a true believer and is convinced that Reich's great work is to be found in his discovery of orgone energy and all that flows from it. For example, he writes, "many aspects that Reich was to note about the interaction between orgone energy and nuclear energy continue today in the interaction between orgone energy and diverse forms of pollution." This part of his transference—or perhaps I should say of his deepest experiences—has not been resolved, although he is able to regard it with some apparent measure of dispassionateness as well. He can, for another example, speak in this way about his strongest conviction: Reich's "paradigm," he writes, "with its unification of man and nature and its energetic model of life and death, holds such possibilities that it behooves us to find out how right or wrong it is. . . . we lose more by failing to pursue orgonomic hypotheses with all due speed should they eventually prove to be correct than we do by testing them thoroughly only to find they are worthless." Balanced and rational as this may appear, it is the balance and rationality characteristic of a true believer, who is pleading for a special cause in which he knows that very few others have either interest or credence. (It isn't clear, incidentally, whether or not Sharaf believes in flying saucers.)

Yet it is precisely by virtue of his explicitness in these connections that Sharaf has been able to write such a good book. For although he does not say so, in writing this biography he has also in some highly significant way been writing his own autobiography as well. Most biographies of any value, from at least *The Life of Johnson* onward, contain large components of autobiography in them, whether these elements are covert or spelled out. So profound is the engagement or identification of a good biographer with his subject that in seeking to reconstruct the life of a considerable personage he is at the same time reconstructing his own. In psychoanalysis this entire set of processes has been formally structurized in the phenomena that constitute the transference, and I suggest that no good psychoanalytic biography can be written that is not deliberately open and conscious about this matter and what follows from it. Because Sharaf is open, explicit, and conscious on these scores, because he has been able to write his own transference into this biography, he has succeeded in creating a plausible, interesting, and useful work. He is to be praised both for his achievement and for the courage it took to pursue it in the way that he did.

■
■
■

**Three**
■ ■

**Plagiarism and Parallel Process: Two Maladaptive Forms of Cultural (or Interpersonal) Transmission**

*Ethel Spector Person, M.D.*

William James maintained that the greatest discontinuity in nature was that between two minds. As he put it,

> Each of these minds keeps its own thoughts to itself. There is no giving or bantering between them. No thought even comes into direct *sight* of a thought in another personal consciousness than its own. Absolute insulation, irreducible pluralism, is the law. It seems as if the elementary psychic fact were not *thought* or *this thought* or *that thought,* but *my thought,* every thought being *owned.* Neither contemporaneity, nor proximity in space, nor similarity of quality in content are able to fuse thoughts together which are sundered by this barrier of belonging to different personal minds. The breaches between such thoughts are the most absolute breaches in nature. Everyone will recognize this to be true, so long as the existence of *something* corresponding to the term "personal mind" is all that is insisted on, without any particular view of its nature being implied.' (1952, p. 147)

We all know what James is talking about. Subjective experience tells us that we cannot enter another's mind. Yet this separateness of mind that each of us experiences may not be as absolute as James suggests. The barrier between minds is perhaps both narrower and more porous than he describes. Al-

I would like to acknowledge the helpful suggestions of Dr. Gerald Fogel, who read an earlier draft of this chapter.

though it is true that experiential reality, as a function of a separate brain, is indeed solitary, the "ownership" of content of mind is partly illusory. It is in looking at how the organization of mind is shaped that we begin to see evidence for the porosity of the barriers separating minds from one another.

The major organization of mind occurs within the first five years of life. Tolstoy knew that "from the child of five to myself is but a step" (quoted in Troyat 1980, p. 15) but that, in contrast, the distance from the newborn baby to the child of five was appalling, the distance from the embryo to the infant an abyss. However, this is not to say that change ceases after early childhood.[1] While there are profound conservative tendencies in the adult personality, there are also greater or lesser proclivities to change. Many observe that the personality undergoes continual changes (or at least refining), and some would go so far as to support Emerson in his contention that people may be more like their peers than their progenitors. But the rate of change in the adult is slower than in the child, and the basic structure of the mind is much more stable in the adult.

Yet when theorizing about how psychic organization comes about in the first place in infancy and early childhood and the degree to which organization and content at those early stages depend on an external or environmental input, we are on uncertain ground. Our knowledge of the mind once structuralization has been achieved is further along than our knowledge about the process of structuralization itself. We have been able to advance psychoanalytic propositions of considerable power and persuasiveness concerning intrapsychic conflict as it appears in the already structured personality. But insofar as we focus on intrapsychic transactions within a structured personality, we are dealing with a relatively closed system and a comparatively static one, the major formative influences having taken place before the mind ever became an object of our scrutiny.

Granted that the primary emphasis in the psychoanalytic approach to the mind has been on the already structured personality (particularly on intrapsychic conflict), there still has always been a subtext concerned with the problem of understanding how structuralization comes about. Libido theory has emphasized the biologically preordained dispositions of development; contemporary theory also focuses on structuralization as a result of the individual's involvement with others and recognizes that such involvements can result in significant change, even relatively late in life.

Cultural transmission (and structuralization) depends not only upon learn-

1. Many lay people believe that analysts deny the possibility of significant change after the age of five. This is obviously untrue. If it were, only charlatans could engage in the practice of psychoanalysis.

ing but also upon the individual's internalization of the external world through imitation and identification. Increasingly, object relations theory has taken on more prominence in psychoanalysis in order to theorize the way real experience shapes the self. In general, interpersonal relationships (and object relations) can be described in two modes: complementary and identificatory.

Complementary interactions refer to reciprocal behaviors—for example, one person soothes or gratifies another who, in turn, is soothed or gratified. In development, it is obviously crucial that the infant and young child be provided with sufficient nurturance and need-gratification to allow for the consolidation of basic trust and core relatedness—in essence, that the infant be provided an environment that allows the personality to develop and unfold.

In contrast, in the identificatory mode, one person comes to resemble the other, taking on his mannerisms, behaviors, attitudes, and moods. In this way, the individual's identity comes to be shaped in conformity with the identity of a significant other. Identification is based on an innate capacity for imitation and mirroring. To imitate means to behave like someone else, and it is a fundamental means of learning. But as Schafer (1968) has pointed out, identification is a broader term than imitation. Imitation may be fleeting, may not involve any significant identification, and need not reflect the wishes or beliefs of the object of imitation; in contrast, identification presupposes some mechanism for either the experiential perception or inference of another's inner feeling and motivational state. In other words, the capacity for knowing something of the internal life of another individual appears to be a prerequisite for complex forms of identification. Sometimes, of course, particularly early in life but also throughout the life cycle, a single relationship comprises both the complementary and identificatory modes.

There may well be a third mode of interaction: an emotional contagion between people. Heinz Lichtenstein (1977) alluded to this form when he spoke of the emotional imprinting of a child by its mother (in which case contagion might be viewed as a precursor of identification). Emotional contagion may play a greater role in early development than psychoanalysts have previously acknowledged, and it may have an ongoing role in adult life.

In order to better elucidate the theme of cultural transmission, I present two maladaptive examples: unconscious plagiarism and parallel process. Both involve a certain mental content (thought or feeling) in one mind that now appears in a second, where it is experienced as having been spontaneously generated, originating there, and not borrowed, stolen, caught (in the sense of contagion), introjected, incorporated, or received from another mind. In unconscious plagiarism, the transferred content is cognitive or artistic: an idea, a phrase, a melody. In parallel process, the transferred content is sometimes a piece of behavior, more often a specific emotion. In unconscious plagiarism one has appropriated a product; in parallel process, one has appropriated a feeling—perhaps even a part of another's self.

A discussion of plagiarism leads to a consideration of the ubiquity of imitation in mental life; a discussion of parallel process, to a consideration of the ubiquity of emotional contagion in mental life. Plagiarism and parallel process appear as distortions of the normal processes of, respectively, imitative learning and intersubjective communication.

## UNCONSCIOUS PLAGIARISM

Unconscious plagiarism is easier to grasp and discuss than parallel process because the transferred material is essentially cognitive rather than emotional or affective. Unconscious plagiarism is a conflictual version of the basic human capacity for unconscious imitation and learning.

In a study of hypnosis, F. J. Evans (1979) found that posthypnotic subjects were able to recall specific information learned during hypnosis but remained unaware of how they had acquired the knowledge. Evans calls this phenomenon *source amnesia* and notes that it is clearly involved in those incidents in which songwriters, novelists, and scientists discover too late that their current endeavor has already been carried out by someone else and was previously known to them but forgotten. I believe that this phenomenon is descriptively true of most of what we learn through imitation. Some kind of imitative capacity is closely linked to many of the ordinary processes of learning. We do not remember how we came by most information or skills; these are retrievable, but not the context in which they were acquired. The particular thing learned or imitated is judged to be important. How it was acquired may or may not be.

Minor and often unconscious borrowing and imitation are probably built into o·'r intellectual apparatus.[2] The transmission of that most elusive of

2. A chilling example of our propensity for imitation was recorded in an interview with Dr. Geschwind, who is a professor of neurology (Miller, 1983): "Several years ago, I saw a patient who had had surgery carried out on his corpus callosum. Splitting of the structure is sometimes carried out on patients who have severe, widespread, and uncontrollable epileptic seizures. Exactly why this works is not altogether clear, but it does work in many patients. The patient whom I saw had undergone this operation and thus the two sides of his brain were disconnected. There was, however, a surprising finding. If you asked him to do something with either his right or his left hand, he would carry out the command. That he successfully carried out verbal commands with the right hand presented no problem, but the successful performance with the left hand was perplexing. Let me explain why. Since the left side of the brain, which is the speech side, was intact in this patient, and since the left side of the brain usually controls the right hand, it

phenomena, a particular cultural sensibility, depends on mechanisms of un-conscious borrowing, imitation, and contagion. Language itself can be seen to evolve as metaphors are borrowed and sequentially modified until they become part of the common tongue. The particular metaphor favored at a given time reveals the cultural sensibility of a period. The first year Ronald Reagan was elected president, it suddenly became popular to use the term "hit the ground running" to indicate a fast start. The military connotation had meaning insofar as it reflected the shared conservative belief that it was time to take an active and even a military stance in the world. Nixon's presidency yields another example. The substitution of "at this point in time" for "now" and "on a daily basis" for "every day" made "bureaucratization" of the language, if not fashionable, at least acceptable and common. This kind of minor unconscious borrowing or imitation is responsible for the diffusion of clothing styles, taste in music, and so forth. Without unconscious borrowing, no fads would ever develop. It is out of this simple kind of borrowing, learning, imitation, and minor identification that a cultural sensibility is constructed, thus forming the context of what we know to be a cultural fact: expression of "drive" takes different forms in different historical periods and cultural milieus.

Creative borrowing goes one step further; it takes place most readily in the prepared mind. An imaginative and creative friend of mine tells me that if he

---

was no surprise that he responded correctly if you asked him to show how he would throw a ball with his right hand. Movements with the left hand are usually controlled from the right side of the brain. Since the right brain has poor language capacities, one would not expect it to understand a command and, therefore, would not expect it to respond to a command to use the left hand. This is not a problem in the normal, since the left hemisphere will understand the command and will transmit the instruction to the right side of the brain. But since the patient's hemispheres were disconnected, the left hemisphere could not fulfill this function. Why then did he carry out verbal commands with the left hand?

"Some observers had drawn the conclusion that the right hemisphere of the patient did in fact understand the commands, but careful observation showed that his successful performance was based on a completely different mechanism. When I asked the patient to show me how he would salute with the left hand, he would say: 'I know just what you want me to do. You want me to do that with my left hand,' and simultaneously, with the utterance of the last phrase, he first saluted with his right hand and then saluted with his left hand. Obviously, a normal who is asked to salute with the left hand does not usually carry out the movement first with the right hand. A few minutes later, I again asked him to salute with his left hand, but I held his right hand in order to prevent him from carrying out the movement with that hand. As long as I held the right hand, he could not carry out the command with the left hand. When the right hand was released, he saluted with it and only then did he salute with the left. Somehow, this patient's left hemisphere had learned, I suspect unconsciously, that it could signal to his right hemisphere non-verbally and thus get it to carry out some acts. In other words, his left hemisphere was treating his right hemisphere as though the right hemisphere was a foreigner who did not understand English, but who responded correctly to gestures" (pp. 131–32).

is engrossed in an author's work—if he and the author "speak the same language" and are interested in the same problems—he may put down the book in midargument at the end of the day, go to sleep, and dream an ending for the book written in the style of that author. If two people are working on the same problem, a chance remark by one may solve an intellectual problem for the other. Insofar as the chance remark leads to a solution for which the second individual has been searching, he may have the subjective impression of having found the solution completely alone, without any outside input or help, and it is surely true that his solution is genuinely creative. But the spark was unconsciously ignited from an outside source.

Unconscious plagiarism is related to imitation, learning, and creative borrowing, but, as pointed out by Helene Deutsch (1965), differs in three fundamental respects: the source is not casually but purposefully and defensively forgotten; the motive can usually be construed as being envious and/or hostile; and the act is not generally genuinely creative or sublimative.

In unconscious plagiarism, an individual believes that he is the author of an idea or invention that he has, in fact, acquired from someone else. It appears that unconscious conflicts and motives have attached themselves to the general process of unconscious learning and imitation. Deutsch (1965) reported a brief vignette of a patient for whom plagiarism was a central problem. Originally a practitioner, her patient found himself shifted into the theoretical end of his discipline, in which a very good friend of his also worked. According to Deutsch, her patient's "latent homosexual aggressiveness against his friend and his burning envy of him underwent repression . . ." and he "now discovered the following complicated method of defense. Through identification on the one hand and aggressive taking away on the other, he appropriated the thoughts of his friend" (p. 252). He had known of his friend's work through publications and private discussions. In order to deny his unconscious plagiarism, he forgot all the prior information and published his friend's ideas as his own. It was not just single thoughts he unconsciously plagiarized; his major creative effort was pieced together from his friend's ideas. Deutsch suggests that such a disruption of mental retentiveness has the same structure as a parapraxis, like forgetting a word.

Yet there is more to unconscious plagiarism than this; by and large the plagiarist is ambitious and narcissistic and consciously or unconsciously can justify his plagiarism on the basis of a feeling of entitlement. In a case from my practice, the fear of unconscious plagiarism (at first reported as an incidental and minor preoccupation) was linked to a series of fragments of conscious fantasies and to a central unconscious one. The patient, an ambitious academic in her early thirties, was modestly successful but somewhat inhibited in her professional activities. She had entered treatment for another reason altogether, but in the course of treatment her longstanding fears of plagiarism emerged, her obsessive preoccupation having been triggered by her discovery of a plagiarized phrase in one of her essays. Each time one of her articles appeared, she sporadically obsessed over the fear that again she would discover she had unknowingly stolen an idea or phrase from someone else's essay, and she dreaded discovery. She was also very proprietary about her own work, frequently suspicious that she herself was being plagiarized by others. Extremely competitive with her peers, particularly women, her admiration of them was generally mixed with envy. It will come as no surprise that she coveted married men and suspected other women of having designs on her own husband. Far into the treatment, she revealed that she sometimes soothed herself to sleep by planning imagined wardrobes for herself, to be composed of items belonging to women she knew, admired, and liked, but of whom she was simultaneously envious. She allowed herself to "confiscate" ten items of clothing belonging to each woman. Even later in the treatment, she revealed what she experienced as a shameful and primitive fantasy: her intestinal tract was inhabited by miniature humans whose meals had to be chosen from the foods she had eaten over the past three days. She was obsessed about what she ate in order to make sure she was providing enough variety for the miniature intestinal creatures. (These creatures were in part unintegrated little "selves," in part derivatives of pregnancy fantasies, but the fantasy was largely an attempted magic resolution of her conflict about desiring a symbiotic relationship and recoiling from it: here, though invaded, she controlled the creatures' sustenance.) Cannibalistic preoccupation and fear of being devoured were unconscious themes that emerged only late in treatment, both in the form of dreams and in transferential fears. Stealing (plagiarism) was related to an early oral preoccupation, to a desire for and a fear of a symbiotic mother, and to pronounced Oedipal jealousy, though the Oedipal material was melded to oral aggressive derivatives.

The patient's earliest life had been lived in tandem with a mother who regarded the patient as special, but she was intrusive and insensitive to the child's actual needs, all the time expecting the patient to grow up to be the successful woman she believed she herself, given the opportunity, would have become. In part, the plagiarism represented an identification with her mother, who had superego lacunae of her own, including a tendency to tell "white" lies and commit other small acts of dishonesty. More important, the plagiarism was emblematic of a major aspect of the patient's core pathology: her feeling of being robbed of her autonomy (gratified only through her submission to her mother and her tacit agreement to live vicariously for her mother) and her reciprocal fantasy of getting her due through entitlement to that which belonged to another. Nonetheless, her unconscious plagiarism perpetuated her symbiotic dependency wishes and prevented her from enjoying the authentically creative aspects of her work.

Perhaps the major difference between imitation and borrowing, on the one hand, and unconscious plagiarism, on the other, is this: in imitation, we forget the source because the source is unimportant; in unconscious plagiarism, we forget the source precisely because it is important. But the borderline between the two is sometimes hard to draw. The flux between creative imitation, borrowing, and unconscious plagiarism are pointed out and well illustrated in Phyllis Greenacre's (1978) account of some aspects of Robert Louis Stevenson's creative life. Stevenson taught himself to write by consciously imitating the style of other writers (a common exercise among writers). He acknowledged conscious borrowing, with modifications, of characters from other works of fiction to use in his own work. As with so many other authors, he felt free to draw inspiration from—or borrow—other writers' devices. But on at least one occasion, he borrowed more than he had suspected. Greenacre tells of Stevenson's experience with *Treasure Island,* recounted in his preface to the book. He knew that the parrot was Robinson Crusoe's, the skeleton Poe's. But when he picked up a copy of Washington Irving's *Tales of a Traveler* with a view to anthologizing it, he was suddenly struck with the knowledge that "the whole inner spirit and a good deal of the material detail of my first chapters . . . all these were there . . . all were the property of Washington Irving" (quoted in Greenacre 1978, p. 531). Yet Stevenson had written *Treasure Island* with the subjective certainty that it was entirely his own inspiration. Such stories are not at all unusual. In a recent *New York Times* article, Garson Kanin declared his ignorance of any similarity in theme between his *Born Yesterday* and Shaw's *Pygmalion* until it was pointed out by reviewers.

As Greenacre suggests, preoccupation with plagiarism is common in groups with creative aspirations; suspicions of plagiarism and fears of one's own unconscious or conscious plagiarism are frequently found together. A good example of this dual preoccupation may be found in Sabina Spielrein's journal entries relating to her intellectual aspirations and her passionate friendship with Jung.

> 26 November 1910: ". . . Yes, the first goal I want to reach is that my dissertation may be so good that it will assure me of a place in the Psychoanalytic Society. Much more important to me is my second study, 'On the Death Instinct,' and there I must admit that I greatly fear that my friend, who planned to mention my idea in his article in July, saying that I have rights of priority, may simply borrow

the whole development of the idea, because he now wants to refer to it as early as January. Is this another case of unfounded distrust on my part? I wish so fervently that might be so for my second study will be dedicated to my most esteemed teacher, etc. How could I esteem a person who lied, who stole my ideas, who was not my friend but a petty, scheming rival? And love him? I do love him, after all. My work ought to be permeated with love! I love him and hate him, because he is not mine. It would be unbearable for me to appear a silly goose in his eyes. No, noble, proud, respected by all! I must be worthy of him, and the idea I gave birth to should also appear under my name." (Quoted in Carotenuto 1984, p. 35)

8 December 1910: "My first goal is to do well on my examination. Especially— plagiarize well! Ugh! for shame! My friend said in parting that I will write an excellent exam because at present I am in league with the devil. May that be true." (P. 37)

Such a dual preoccupation ought not to surprise us. Mutual pilfering is quite common in intellectual discourse. More important, plagiarists, of both the conscious and unconscious varieties, have not only the impulse to take what belongs to another but the retaliatory fear either of being plagiarized in turn or of being discovered, exposed, and disgraced.

The mechanisms of imitation alert us to a general mode of intersubjective transfer. Cognitive material is passed from mind to mind, but this is only possible because the same potential for cognitive processing exists in different minds. The second mind is, by its nature, able to recognize, process, and utilize the cognitive material. In source amnesia, "forgetting" the context in which learning took place occurs because the context is inessential. This mechanism, however, secondarily helps to maintain the illusion of the complete separation of mind and to downplay intellectual indebtedness. (And, of course, this mechanism is more prominent in cultures such as our own that value radical individuality and originality.)

In imitation, the original source is an inspiration to thinking and may or may not be acknowledged; in plagiarism the source substitutes, at least to some degree, for original thinking and is denied. Imitation and borrowing are necessary components of the creative process, but plagiarism serves conflicting and defensive ends.

## PARALLEL PROCESS

Although plagiarism and parallel process are alike in certain formal ways— that which is in one mind is subsequently claimed by another as its own—

there are also significant differences. First, plagiarism is generally viewed as active, while in parallel process one sees the therapist as having been "infested" with a foreign body. This view is related to the fact that the benefit in plagiarism is clear, whereas any comparable purpose in parallel process is obscure. However, the difference between active and passive, between stealing and contagion, may be in the eye of the beholder. The second and major difference is that what is reproduced in parallel process is not another person's cognitive product but part of his behavioral and affective life. My tack is to present the major psychoanalytic formulations of parallel process as they apply to the supervisory process. However, parallel process ought to be viewed in a broader context; it is a window through which to explore aspects of intersubjectivity, affect transmission, and the internalization of a dyadic object relationship.

What we call parallel process was first described by H. F. Searles in 1955, although he called it *mirroring* (reported by Caligor 1981). Searles observed that the supervisor experiencing a particular emotion during the supervisory hour ought to be alert to the possibility that this was due not to a classic countertransference reaction but was a *"reflection* of something which had been going on in the therapist-patient relationship and, in the final analysis, in the patient" (1955, p. 136). Searles presented examples of how the therapist identified with his patient and enacted the role of the patient in supervision. Both the patient's enactment and the therapist's own reenactment took place outside the consciousness of the therapist. Having intuited and identified this extraordinary yet common phenomenon, Searles apparently used his observation primarily to facilitate supervision, not dwelling on its underlying mechanism, though he believed the mechanism might have relevance to "human relationships in general" (p. 146).

Most clinicians have followed Searles in this insight into parallel process without examining the phenomenon for its larger implications. Parallel process has been regarded as the repetition between therapist and supervisor of an interaction that had previously taken place between the therapist and his or her patient. As such, parallel process is viewed predominantly as a disruptive phenomenon except insofar as it provides an explanation for a particular difficulty that arises between therapist and supervisor; there may be some benefit insofar as parallel process is revelatory of a previously unnoted reaction of the patient in therapy. Unfortunately, the focus on the largely negative impact of parallel process appears to have inhibited any extensive investigation into parallel process as a phenomenon itself in urgent need of explanation. Only gradually have analysts come to focus on the rather amazing mimicry in parallel process and the implications for its role in interpersonal relationships and internalization.

R. Ekstein and R. S. Wallerstein (1972) propose that the enactment or mirroring seen in parallel process may go in two directions: "The development of the professional self of the student depends on his specific and unique ways of seeking help and of helping—two faces of the same coin that have a definite functional relationship to one another" (p. 178). Further, "it is as though we work with a constant 'metaphor' in which the patient's problem in psychotherapy may be used to express the therapist's problem in supervision—or vice versa" (p. 180).[3] In essence, then, they suggest that parallel process can occur in the therapist's response to the patient in a mirroring of the supervisor's response to the therapist, and not just the other way around.

Many of the questions Eckstein and Wallerstein raise pertain to the essential riddle of the meaning of parallel process and our continuing reluctance to understand it. The authors point to therapists' and supervisors' strong belief that parallel process is atypical, an aberration rather than the rule. "This *parallel process* carries with it a never-ending surprise element as if we should not expect things to turn out as they usually do, as if the occurrence of such parallels is chance rather than the rule. The surprise, we believe, depends on the teacher's perhaps irrational expectation that the teaching and learning of psychotherapy should consist primarily of rational elements" (p. 177). By recognizing parallel process as a normal part of the experience, not as a problem inherent in a particular therapist, Ekstein and Wallerstein urge us to attempt an understanding of the phenomenon, not simply to make use of it in supervision. I agree with Ekstein and Wallerstein that parallel process does *surprise* us by being the rule rather than the exception. But by attributing our surprise to the expectation that supervision is rational, they gloss over the underlying nature (or meaning) of parallel process.

To the best of my knowledge, J. A. Arlow (1963) was the first to attempt to introduce a psychodynamic explanation for parallel process, and he proposed what might be considered the classic explanation to date. He reported on several instances in which a therapist in supervision with him enacted something that had previously been enacted by the therapist's patient in the treatment situation. He felt that these examples demonstrated in a clear-cut fashion how, during the supervisory session, the therapist, in presenting the material, unconsciously shifted his role from reporting the data of his experi-

---

3. If I read Ekstein and Wallerstein correctly, they identify the therapist as the pivotal figure and suggest that he will play out different roles of his central conflict or governing metaphor depending upon "the differing relationships assumed toward the hierarchical structuring upward (being supervised) and downward (doing therapy)" (p. 182).

ence with the patient to experiencing the experience of the patient. That is to say, during the supervisory session, one could see evidence of a "transient identification of the student with his patient" (pp. 578–79). Arlow believed that the identification derived from a "community of resistance of defense mechanisms" between therapist and patient or from a community of shared fantasy wishes.

In contrast to Ekstein and Wallerstein, Arlow shifted the focus from the dynamic involving the therapist's own feeling about teaching and learning to a more general question, that of the transmission by the therapist through his own behavior of a communication from the patient. He draws an analogy between empathy in the therapy situation (which he suggests is based on a transient identification with the patient) and parallel process in the supervisory situation (which he also sees as resting on a transient identification of the therapist with the patient—one that surfaces during the supervisory session). Arlow suggests that the therapist may borrow either a defensive pattern of acting out or some wish-fulfilling fantasy from the patient. He also suggests that if one looks closely at what the therapist is reporting when he enacts an episode of parallel process, it turns out to be material that required him to make an interpretation, which he failed to do. As Arlow puts it, "there are two aspects of the process of empathy—the id aspect, and the ego aspect" (p. 585). In essence, he argues that parallel process represents a form of aborted empathy. The therapist has identified with the patient but cannot make the necessary interpretation because he has lost his observing ego due to overidentification with the patient. Not a symptom of countertransference, according to Arlow, this identification is based on a preexisting correspondence between a characteristic of the patient and one of the therapist. The therapist is unaware of the characteristic in the patient because he shares it. To this degree, Arlow does conflate countertransference or a blind spot with parallel process. Even so, we are still left with the question of why this should not just emerge as a blind spot but must perforce be acted out.

D. M. Sachs and S. H. Shapiro (1976) extend Arlow's consideration of parallelism as a form of impotent empathy. They compare the similarities and differences between the dynamics of transference in the treatment situation with parallel process in the three-tiered patient-therapist-supervisor interaction.

As they point out, the theoretical basis for understanding transference may be found in Freud's observation (1914) about the complementary relationship between repeating and remembering: "We may see that the patient does not *remember* anything of what he has forgotten and repressed, but *acts* it out. He reproduces it not as a memory but as an action" (Freud, p. 150).

Transference is understood to represent a piece of the patient's past emotional experience carried forward in the present and directed at objects in the present (the transference objects) who are stand-ins for the original objects of these emotions. Consequently, transference "provides the analyst with a dramatic portrayal of the patient's past" (Sachs and Shapiro 1976, p. 405).

Parallel process is a different kind of remembering, and it too has a complementary relationship with repeating. Sachs and Shapiro refer to Hans Loewald's discussion (1973, unpublished) in which he distinguished between two forms of remembering, what he called the *enactive* and the *representational.* Representational refers simply to verbal remembering. In contrast, the enactive type of remembering is, as the name suggests, characterized by acting out through a process Loewald has referred to as *identificatory reproduction.* According to Sachs and Shapiro, "Loewald gives the example of a patient who alternated between reporting how his father treated him (representational memory) and acting toward the doctor the way his father treated him (identificatory reproduction)." As they correctly point out, Loewald's contribution enlarges Freud's concept of remembering by repeating. In the more familiar mode of transference, the analyst becomes the stand-in for the original object (in Loewald's example, the father); in identificatory reproduction, the patient himself takes on the behavior and attitudes of his infantile object (in this example, his father) and treats the analyst as his own (the patient's) infantile self. (Although identificatory reproduction is one form of transference, in this context I am going to use the term *transference* as distinct from *identificatory reproduction.*) In transference, one transfers one's feelings and wishes from one object to another; in identificatory reproduction, one incorporates the perceived or inferred feelings and motives of an object into oneself. Parallel process can be described as a form of identificatory reproduction with this difference: it reproduces something from the present, not from the past (as is the case with Loewald's example). With parallel process, it is as though we are witness to some form of internalization taking place before our very eyes.

Sachs and Shapiro noted several kinds of "remembering by repeating" in their supervisory group, but by far the most common could be classified as identificatory reproduction. In other words, they found that parallel process was more prominent than transference in the supervisory situation. By linking parallel process to identificatory reproduction, they accurately describe what transpired. They do not, however, address the question of the mechanism and the motive for identificatory reproduction in parallel process (and in life).

Transference and parallel process have in common the fact that both are enacted in a state of unawareness, but they differ greatly in what they reveal about modes of interpersonal interactions. In transference, we see how the past profoundly influences the present and how significant memories and predispositions are enacted in the present with the patient maintaining his own role in the reenacted drama. In transference, the emphasis is on what the monadic mind (already structuralized) brings to an interpersonal encounter in the present.

In contrast, parallel process illuminates the contemporaneous change that occurs in one mind upon exposure to another mind. Parallel process, as described in the literature on supervision, appears to have the potential for "demonstrating" if not "explaining" emotional contagion. If one looks at the therapist's responses, countertransference represents a complementary response, while parallel process is a duplication of the patient's response—not a reciprocal response but a cloned one. This is similar to Racker's distinction between two kinds of countertransference: concordant and complementary. In a sense, transference (in the narrow definition) confirms a paradigm of mind as discontinuous with other minds, whereas parallel process suggests both a historical and a contemporary contagion from one mind to another, a channel through William James's breach mentioned earlier. The question is how to understand such a transfer of state of mind.

To understand parallel process one must try to grasp the conditions prerequisite to its occurrence. Sachs and Shapiro suggest that "the therapist's narcissistic vulnerability may lead to an identification with the patient as aggressor." Although they believe that identification with the aggressor is one kind of identification that leads to enactment (parallelism) rather than verbal reproduction, they do not specify what other mechanisms or motives for parallelism may exist. I believe that the different mechanisms Schafer describes in respect to hostile introjects may well inform parallel process as well. These include masochism—wishing to destroy the bad object by cannibalistic incorporation and then fantasizing deserved punishment by the vengeful incorporated object—but many others as well (Schafer, p. 114), not all of them with negative connotations.

Although most analysts would concur that transference in its most intensely developed form is seen in the treatment situation, I think many would also agree that transferencelike reactions are common in life and determine relationships in the real world. In fact, the brilliance of the concept of transference is that it is so useful in conceptualizing many disparate phenomena: hero worship, religion, and so on. The question is whether parallel process has the same potential for enactment in the extrasupervisory situation. It would be odd indeed, to discover that, in contrast to transference, parallel process was a psychic phenomenon that found expression only in the supervisory experience!

I suspect that phenomena akin to parallel process take place in everyday life with great regularity, not just in the patient-therapist-supervisor triad, although the original recognition of the phenomenon was made in that context. I am suggesting that manifestations of contagion, parallel process, or simply mirroring are probably as widespread as those of transference, but we have not yet begun to look for them systematically. Parallel process clearly belongs to the family of identificatory reproductions. M. G. Dorman's (1976) example of identificatory reproduction portrays a patient speaking in the voice of his father. I find this a telling example, given that it is something commonly reported by patients: those frequent occasions of horrified insight when a patient discovers that he or she speaks in the voice of the parent. (This is surely the complaint of many a female patient devastated upon hearing herself addressing her own child in the manner—and with the voice—of her own mother.) Identificatory reproduction can be usefully viewed as a ubiquitous/universal process in human (intrapsychic and interpersonal) affairs, though it has been studied primarily in the context of the analytic situation.

Parallel process appears to be a very specific form of intrapsychic modification, one based on emotional contagion and identificatory reproduction. It is an unconscious communication in which one person takes on affective and behavioral characteristics (and possibly the motivational states) of the other (or, as Arlow would have it, an already preexisting defense or wish, similar to the patient's, is released through some kind of resonance). In parallel process, as observed in supervision, there is an opportunity to examine identificatory reproduction. The supervisor must try to ascertain whether or not the mimicked behavior on the part of the therapist is restricted to the supervisory sessions—or, for example, whether it infuses the therapist's personal analysis as well, or any interaction other than that of supervision. Whether or not the response is as specific as has been assumed will be a clue in understanding its motive and mechanism. Psychoanalysts must also try to verify Arlow's contention that there is a preexisting community of defenses or wishes. Indeed, the motives in parallel process may be more complex than have yet been discovered. The possibility for multiple function—adaptation as well as maladaptation—of these mechanisms in the service of personal and/or cultural growth rather than just as "substitutes" for mature psychic structure or creative synthesis must be considered.

Just as imitation can only occur because the same potential for cognitive processing occurs in different minds, identificatory reproduction can occur only because all people have the same potential to experience a range of emotions and motivations. It is this similarity that allows for empathy. The unconscious "transfer" of a motivational affective complex can probably occur only because, fundamentally, self-representations and object representations often overlap—hence the case in which a person may assume either the masochistic or sadistic role with equal facility. Such a fluctuation (as in sadomasochistic relationships) suggests that the internal representation of an object relationship sometimes takes place in such a way that either role may become attached, however briefly, to self-representation. One of the puzzles in parallel process and in identificatory reproduction is the time delay—in the latter case sometimes a matter of years—between an experience and its enactment in the identificatory mode.

## DISCUSSION

Although plagiarism and parallel process may be examples of maladaptive behaviors, they are nonetheless valuable for what they tell us about the human's ongoing capacity to utilize the external world in order to effect internal modifications. There is relative intrapsychic stability later in life, but just as there is a channel for cognitive transaction, so too is there a channel for emotional contagion and transformation that allows for continuing change. Such a mechanism is clearly adaptive. The human mind appears to be structured to ensure continuity and stability while still allowing for change. (An analogy to language may be instructive. Although the capacity for mimicry, imitation, and reproduction of specific sounds may be at its height during a relatively early period in life, nonetheless, a second language may still be acquired later on.)

Certain modes of communication similar to parallel process—empathy and love, for example—seem to encompass more than a recognition or reaction to someone else's emotional life. Both empathy and love depend not just on emotional recognition but also on some form of contagion or mirroring and on identification as well. Both are experienced by the participants as magic moments. They may be experienced as magical because they momentarily break down the insulation that we feel surrounds the privacy or the isolation of our individual consciousness or because they appear to have the capacity to transform us. (It may be in these moments that the capacity for intrapsychic change is heightened.) Nonetheless, both empathy and love differ from parallel process in several important ways: they are consciously experienced, and they maintain the distinction between the self and the other, notwithstanding the strong identifications engendered.

Psychoanalysis traditionally focuses on intrapsychic life once structuralization has occurred. What has not yet been formulated is an exhaustive interface theory that speaks to the issue of how the outside world is internalized, both in the first five years of life and as a continuing mode throughout life. Current theories of identification and internalization are incomplete. The transmission of affect and motivation—and what Lichtenstein has called identity imprinting—remains more of a mystery than the transmission of cognitive data. Any understanding of parallel process (and identificatory reproduction) must ultimately rest upon a theory of affect: its transmission, reception, and decoding. In particular, those conditions that lead to a resonant (or parallel) response rather than a complementary one must be explored.

## References

Arlow, J. A. 1963. The supervisory situation. *Journal of the American Psychoanalytic Association* 11 (3):576–94.

Basch, M. 1983. Empathic understanding: A review of the concept of some theoretical considerations. *Journal of the American Psychoanalytic Association* 31:101–26.

Bromberg, P. M. 1982. The supervisory process and parallel process in psychoanalysis. *Contemporary Psychoanalysis* 18:92–111.

Buie, D. H. 1981. Empathy: Its nature and limitations. *Journal of the American Psychoanalytic Association* 29:281–307.

Caligor, L. 1981. Parallel and reciprocal processes in psychoanalytic supervision. *Contemporary Psychoanalysis* 17:1–27.

Carotenuto, A. 1984. *A secret symmetry: Sabina Spielrein between Jung and Freud: The untold story of the woman who changed the early history of psychoanalysis.* Paperback ed. New York: Pantheon Books.

Deutsch, H. 1965. *Neuroses and character types: Clinical psychoanalytic studies.* New York: International Univ. Press.

Dorman, M. G. 1976. Parallel processes in supervision and psychotherapy. *Bulletin of the Menninger Clinic* 40:3–104.

Ekstein, R., and Wallerstein, R. S. 1972. *The teaching and learning of psychotherapy.* Rev. ed., 177–96. New York: International Univ. Press.

Emerson, R. W. [c. 1929]. *Emerson's essays,* with an introduction by Irwin Ednan. New York: Harper Colophon Books.

Evans, F. J. 1979. Contextual forgetting: Posthypnotic source amnesia. *Journal of Abnormal Psychology* 88:556–63.

Freud, S. 1914. Remembering, repeating, and working-through (Further recommendations on the technique of psychoanalysis). *Standard Edition,* 12:147–56. London: Hogarth Press. 1958.

Gediman, H. K., & Wolkenfeld, F. 1980. The parallelism phenomena in supervision: Its reconsideration as a triadic system. *Psychoanalytic Quarterly* 49:234–55.

Greenacre, P. 1978. Notes on plagiarism: The Henley-Stevenson quarrel. *Journal of the American Psychoanalytic Association* 26:507–39.

James, W. 1890. The stream of thought. In *The principles of psychology.* Reprinted in *Great books of the Western world.* Vol. 53, *William James.* Chicago: Encyclopaedia Britannica, 1952.

Lichtenstein, H. 1977. *The dilemma of human identity.* New York: Aronson.

Meissner, W. W. 1971. Notes on identification II: Clarification of related concepts. *Psychoanalytic Quarterly* 40:277–302.

_____. 1972. Notes on identification III: The concept of identification. *Psychoanalytic Quarterly* 41:224–60.

Miller, J. 1983. *States of mind.* New York: Pantheon.

Racker, H. 1972. The meanings and uses of countertransference. *Psychoanalytic Quarterly* 41:487–506.

Sachs, D. M., and Shapiro, S. H. 1976. On parallel processes in therapy and teaching. *Psychoanalytic Quarterly* 45:394–415.

Schafer, R. 1968. *Aspects of internalization.* New York: International Univ. Press.

Searles, H. F. 1955. The informational value of the supervisor's emotional experiences. *Psychiatry* 18:135–46.

Stern, D. M., Barnett, R. K., and Spieker, S. 1983. Early transmission of early affect: Some research issues. In *Frontiers of infant psychiatry,* ed. J. Call, E. Galenson, and R. L. Tyson. New York: Basic Books.

Troyat, H. 1980. *Tolstoy.* Trans. N. Amphoux. New York: Harmony Books.

■ ■ ■
# PART 2　　　DRIVES AND DESIRES

# ■
# ■
# ■

# Introduction
*Arnold M. Cooper, M.D.*

his section on drives and desires addresses one of the core problems of Freud's metapsychology—in fact, one of the core problems for any depth psychology. Put simply, how is behavior initiated and steered? Freud's theories of motivation are complex, shifting, sometimes contradictory, and his clinical data do not always fit neatly into his theoretical propositions. Two ideas are central to his psychoanalytic thinking about motivation. The first is the notion that the individual initiates action out of his own organism: he is the spontaneous organizer of behavior rather than a simple responder to stimuli. Freud formulated this concept in his theory of the drives, stating that the root of behavior lies in the body's demand upon the mind for work. The body propels the mind into action. He described the sexual and later the aggressive drive. Stated in its simplest form, the theory says that any human behavior can be reduced to derivatives of those two bodily rooted drive states.

His second proposition is the pleasure-unpleasure principle. That is, all behavior aims at maximizing pleasure and avoiding pain. This concept describes an emotional compass for the drives; drive energies are directed in accord with this pleasure-unpleasure principle, in effect making a psychological statement of the concept of adaptation.

The growth of psychoanalytic clinical experience and changing modes of formulation have led later generations of psychoanalysts to look to additional or alternative ways of understanding what initiates action and what determines the aim and object of any action. Freud himself recognized that the pleasure-unpleasure principle, seemingly vast and all-inclusive, fit poorly in the instances of the dreams of traumatic neurosis, the problems of masochism, and the negative therapeutic reaction. He formulated an instinctual repetition compulsion and described a group of behaviors that were "beyond the pleasure principle" to try to understand events that did not conform to his seemingly basic principle. As Freud's experience grew, he developed his ideas on narcissism, the structural point of view, and the second theory of anxiety in addition to the dual-instinct theory. Each of these concepts carried implications that made Freud's original drive concept seem less adequate.

Freud was also troubled by his inability to outline a physiology for aggression as a drive, similar to the physiology that he could at least imagine would one day be outlined in terms of hormonal activity as the bodily basis for sexuality as a drive. Others chose simply to regard aggression as a response to frustration rather than as a drive. Freud's grand conceptions of Eros and Thanatos as the ultimate drive principles reflected his difficulties in fitting the clinical data to his metapsychology. For these and other reasons, the metapsychology as well as the clinical concepts of motivation became increasingly unclear.

Today there are competing ideas concerning multiple motivators of behavior and their interacting effects. For example, self psychologists view behavior as originating out of the innate propensities of the developing self to realize its own potential. Narcissism, first seen as an aspect of libido, then as an additional drive source, was finally conceived by Kohut as the ultimate drive.

Object-relations theorists see behavior as a consequence of the need to project onto the external world aspects of the internalized representational world. This internal world, in turn, is a result of attachment needs, self and object representations, and the affects associated with them. Although some object-relational analysts have tried to make their views consonant with Freud's definition of drive, I think they are stretching the definition beyond recognition.

Ego psychology suggests that many behaviors originate out of the ego's autonomous activities and the ego satisfactions inherent in them. These constitute yet another source of behavior. Sandler, among others, has pointed to the needs for safety and satisfaction as powerful motivators of behavior that are not drive-determined.

The hermeneutic view suggests that psychoanalysts should think entirely in terms of psychological wishes, abandoning biological drives, and, further, that much of behavior is designed to maintain narrative coherence concerning one's self and one's relations to objects. Today, almost but not quite everyone seems willing to give up the energic metaphors that Freud regarded as central to his metapsychology and that a generation of psychoanalysts took as the touchstone of analytic conviction.

I could expand the list of possible motivational sources, but I leave that to the individual authors in this section. Psychoanalysts are, perhaps unfortunately, a long way from the aesthetically more pleasing, grand, encompassing conceptions with which Freud began. Physicists must have felt the same as their beautiful unified theories collapsed with the discovery of more and more particles that didn't obey the rules. In these situations, whether in physics or in psychoanalysis, one is forced to put philosophy aside and look to theories that are closer to the data.

The authors included in the following pages help to clarify the numerous puzzles now confronting psychoanalysts in their attempt to understand motivation and point to the future directions of this topic for the next hundred years.

# Four

■ ■

■
■
■

# Instinct and Affect

*Aaron Karush, M.D.*

T he need to reconcile hypotheses of instinct and affect has plagued the development of psychoanalytic theory almost from its beginning. The debates continue, however, and a primary focus of this chapter will be discussion of changes in affect theory, as distinct from the original emphasis on instinctual drives, as central motivating forces in human behavior. The position taken here is that the core problems of psychoanalysis are not instinctual in the classical sense but are better formulated as vicissitudes of the emergency emotions of fear, rage, guilt, and so on, coupled with social influences that also figure strongly in the development of personality and psychopathology.

An analysis of debatable issues properly begins with definitions of instinct and affect. That may not be easy. Difficulties in that regard were apparent during the early years of Freud's work in his uncertainties about distinguishing clearly between the clinical data that he believed defined instinct and the data that referred to affect. It was not acknowledged for a long time that instinct and affect are reflected in very different mental events and processes and require different frames of reference with which to identify and analyze them.

Freud's failure to differentiate between instinct and affect as explanatory hypotheses created a persistent source of confusion that was perpetuated by his disciples for many years. Because affect was defined in terms of instinct, it was reduced to a position of functional subordination. The concept of instinct, being removed from direct observation in man by its essential nature, promoted reliance on metapsychological theories of explanation that were based mostly on untestable assumptions and postulates.

Affect, on the other hand, is a clinical concept that is more directly related to observable phenomena. It is possible, therefore, to account for many more mental processes, and especially mechanisms of defense, as derivatives of affect rather than instinctual energy. Affect can explain the origins, nature, and aims of defenses. It can help to unravel how defense mechanisms disguise and distort the actual content of thought and of affective states and render their associated ideas unconscious. Finally, the theory of affects may clarify the processes by which defenses are transformed into normal mental functions when their pathological contents have been neutralized. What traits of personality and character, for example, can replace the pathological action of projection, isolation, reaction formation, or any of the other defensive mechanisms with which we are familiar?

It is possible that the great discoveries of psychoanalysis that have been attributed to the libido theory, such as the concept of the dynamic unconscious from which motivating needs are activated, represent to a considerable extent derivatives of affects and not instinctual drives and their energies. The data of dreams, parapraxes, and other symptomatic behaviors largely reflect the influence of affects, and it may not always enlarge our understanding to restate them in the complex terms of instinct. In retrospect, it seems that Freud often relied upon the manifestations of affects and their mutations in his efforts to confirm metapsychological assumptions. When he obtained corroborative pieces of evidence, he chose to refer to them as "vicissitudes of instinct" and not affect. He thus removed the issue from the realm of observation and discovery to the realm of postulation and assumptions that have been borrowed from questionable suppositions of other sciences. The result, I think all too often, has been to draw conclusions that cannot be justified by the premises and, worse, that may block the path to new knowledge. It was not until Freud introduced the structural hypothesis and altered some parts of his theory of instincts that he opened up a place for a meaningful psychoanalytic theory of affect.

In 1915 Freud defined instinct in "The Instincts and Their Vicissitudes" as "the psychical representative of the stimuli originating from within the organism and reaching the mind." Instinct, he said, can never be conscious; it can only be represented in both consciousness and unconsciousness by an idea. But, he added, such an idea is not the only representation possessed by an instinct. It has a second component, which he called a *charge of affect,* representing that part of the instinct that "finds proportionate expression, according to its quality, in processes which become observable . . . as affect."

By combining the ideational component of instinct with affect which supposedly supplied an energic charge that activated mental processes and behavior, Freud left a legacy of ambiguity and contradiction. It has impelled a generation of analysts to develop tortuous explanatory concepts in an attempt to bridge the gap between an idea's compulsion to repeat itself as an "instinct" and the energic "charge of affect" that propels mental activity and behavior. Freud seemed to convert affect into an energic handmaiden of an assumed repetitive life force that governs responses to internal needs and to social imperatives beyond adaptation.

It is a tribute to Freud's genius as a scientist that he ultimately recognized the flaw in the original instinct hypothesis when he said that instinct is a concept with shadowy derivatives of which we get at best only glimmers in fantasy and imagery, in dreams and in motivated behavior. Affect is not, as is instinct, a theoretical construct invented to explain phenomena in terms of assumed fundamental life processes that are then equated with instinctual drives. Another way to put it is that instinct is a symbol for psychological events; affect is a signal of those events that can announce danger or the promise of pleasurable gratification of a wish. The essential nature of the events in question can be accounted for ultimately in neurochemical terms that are beyond the province of psychoanalysis.

Affects are signals that may or may not be accurate when they give notice of such psychic events as painful conflicts of motivation, the anticipation of danger, the arousal of guilt, the need for self-punishment, the threat of hostile aggressive intent toward significant objects, a self-threatening sense of hopelessness and helplessness, and so on. Affects are signals that can arouse psychic efforts to ward off the undesired effects of the events, whether accurately perceived or not.

The concept of drive remains useful to categorize primary appetitive and recurring needs such as those for food, warmth, sexual gratification, and object attachment, to name the most common and recognizable. The value of our psychodynamic theory of mental processes depends largely upon its ability to treat those processes as psychical means by which adaptive ends are served rather than as instruments for defining the basic transactions of life itself as they presumably influence the mind, a goal I see as grandiose and beyond our means to confirm. Affects are an integral part of such psychic processes even though they are a more modest tool than instinct to explain human behavior. There are other autonomous ego functions beyond affect, such as the capacity to contrive languages for interaction with others, as Hartmann and others have emphasized, which cannot be explained by drive theory but must be viewed separately from hypothetical instinctual forces. Affects do not account for language, but they play a key role in the defensive uses to which language and words can be turned.

Modern efforts to clarify the ambiguities that arise when instinct is made responsible for affect became possible when Freud acknowledged, in his new theory of anxiety, that the affect of anxiety was not a product of repressed libido but was simply a signal of danger.

Many authors have struggled to harmonize drive theory with an acceptable theory of affect by clinging in some measure to the instinctual frame of reference. A brief review of some of their approaches may help to explain the relatively slow evolution of scientific precision in psychoanalytic theory-building. Apart from Freud himself, I shall refer mainly to the contributions of Rapaport, Jacobson, Lewin, and Fenichel as representatives of earlier commentators.

Rapaport's views in the 1950s were typical of the more serious attempts to unify the concepts of drive and affect. In a review of the history of psychoanalytic theory, he identified three phases in which instinctual drives and affects were presumably treated in different ways, while continuing to bind affect to instinct.

Phase one, said Rapaport, equated affect with quantities of psychic energy defined as *drive cathexis.* In this early period of the libido theory, Freud suggested that symptoms were created because undischarged affects remained attached to pathogenic fantasy and found another outlet for discharge through conversion symptoms. In what might be called a neurological and energic theory, anxiety was regarded simply as the result of "dammed-up" libidinal energy.

Phase two, according to Rapaport, reflected a stage in which economic theory was more prominently established as metapsychology. The central factor became the concept of drive cathexis. In the *Interpretation of Dreams,* Freud had treated affects as motor and secretory processes of discharge that were controlled by ideas in the unconscious. Affects were conceived therefore to be released by unconscious wishes. The emphasis during this second phase changed and affects were now considered to be safety valves for the discharge of drive energy.

In his paper "Formulations Regarding the Two Principles of Mental Functioning," Freud distinguished the reality and pleasure principles and two corresponding modes by which inner tension could be reduced. He now considered affect discharge to be the responsibility of the pleasure principle, while action was the province of the reality principle. Action sought to change the external environment so as to make the object of a drive available; affect discharge, on the other hand, dealt with the inner world concerned with gratification of wishes. Rapaport interpreted this to mean that "affect-discharge is then the short-cut to tension-decrease, while action is the realistic detour to it." Taken together with its ideational component, the affect charge also constituted for both Freud and Rapaport the basis of drive representation.

Clearly in this discharge theory all affects, and especially the anxiety affect, were reduced to the status of vicissitudes of drive. Although Freud's earlier toxic or transformation hypothesis remained ascendant, it no longer held that *all* undischarged affects could be changed into anxiety but only that repressed drive-cathexis might still be transformed into anxiety. The affect theory of the second phase viewed the expression of affects in the form of symptoms as the result of partial and incomplete discharge of accumulated drive-cathexes because their direct discharge by action could not take place. In summary, the second phase theory of affect was both an economic one based on "cathexis" of drive energy and a dynamic one based on "conflict."

Phase three was dominated by Freud's structural and dual instinct theories. It appeared to Rapaport that, despite great strides toward a fuller understanding of mental processes and defense mechanisms, affect theory had remained incomplete and "scanty." In retrospect, his pessimism is surprising since, in fact, Freud had rerouted affect theory to a more productive track. Freud acknowledged anxiety as a prototype for all affects to be a signal of danger, of perceived reality, and not a by-product of obstruction to the discharge of instinctual energy. The issue now proved to be the ego's mastery of the process of "taming" affects, perhaps by changing them into signals that could lead to realistic actions.

Structural theory, having established affects as ego functions, changed their significance from being "safety valves" to being signals by the ego of anticipated future experiences. The taming of affects was also acknowledged to be the ego's task as it was responsible for the mental processes that modulated affective intensity and regulated an affect's choice of objectives.

The taming process and how to bring it about has become the proper concern of psychoanalytic theory. Continued concern with instinct and energic concepts has not brought a solution closer. When Rapaport presented his complex conceptualization of the taming process, he clung to assumptions that belonged to the first two phases of developing theory about energy and cathexis. This is how he summed up his confusing views of affects and drives:

> The theory of affect integrates three components: 1) *inborn affect-discharge channels* and discharge-thresholds of drive cathexis; 2) the use of these inborn channels as *safety valves and indicators of drive tension,* the modification of their thresholds by drives and derivative motivations prevented from drive-action, and the formation thereby of the drive representation termed *affect-charge;* and 3) the progressive "taming" and advancing ego-control in the course of psychic structure-formation, of the affects which are thereby turned into *affect signals* by the ego.

It was not surprising that Rapaport admitted pessimistically, "The complexity of the phenomena and of the theoretical implications of affects . . . makes a definitive formulation of an up-to-date psychoanalytic theory of affects certainly ill-advised, if not impossible."

Apart from Rapaport's recognition that Freud had restated the nature, origin, and function of affects as signals that were set in motion by the ego, his continued insistence on accounting for affects by using the language of the energic hypothesis of instincts and their cathexes failed, as he himself said, materially to advance our understanding of affects and how to "tame" them. If affects are treated as autonomous ego functions whose origins are separate from drives, it becomes possible to discover the many ways in which affects interact and influence the operations of other ego processes.

Another major contribution to the subject was that of Edith Jacobson in 1953. She offered an interpretation of the relationship between instinctual drives and affects that is closer to current views than that of Rapaport.

Jacobson considered affect and emotion to be synonymous. "Feeling" refers to subjective experience, while affect and emotion represent a psycho-physiological set of reactions. The gist of Freud's structural theory as it concerned affect assumes two forms. Anxiety is first of all not the result of repression but is the motor that produces it. Second, anxiety arises in the ego as an autonomous organization of functions. Freud believed that affect is physiologically established as a reaction to the trauma of birth and is later reproduced psychologically in the ego as a signal of a danger situation. Freud, as Jacobson interprets him, seemed to regard affects as inherited, as having once been purposeful and adaptive reactions to traumata. By this Jacobson meant that affects are the manifestations of ego responses to instinctual drives. She speculated that affects could be classified according to whether they "corresponded to instinctual discharge processes" or "represent[ed] ego responses."

Although Jacobson objected to Edward Glover's earlier classification of primary and secondary reactive affects, in many respects her views described affects as having instinctual origins in the id and serving adaptive purposes of the ego. Her approach, like Rapaport's, was an effort to bridge the gap between drive and affect and to integrate them into Freud's structural and adaptational frame of reference—an effort that did not satisfactorily resolve their contradictions.

Apart from this methodological objection, my own view is sympathetic with her emphasis upon the adaptive function of affect and its subordination to the ego's control. Jacobson's stress on adaptation in her treatment of affect highlighted the difference between instinct and affect.

Bertram Lewin also reviewed the confused approach to defining the nature of affect and in "characterizing the relation of emotion and illness." He traced the origins of the problem to pre-Freudian conceptions, going back to the ancient Greeks, who "did not clearly distinguish semantically between perceptions, knowledge, feeling and action." As for early Freudian ambiguity in distinguishing emotion or affect from instinct, Lewin chose to accept Rapaport's idea of affect charge as empirically useful in explaining the separation of the component idea of an affect from the "appropriate" affect charge by the processes of repression and isolation. That it was empirically useful was true, for a time. Freud's statement that an affect is always a conscious manifestation presumably accounts for the capacity of repression and isolation to inhibit the discharge of an affect or to separate the affect charge from the ideational content by displacement. Lewin carefully avoided getting bogged down in the issue of instinct and its supposed control of subordinate affect.

Otto Fenichel, on the other hand, openly expressed reservations about the instinct theory in both its original and in its later form as the dual-instinct theory. He also rejected the concepts of fusion and defusion with which Freud supported the dual-instinct theory. As he noted, the first theory of instincts "was overthrown by the discoveries concerning narcissism." Fenichel suggested that Freud clung to the older libido theory that preceded the dual-instinct hypothesis because the libido theory "reflected the theory of repression." Fenichel also dismissed the validity of the dual-instinct theory that Freud proposed to replace the failed libido theory.

Fenichel went on to discuss affect in depth as a reflection of the ego. He separated the concept of affect from emotion, which he defined as "the feeling sensations themselves," and he considered affect to be "the outcome of those sensations, the discharge phenomena." Fenichel assigned affect to the biological sphere but without referring directly to instinct. The implication remains that Fenichel adhered to Freud's original energic conception of the charge of affect as a component of instinctual drive. Fenichel's contribution to a modern psychoanalytic theory of affect nevertheless deserves to be considered one of the first major deviations from strict adherence to the instinct theory that opened the way to a changed affect theory.

Moving to more recent discussions, Charles Brenner, Joseph Sandler, Otto Kernberg, André Green, and several psychoanalysts at the Columbia Psychoanalytic Center (including myself) illustrate some of the more modern approaches to the instinct-affect dilemma.

Brenner tried to avoid what he considered to be twin pitfalls in previous discussions of affect theory: first, that affects are constant and identifiable mental phenomena; and, second, that affects are an aspect of instinctual discharge. He urged that discussions of affect be more firmly rooted in clinical data. Brenner assumed that anxiety, for example, is "not merely an unpleasant sensation, but . . . includes ideas as well." Affects in general consist of mental phenomena that include pleasant and/or unpleasant sensations and ideas that embrace "thoughts, memories, wishes, fear."

Brenner went on to note that we do not know what, if any, is the developmental history of pleasurable and unpleasurable sensations. On the other hand, ideas "are wholly dependent on ego development and ego functioning." He concluded that "the evolution of affect is an aspect of ego development" and that few psychoanalytic authors have related affects to ego functions and development, repeating instead Freud's emphasis on affect as an instance of instinctual discharge. He quoted Bertram Lewin and Max Schur in particular as having underscored the significance of the ideational components of affect.

Brenner's paper marked a fundamental shift from the earlier rigid adherence to the energic hypothesis of instinct theory. It is a major contribution toward a psychoanalytic theory of affect that is free of limitations imposed by early Freudian conceptions.

Joseph Sandler has also reconsidered the role of affects in psychoanalytic theory and made a serious effort to confront the problems of creating a scientific affect theory. He pointed out that before 1897 Freud had made affects crucial to his theory by relating the origin of affects to trauma and by making such affects responsible for the production of symptoms. Shortly afterward, as Sandler stated, Freud began to neglect affects in favor of libidinal instincts. It was not until 1923 that affects were partly reinstated by the structural theory. Sandler then proposed that the theoretical problems involved in emotions could be clarified only if a sharp distinction were made between somatic activity and subjective experience, a position quite different from that of Brenner and others. Sandler did not fully elaborate his affect theory, however, and did not establish the nature of the bridge between the somatic and psychological aspects of emotion.

Otto Kernberg in his recent discussion was somewhat ambiguous in suggesting that unconscious conflicts, in part at least, arise "under the impact of a determined drive derivative (clinically, a certain affect disposition)." He appears to treat affect disposition as a reflection of instinctual discharge or as its clinical equivalent. Although Kernberg works clinically with affects as separate entities, he mixes the clinical concept, affect, with a metaphoric conception of instinctual drive in his construction.

The founders of the Columbia Psychoanalytic Center made significant contributions to the instinct issue in psychoanalytic theory during the critical controversies of the 1930s and 1940s. Sándor Radó in particular focused upon the emergency emotions of fear, rage, and guilt and in the process discarded some aspects of the libido theory. He found similar fault with the awkward corrective formulations of such ego-psychology psychoanalysts as Heinz Hartmann, Ernst Kris, Rudolph Loewenstein, and others. He may have overreacted and oversimplified the complexities of unconscious mental processes, but he squarely confronted the instinct-affect argument. Abram Kardiner added another dimension to psychoanalytic theory with his analysis of the dynamics of parenting and family interreactions in primitive societies and in modern cultures. He presented new data that further weakened the basic assumptions of instinct theory that personality developments were primarily genetic formations. Kardiner believed rather that emotional constellations were created by the psychodynamics fostered by the customs and mores of differing social organizations.

In 1959, Kardiner, Aaron Karush, and Lionel Ovesey published their critique of the theory of instincts and in the process reemphasized the primary importance of affects in shaping psychoneuroses and personality disorders

The papers began with a methodological examination of the construction of the libido theory. The authors accepted the basic principle that psychoanalytic knowledge represents a fusion of observable phenomena with explanatory assumptions or postulates that help to define interrelationships among the data of behavior. Scientific postulates, to be useful to theory building, are built around a conceptual framework that, one hopes, will open the way to fresh observations that ultimately verify or refute the original assumptions. In this way we obtain new knowledge. Assumptions that have been useful at one stage of scientific inquiry, however, may unfortunately prove at a later phase incapable of further verification or refutation. The discovery and application of new data to our theory is then blocked. No matter how attractive the assumptions of the libido theory may have been and no matter how much new knowledge of psychic development and of pathological processes it made possible, the authors felt that, after a certain point, some changes were called for.

That Freud accomplished so much with the libido theory, despite its limitations, remains a major miracle. Its great value to the creation of a solid store of knowledge is not diminished by the recognition that certain changes are desirable. One of the problems has been that assumptions supporting the instinct theory have come to be treated as if they were equivalent to hard data. An example is the body of assumptions implicit in the energic hypothesis that has become a metaphor for quantification and even for explaining developmental processes. As other authors cited earlier have recognized, a serious impediment has been fostered by the energy concept to the development of a psychoanalytic theory of affects that is distinct and separate from instincts and their assumed energies.

Somatization has also received typical energic explanations that block the emergence of new and possibly more productive hypotheses. Another relatively neglected area of study involves the interaction between affect and symbolic language for the operation and content of defensive mental processes. Symbolic thought and the mental representation of affects by metaphors may not only bridge the gap between mind and body but may explain how affects stimulate specific defenses that mask certain conflicts. No assumptions are holy; whether such new postulates concerning the significance of affects in causing psychoneuroses will prove valid remains to be seen.

Reports of two panels were published in 1968 in the *Journal of the American Psychoanalytic Association,* one of which discussed the theory of instinctual drives in connection with recent developments, the other of which reviewed the efforts to create a psychoanalytic theory of affects (Dahl 1968; Löfgren 1968). The panel on instinctual drives revealed much the same kinds of split positions as I have described. The discussion of affects also tended to become involved in the energy question, about which differing opinions were expressed. Brenner presented the view that it was necessary to distinguish affect from the energic hypothesis of instinctual discharge. Schur's paper was described by the reporter as an attempt at "a further development and reformulation of Freud's emphasis on the economic aspect of metapsychology in order to construct a theory of affects." Schur also restated Freud's signal concept by making the cognitive component an integral part of affects; he also extended the signal concept from anxiety to other affects and made invalid the objection to the idea of unconscious affect. Although no final agreement was reached, a genuine effort was in progress toward accepting affect as an ego function and not as the route for instinctual discharge of energy.

André Green wrote a review of affect and instinct in 1977 that covered much the same ground as had other authors in describing Freud's changing hypotheses about affect and instinct. At first, Freud had referred to affect as a quantum of energy that accompanies the events of psychic life, a definition that really excluded affect from a dynamic role in the creation of mental processes, wishful fantasies, and other psychic contents. Freud limited the ego's functions to moderating the impact of affects when they threatened disorganization. It did so by specific actions that discharged energy and at the same time linked the affects to related mental representations by associative psychical activity.

Green went on to describe some of Freud's changing theories of the place of affect in mental function, which have been summarized by others. He suggested that Freud distorted the significance of affect in order to preserve his energic hypothesis, which enabled him to treat normal and pathological behavior as reflections of instinctual development. Freud, said Green, "describes three possible vicissitudes of quantity . . . : 1) the suppression of the instinct so that no trace of it is found; 2) the appearance of an affect which is in some way or another qualitatively coloured; and 3) the transformation into anxiety of the psychical energy of the instincts." Affect thus became a by-product of instinctual energy that seeks discharge.

Freud did not remedy his wishful hypothesis of instinct as opposed to affect until compelled to solve the problem of narcissism. He did ultimately grapple with the overwhelming evidence that affects were adaptive reactions to events rather than a road for the escape of instinctual energy. Freud began to turn matters right side up with his final theory that anxiety was a response to danger and not the incidental product of repressed libidinal energy.

Green concluded with a challenging hypothesis to the effect that the importance of the new theory lay in Freud's having to displace his accent from the Oedipus complex and its corollary of castration anxiety onto separation anxiety. The mother loomed more than the father, according to Green, as an object who most influenced development and the loss of whom is the primary cause of early childhood anxiety. By protecting against overwhelming painful stimuli, by supporting the child, and by presentating herself as a primary model for identification, she also became the archetype for the preferred defenses to be chosen by the child in the future.

Surprisingly, Green continued to regard affect, partly, at least, as an indicator of drive activity. Freud had granted affect the possibility of unconscious function, but Green concluded that, although affects could be conscious or unconscious, only thought representations had preconscious status linking them to language.

The latter is an interesting but questionable postulate. It appears to make language independent of influence or use by affects. It seems more accurate to recognize that affects are, from the beginning, intimately involved in the development of language usage, which in turn helps to regulate the functions of defense. The fundamental autonomy of language acquisition, however, is not impaired by affects.

On the whole there is little to quarrel with in Green's delineation of the independence of affect from drive.

What, finally, is to be gained by the hypothesis that affect is an autonomous ego function that can regulate mental processes and behavior independently of instinctual drives? Justification for separating the two concepts functionally and dynamically can be found at several levels of discourse. Treatment of affect as an ego function discloses its integral part in the signaling apparatus that adapts us to coming events. It also provides broader opportunities for the study of the integration by affects of primary and secondary mental processes. The interactions that result may be responsible for behavioral responses that range across the whole spectrum of normalcy and psychopathology.

Among areas of special interest is the susceptibility to symbolic expansion of meanings in affect signals and even proneness in some cases to gross distortion of those signals in psychoneurosis and psychosis. Affects not only send us signals but simultaneously arouse somatic readiness for action. How this process can go awry due to developmental or genetic predisposition has always been the focus of psychoanalysis. That affective excitation was considered to be essentially a manifestation of instinctual drive created premature closure to more penetrating clinical investigation of the processes involved.

Another area of mysterious activity by affects remains that of somatization, ranging from oedipal conversion to preoedipal conversion reactions.

In concluding this compressed version of so highly a controversial subject as that of instinct versus affect, it may help to remember that we are still in a transitional phase of psychoanalytic theory-building. Tempting new theories will present themselves, whose usefulness remains to be proven. In the meantime, unpleasant as it may seem to live with uncertainty, it may be that the journey will matter even more than the arrival. New hypotheses can be suggested that may underscore my point.

The evidence of past experience indicates that the concepts of instinct and energy are best set aside, at least for the time being, in favor of an extended view of the significance of affect and language symbols in the selection and shaping of mental contents as well as in the choices and aims of the mental processes that underlie thought and behavior.

Thought processes may be said to exist in a "sea" of affects, both pleasurable and unpleasurable. The first hypothesis to be offered about the source and dynamic range of influence of affect upon psychic processes can be stated simply. It postulates that all language signs that designate subjects and objects, that is, nouns, and signs that express an act, event, or mode of being, that is verbs, possess an affective component that impels toward action. Affects, in other words, are bound to ideas that identify their aims and urge the subject to achieve them by action. Through those ideas, affects maintain a state of readiness to act, whether that aim is incorporative in intent, self-protective in the form of flight, or an act of aggression and riddance of an offending object. A perception that is organized around images created by any sense organ can signal the possibility of gratifying a need or, contrariwise, the approach of danger. The preexistent state of excitability that language signs have created provides a readiness for prompt response to the prevailing affect.

A second hypothesis suggests that affects can be divided into signal affects and symbol affects. Signals announce the imminence of events; symbols explain their meaning for the welfare and security of the subject. Each class of affect can induce and motivate different mental processes and behaviors. Signal affects are more dramatic and peremptory. Symbol affects activate affective memories that provide conscious or unconscious associations to signals that may either be anticipated or actually received in the future. In recent years, psychoanalysis has been more concerned with signal anxiety which reflects the functioning of the ego, and with chronic guilt, which is a symbol affect of psychic conflicts that arise out of superego functions. The long-term significance of characterological traits that derive from the pursuit of pleasure has been largely neglected. Psychoanalytic theory has also misconstrued the connections between psychoneurosis and faulty anticipation of the future, which may be the product of misleading affect states, by assuming that instincts and their repetition compulsion are responsible.

A third hypothesis holds that figures of speech, especially such tropes as metaphor, metonymy, and synecdoche, have the power to modulate peremptory affects—with uncertain success, to be sure. When somatic metaphors fail in their task of neutralizing affects of anxiety, rage, and guilt, they can bear the responsibility for certain types of somatization.[1]

In any case, it is no longer sufficient to define psychoanalysis solely as a

1. A fuller discussion of the subject of somatization will be published elsewhere.

psychology of motivation and to describe its subject matter as consisting only of the nature and vicissitudes of motivational conflict. Both are of fundamental import, but we must extend our concern to unraveling the complex psychic processes and mechanisms that are set in motion by motivational conflicts and affects. A central hypothesis in this regard asserts that affects and language signs that name and transmit the meanings of affects and the feelings that affects generate in a subject are primarily responsible for the choice and even the enactment of defenses and reparative functions. As Brenner has emphasized, both ideas and exciting feeling states are combined in the representation of an affect. The composite of the two elements need not be arbitrarily split by an assumption of instinctual energy or charge of affect in order to confirm the biological roots of psychoanalysis. Affect and the capacity for language are, after all, also biological processes central both to psychoanalytic theory and to its application in therapeutic analysis.

## References

Brenner, C. 1974. On the nature and development of affects: A unified theory. *Psychoanalytic Quarterly* 43:531–56.

Dahl, H. 1968. Report of APA panel on "Psychoanalytic theory of the instinctual drives in relation to recent developments." *Journal of the American Psychoanalytic Association* 16:613–37.

Fenichel, O. 9153. Critique of the death instinct. In *Collected Papers of Otto Fenichel.* First series. Ed. H. Fenichel and D. Rapaport, 363–72. New York: W. W. Norton.

———. 1954. The ego and the affects. In *Collected Papers of Otto Fenichel.* Second series. Ed. H. Fenichel and D. Rapaport, 215–27. New York: W. W. Norton.

Freud, S. 1911. Formulations regarding the two principles of mental functioning. *Standard Edition,* 12:218–26. London: Hogarth Press, 1958.

———. 1915. Instincts and their vicissitudes. *Standard Edition,* 14:117–40. London: Hogarth Press, 1957.

———. 1915. Repression. *Standard Edition,* 14:146–58. London: Hogarth Press, 1957.

Green, A. 1977. Conceptions of affect. *International Journal of Psychoanalysis* 58:129–56.

Jacobson, E. 1953. Affects and their pleasure-unpleasure qualities. In *Drives, affects and behavior,* ed. R. Loewenstein, 1:38–66. New York: International Univ. Press.

Kardiner, A., Karush, A., and Ovesey, L. 1959. A methodological study of Freudian theory. *Journal of Nervous and Mental Disease* 129, no. 1:11–19; no. 2:133–43; no. 3:207–221; no. 4:341–56.

Kernberg, O. 1980. *Internal World and External Reality.* New York: Aronson.

Lewin, B. 1965. Reflections on affect. In *Drives, affects and behavior,* ed. M. Schur, 2:23–37. New York: International Univ. Press.

Löfgren, L. B. 1968. Report of APA panel on "Psychoanalytic theory of affects." *Journal of the American Psychoanalytic Association* 16:638–50.

Rapaport, D. 1953. On the psychoanalytic theory of affects. *International Journal of Psychoanalysis* 34:177–98.

Sandler, J. 1972. The role of affect in psychoanalytic theory. In *Physiology, emotions and psychosomatic illness*, Ciba Foundation 8, n.s. Amsterdam, N.Y.: Assoc. Scientific Pub.

# Five

## Toward a Reconsideration of the Psychoanalytic Theory of Motivation

*Joseph Sandler, M.D.*

T he topic of motivation is an extraordinarily difficult one to study and has preoccupied psychologists for many years. One of the major diffi- culties has been that neither in the field of general psychology nor in the more specific area of psychoanalysis is there agreement on what a motive really is. And even when we turn to the relatively restricted area of psycho- analytic theory, we find that we cannot be sure whether the term *motive* refers to drives, drive derivatives, affects, feelings, needs, wishes, aims, inten- tions, reasons, or causes. The term possesses the quality of elasticity to a remarkable degree, and its meaning is highly dependent on the context in which it is used. It reflects a multidimensional concept. Such concepts, I have commented elsewhere,

> play a very important part in holding psychoanalytic theory together. As psycho- analysis is made up of formulations at varying levels of abstraction, and of part- theories which do not integrate well with one another, the existence of pliable, context-dependent concepts allows an overall framework of psychoanalytic the- ory to be assembled. Parts of this framework are rigorously spelled out, but can only articulate with similar part-theories if they are not tightly connected, if the concepts which form the joints are flexible. Above all, the value of such loosely jointed theory is that it allows developments in psychoanalytic theory to take place without necessarily causing overt radical disruptions in the overall the- oretical structure of psychoanalysis. The elastic and flexible concepts take up the strain of theoretical change, absorbing it while more organized newer theories or

part-theories can develop. . . . Such an approach to psychoanalytic concepts regards each as having a set of *dimensions of meaning*, as existing in a meaning-space, in which it moves as its context and sense changes. (Sandler 1983, p. 36)

It follows that, in addressing oneself to the concept of motivation, one has to consider, so to speak, a meaning-space rather than a point in such a space. There are many paths one can take in exploring the meaning of the concept. The one I shall describe is that which reflects my own struggles with the concept. These conceptual struggles were for the most part not explicitly connected with the theory of motivation but were, rather, implicit in much of the work reported by my close colleagues and myself. In retrospect; it seems clear that our own preoccupations were in many respects the same as those which occupied the minds of many of those associated with the Columbia Institute, mainly Radó and Kardiner, although our solutions to the problems concerned were, I think, rather different.

Having given myself license to be imprecise, I want to take as a starting point a story that may give some indication of what it is I want to discuss. Some time ago—in 1959—I had the opportunity to present a paper to the British Psycho-Analytical Society. The paper consisted of two parts. The first was a theoretical discussion of what was referred to as a background feeling of safety; the second was a short account of some analytic work with a woman I had commenced treating some nine years previously who had been, in fact, my first control case. The first, theoretical part of my paper (which was later published as "The Background of Safety," 1960a) is summarized as follows:

> The act of perception [can be regarded as] a very positive one, and not at all the passive reflection in the ego of stimulation arising from the sense-organs; . . . the act of perception is an act of ego-mastery through which the ego copes with . . . excitation, that is with unorganized sense data, and is thus protected from being traumatically overwhelmed; . . . the successful act of perception is an act of integration which is accompanied by a definite *feeling of safety*—a feeling so much a part of us that we take it for granted as a background of our everyday experience; . . . this feeling of safety is more than a simple absence of discomfort or anxiety, but a very definite feeling quality within the ego; . . . we can further regard much of ordinary everyday behaviour as being a means of maintaining a minimum level of safety-feeling; and . . . much normal behaviour as well as many clinical phenomena (such as certain types of psychotic behaviour and the addictions) can be more fully understood in terms of the ego's attempts to *preserve* this level of safety. (P. 352)

The feeling of safety or security was, I argued, something positive, a sort of ego-tone. It was more than the mere absence of anxiety, and as a feeling it could become attached to the mental representations of all sorts of different ego activities. Because of this it was possible to postulate the existence of safety signals in the same way we do signals of anxiety. I suggested that the safety signals were related to such things as the awareness of being protected by the reassuring presence of the mother. The paper ended with the suggestion that we could see, in what had been described, the operation of what could be called a *safety principle.*

> This would simply reflect the fact that the ego makes every effort to maintain a minimum level of safety feeling . . . through the development and control of integrative processes within the ego, foremost among these being perception. In this sense, perception can be said to be in the service of the safety principle. Familiar and constant things in the child's environment may therefore carry a special affective value for the child in that they are more easily perceived— colloquially we say that they are known, recognizable, or familiar to the child. The constant presence of familiar things makes it easier for the child to maintain its minimum level of safety feeling. (P. 355)

The second part of the paper (published under the title "On the Repetition of Early Childhood Relationships in Later Psychosomatic Disorder," 1959) described the case of a woman of thirty-five who had been referred for sexual difficulties, more specifically for the symptom of vaginismus. She was able to have a good analysis, as her sexual problems readily transferred themselves to the whole area of communication in the analysis. She had an obstinate though intermittent tendency to silence, and I commented,

> It soon became clear that this paralleled, on a psychological level, the physical symptom of vaginismus. The similarity between the two was striking, and it seemed as if she suffered an involuntary spasm of a mental sphincter. In time we could understand something of her inability to tolerate penetration of a mental or physical kind, and as the silence disappeared in the course of analysis, so there was an easing of her physical symptom. It became clear that she wished me to attack her, to make her speak and to force my interpretations upon her. She was able to recall how her sexual fantasies in childhood had been rape fantasies, and the thought of being raped . . . had been a very exciting one. (Pp. 189–90)

I noted at the time that a central feature of her personality was her intense masochism and a highly sexualized need for punishment. The analysis resulted in the disappearance of the vaginismus and a general lessening of the patient's need to do damage to herself.

Four years after she stopped treatment, I heard from my patient again. She was very anxious, as her husband, from whom she had separated, had been threatening suicide if she did not rejoin him. She started treatment again, and I saw her for a year. She did not have her vaginismus, but it transpired that she had another symptom. She was now mildly but noticeably deaf. At the time I noted that it seemed "that this new symptom derived from the same unconscious processes which had led to her vaginal spasm" (p. 193). In spite of working through all this material again, her deafness persisted. However, an understanding of her deafness occurred suddenly and rather unexpectedly. I suddenly became aware that my need to talk loudly so that she could hear me also caused me to shout pedantically, as if to a naughty child. This realization led me to the understanding that

> by being deaf she could force me to shout at her as her grandmother had done when she was very small. It became clear that she was unconsciously recreating, in her relationship with me, an earlier relationship to the grandmother, who had been, in spite of her unkindness to and constant irritation with the patient, the most permanent and stable figure in [her] childhood. (P. 193)

After working through feelings of loss for her grandmother and the need to re-create her presence in many different ways, the woman's hearing improved.

I took the position in this paper that my patient was not only obtaining masochistic gratification through her symptoms but was defending against an intense fear of abandonment by re-creating a feeling of the physical presence of the grandmother, "whose mode of contact with the child had been predominantly one of verbal criticism or of physical punishment" (p. 193). I added that "the pain and suffering was the price she paid for a bodily feeling of safety, for the reassurance that she would not undergo the miserable loneliness and separation which characterized her first year of life" (pp. 193–94).

The week after I presented this paper, I received the following letter, dated March 1, 1959, from Anna Freud in reply to a short note of mine:

> Dear Dr. Sandler,
>
> It was very nice of you to write after the lecture. I really felt that I should write and excuse myself for not having taken part in the discussion. The explanation was that I did not feel quite in agreement with various points and I thought it would be much more profitable to discuss that in private than in front of the whole Society.
>
> Actually, I liked the first, namely the purely theoretical part of your paper very much. Your description of a background feeling of safety brought about by the correctness of perception was very convincing. It also reminded me very vividly of an experience with a former patient of mine, a severe alcoholic who lost all control of reality and himself when drunk, or after a drunken bout. A psychiatrist in whose care he had been before analysis had taught him to recover control by merely verbalizing his perceptions of reality, for example: "this is a table," "this is

a stone in the pavement," etc. He reported that this had been a real help to him. I believe many patients do similar things spontaneously when under alcohol, drugs, or in fever states: they test the correctness of their perceptions for reassurance about their own intactness. And, like all defences, this can become greatly over-emphasized.

I felt quite differently when it came to the second, clinical part. I think what your patient tried to reactivate with the symptom of deafness was not the familiar perception of the Grandmother's voice but the familiar masochistic pleasure to which she had become accustomed. There seems to me a world of difference between the mild, all-pervading "functional" pleasure of perception and a drive, an instinctual urge, such as the one for passive, masochistic experience. The latter is an id-urge and, as such, can set action in motion; the former is nothing of the kind, i.e., does not belong to the instinct world. To minimize the difference between the two concepts seemed to me a very dangerous step, namely a step from our instinct-psychology to an ego psychology independent of the drive-world.

I hope you do not mind me being so outspoken about my objections. I bring them up just because I liked the theoretical part.

Yours sincerely,

Anna Freud

Anna Freud was, of course, quite correct in her view that the pleasures associated with direct instinctual gratification have a quality markedly different from what she referred to as "mild, all-pervading 'functional' pleasure." And, without doubt, her major concern was, as she put it, the possibility of the dangerous step "from our instinct-psychology to an ego psychology independent of the drive-world." I think we can understand this very well in view of the need psychoanalysis has had, throughout its history, to protect its basic notions from those who wished to minimize the importance of infantile sexual and aggressive drives as well as the central role of persisting impulses of this sort in adult life.

I must confess that although I felt somewhat abashed by Anna Freud's comments, a niggling feeling remained that neither of us had really come to grips with the problems involved in the disagreement between us, and it is only now, some twenty-five years later, that I find myself able to be somewhat more precise about where these problems lie. In what follows, I shall attempt to work toward a suitable response to Anna Freud's comments and shall do this by a somewhat less than direct route.

In 1960, the year following the presentation of this paper, I found myself referring, in a paper entitled "On the Concept of the Superego" ( 1960b), not only to feelings of safety but also to feelings of well-being and self-esteem.

Certainly this was under the influence of such writers as Edith Jacobson, Edward Bibring, and Annie Reich. In connection with such feelings it was possible to comment, for example, on the topic of identification as follows:

> If we recall the joy with which the very young child imitates, consciously or unconsciously, a parent or an older sibling, we can see that identification represents an important technique whereby the child feels loved and obtains an inner state of well-being. We might say that the esteem in which the omnipotent and admired object is held is duplicated in the self and gives rise to self-esteem. The child feels at one with the object and close to it, and temporarily regains the feeling of happiness which he experienced during the earliest days of life. Identificatory behavior is further reinforced by the love, approval, and praise of the real object, and it is quite striking to observe the extent to which the education of the child progresses through the reward, not only of feeling omnipotent like the idealized parent, but also through the very positive signs of love and approval granted by parents and educators to the child. The sources of "feeling loved," and of self-esteem, are the real figures in the child's environment; and in these first years identificatory behaviour is directed by the child toward enhancing, via these real figures, his feeling of inner well-being. (P. 151)

I went on to suggest that the same feelings can be obtained through compliance with the precepts of the superego introject, or by identification with that introject, and wrote that, in contrast to such unpleasant feelings as guilt and unworthiness,

> an *opposite* and equally important affective state is also experienced by the ego, a state which occurs when the ego and superego are functioning together in a smooth and harmonious fashion; that is, when the feeling of being loved is restored by the approval of the superego. Perhaps this is best described as a state of mental comfort and well-being. . . . It is the counterpart of the affect experienced by the child when his parents show signs of approval and pleasure at his performance, when the earliest state of being at one with his mother is temporarily regained. It is related to the affective background of self-confidence and self-assurance. . . . There has been a strong tendency in psychoanalytic writings to overlook the very positive side of the child's relationship to his superego; a relation based on the fact that it can also be a splendid source of love and well-being. It functions to approve as well as to disapprove. (Pp. 154–55)

On looking back at that paper it now seems clear to me that I was struggling to deal with a conflict over my deep conviction that, in addition to the drives, psychoanalytic theory had to take account of strong motives that were not instinctual drive impulses. In this connection I was, I think, beginning to be involved in much the same sort of problem that concerned Harry Stack Sullivan and Karen Horney, Radó, Kardiner, and others. But my way of dealing with the conflict was to do what was perhaps rather more commonly done—that is, to follow Freud in making use of his own solution to this theoretical conflict by shifting the emphasis from the drive impulse itself to the hypothetical energies regarded as being derived from the drives and making the assumption that such energies entered into all motives. I wrote, for example, that in identification with another person "some of the libidinal cathexis of the object is transferred to the self" (1960b, p. 150). And in a footnote in that paper I commented that

> the problem of what it means to "feel loved," or to "restore narcissistic cathexis," is one that has as yet been insufficiently explored. What the child is attempting to restore is an affective state of well-being which we can correlate in terms of energy, with the level of narcissistic cathexis of the self. (P. 149)

But, having said this, I then put drive energies to one side and talked again about feeling states.

> Initially this affective state, which normally forms a background to everyday experience, must be the state of bodily well-being which the infant experiences when his instinctual needs have been satisfied (as distinct from the pleasure in their satisfaction). This affective state later becomes localized in the self, and we see aspects of it in feelings of self-esteem as well as in normal background feelings of safety. . . . The maintenance of this *central affective state* is perhaps the most powerful motive for ego development, and we must regard the young child (and later the adult) as seeking well-being as well as pleasure-seeking; the two are by no means the same, and in analysis we can often observe a conflict between the two. (P. 149)

This connection between the state of well-being and libido distribution was reiterated—but now, I think, with more manifestly mixed feelings—in a paper entitled "Psychology and Psychoanalysis." But there was also more emphasis placed on the child's object relationships.

> From a psychological point of view it makes a great deal of sense to speak of the child's feeling of well-being as located in his self representation, when a particular representational relationship exists between the self and mother representation. We can then link the state of the child's libido with the particular relationship of the two images at the time—those of himself and of the loving parent. (1962, p. 97)

This theme was reflected in a paper published more or less simultaneously with B. Rosenblatt under the title "The Concept of the Representational World" (Sandler and Rosenblatt 1962) in which, among other things, feelings of well-being were linked—simply through force of habit and quite unnecessarily—with the notion of the narcissistic libidinal cathexis of the self representation. The year after, two colleagues and I discussed the concept of the ideal self in "The Ego Ideal and the Ideal Self" (Sandler, Holder, and Meers 1963). There we said that

> one of the shapes which the self representation can assume is that which we can call the *ideal self,* i.e., that which, at any moment, is a desired shape of the self— the "self-I-want-to-be." This is that shape of the self which, at that particular time, in those circumstances, and under the influence of the particular instinctual impulse of the moment, is the shape which would yield the greatest degree of well-being for the child. It is the shape which would provide the highest degree of narcissistic gratification and would minimize the quantity of aggressive discharge on the self. The ideal self at any moment is not necessarily simply that shape of the self which represents instinctual impulses as being fulfilled but will be determined as well by the child's need to gain the love and approval of his parents or introjects, or to avoid their disapproval. (Pp. 152–53)

It must be clear by now that the states of safety and well-being considered in all these papers must be intimately connected with the problem of motivation, although it was not explicitly referred to. A motivational statement is implicit, for example, in such remarks as

> the construction of the ideal self, and the efforts to attain it, constitute an attempt to restore, sometimes in a most roundabout way, the primary narcissistic state of the earliest weeks of life. But the effort to attain the ideal self is not always successful. If the individual cannot change the shape of his self so as to identify it with his ideal self, then he will suffer the pangs of disappointment and the affective states associated with lowered self-esteem. (Sandler, Holder, and Meers 1963, p. 156)

This statement contains references to two sets of motivating forces. In the first place, there is the attraction of the ideal self, of the set of good feelings that accompany identification with one's own ideal of the moment. But, second, there is also the motivating power of the feelings that accompany the discrepancy between the representation of the so-called actual self—the "self-of-the-moment"—and the representation of the ideal self at that moment. I should mention that the concept of the ideal self was redefined soon after this as the "ideal state," as the wished-for state of affairs at any given time may involve more than a representation of the self, as in the representation of a wished-for self-object interaction. The presence of an ideal object may be just as much a part of the ideal state as the ideal self. The emphasis on object relationships was increasing, while the strain of bringing the energy theory into the picture in order to reduce all motivation to drives and drive-derivatives was becoming too great. In 1964 W. G. Joffe and I presented our thoughts on this topic at the midwinter meeting of the American Psychoanalytic Association in New York. (This paper, "On Skill and Sublimation," was not published until 1966.) We suggested that sublimation might be better dealt with by "a theory of displacement and affect change rather than [by] one of energy transformation" and commented as follows:

> The fact that the functioning of the ego apparatuses yields pleasurable feelings means that we have a whole hierarchy of affective feeling tones within the ego, associated with the hierarchy of ego functions and apparatuses. These range from crudely sensual experiences to feelings of safety and well-being and the more subtle feeling which Hartmann has called "positive value accents." . . . the component which differentiates constant object relationships from need-satisfying ones is a contribution of the ego, an additional affective ego value which we could describe in such terms as "non-sensual love," "esteem for the object," etc. This is not the same as the aim-inhibited instinctual components. (P. 343)

Now, however, we can find more specific reference to "motive forces" and to what was referred to as ego motivation. We said,

> We have suggested that there is a hierarchy of positive feelings which the ego is capable of experiencing. Similarly we could postulate a hierarchy of "unpleasures" of all gradations. If we take the view that the ego functions to maintain a positive feeling of well-being in the self, then the experiencing of any degree of unpleasure will set in motion the adaptive and defensive functioning of the ego apparatuses. This homeostatic view enables us to consider the dynamics of independent ego functioning in the light of motive forces associated with the various ego apparatuses, which have as their aim the avoidance of unpleasure and the preservation of well-being. We can thus contain a theory of ego motivation within a structural framework. These motive forces can be seen as "demands for work" (similar to that imposed by the drives) on the ego apparatuses. This "demand for work" is again quite different from the energy which powers the apparatus. (Pp. 343–44)

(It may be of some interest that the discussion at this American Psychoanalytic Association meeting became rather heated, and Joan Fleming, who was in the chair, permitted it to run some hours over time. Heinz Hartmann cordially disagreed with our ideas, but Rudolph Loewenstein warned us most emphatically that we were treading an extremely dangerous path that could only result in our ruination. Looking back, I can only say that what we had to say at that meeting must have aroused substantial anxiety in our listeners as well, of course, as in ourselves.)

Soon after, in a consideration of depression in childhood (Joffe and Sandler

1965), we made extensive use of the concept of pain as a motivating factor in mental life, pain as an affective state or as a potential state that could be defended against. Pain was connected with a discrepancy between what we called the actual (or current) state of the self on the one hand and an ideal state of well-being on the other. To quote:

> "Ideal" in this context refers to a state of well-being, a state which is fundamentally affective and which normally accompanies the harmonious and integrated functioning of all the biological and mental structure. . . . The striving towards the attainment of an ideal state is basic in human development and functioning. It represents the feeling component which is attributed to the state of primary narcissism. Much of the dynamics of ego functioning can be understood in terms of the ego's striving to maintain or attain a state of well-being, a state which even in the child who has been unhappy from birth exists as a biological goal. Freud put it: "The development of the ego consists in a departure from primary narcissism and gives rise to a vigorous attempt to recover that state." The ideal state of well-being is closely linked with feelings of safety and security. It is the polar opposite of feelings of pain, anxiety or discomfort, and bears the same relation to these as the state of physical satiation and contentment in a small infant bears to the unpleasure of instinctual tension. The attainment of this state may follow or accompany successful drive-discharge, but there are circumstances in which drive-satisfaction does not lead to the development of well-being, but rather to the experiencing of its opposite, as in states of mental conflict.
>
> In this there is a qualitative difference between the systems id and ego. The drives are characterized by states of tension and demands for discharge (and the body-pleasures associated with such discharge) which change in the course of development. The dynamics of ego functioning appear to be much more related to the maintenance of affective states of well-being which do not change as grossly in the course of development (although the ideational content associated with the ideal state may change markedly). . . . we shall use the term ideal state to refer to the affective state of well-being, and the term ideal self to denote the particular shape of the self representation at any moment in the individual's life which is believed, consciously or unconsciously, to embody the ideal state. As the representational world of the child becomes increasingly structured, his system of self representations includes images which reflect affective states of well-being. The "ideal self" derives its content not only from affect representations, but also contains ideational components which originate from various sources. These sources include memories of actual states of well-being previously experienced, or of fantastic or symbolic elaborations of such states. The elaborations in fantasy may subserve defensive functions, in which case we may get magical and omnipotent components in the ideal self. The specialized form of ideal which ensues when the child needs to aggrandize himself for the purpose of defence can be referred to as the "idealized self," but it should be borne in mind

that idealization is only one possible source of the content of the ideal self. Similarly, where the ideal self is based on identification with an admired object, we can distinguish between qualities which the child attributes to the object because of its infantile perception of the object at that time, and those which are attributed to the object representation in fantasy. (Pp. 397–98)

The relation to the object was seen as being of crucial importance in the attainment and maintenance of an ideal state. We said,

> Object love, like the whole development of the ego, can be seen as a roundabout way of attempting to restore the ideal primary narcissistic state. The perception of the presence of the love object when its presence is expected is, moreover, a source of feelings of well-being and safety. . . . And this is true even when the object is fulfilling no drive-reducing role. It is clear that if the presence of the object is a condition for a state of well-being in the self, then loss of the object signifies the loss of an aspect of the self, of a state of the self. One might say that for the representation of every love object there is a part of the self representation which is complementary to it, i.e., the part which *reflects the relation to the object,* and which constitutes the link between self and object. We can refer to this as the object-complementary aspect of the self representation. (Pp. 398–99)

An attempt to look more closely at the concept of narcissism (Joffe and Sandler 1967) included an extensive discussion of the relation of affects to the energy theory; we remarked that

> from the moment the infant becomes a psychological being, from the moment it begins to construct a representational world as the mediator of adaptation, much of its functioning is regulated by feeling states of one sort or another. The demands of the drives, and the reduction of these demands, have a major influence on feeling states, *but they are not the only influence.* Feeling states are produced and influenced by stimuli arising from sources other than the drives, for example, from the external environment; and *it is an oversimplification to assume that the vicissitudes of the development of affects are a direct reflection of the vicissitudes of the drives.* (P. 62)

We went on to say,

> Freud drew attention to the function of the affect of anxiety as a signal which initiates special forms of adaptive activity, and we believe that there is a strong argument in favour of the idea that all adaptive activity, defensive or otherwise, is instigated and regulated by the ego's conscious and unconscious scanning and perception of changes in its feeling states. We can assume that, from the very beginning of life, the development of the individual is influenced not only by the search for pleasurable experiences and the avoidance of unpleasurable ones. The striving to attain states that embody feelings of well-being and safety are . . . of

cardinal import. . . . During the course of development affective experiences become increasingly integrated with ideational content, and aspects of both self and object representations become linked with affective qualities, often of the most complicated sort. In this connection, the notion of an *affective cathexis* of a representation becomes meaningful and valuable; and affective cathexes can range from the most primitive feelings of pleasure and unpleasure to the subtle complexities of love and hate. (P. 63)

We then gave a definition of narcissistic disorder related to the need to deal with a latent threatening state of pain by particular sorts of defensive and adaptive maneuvers. Perhaps of interest in the present context is the re-introduction in that paper of the idea of a cathexis of *value* (mentioned in our previous paper on sublimation: Sandler and Joffe 1966):

> By "value" . . . we do not refer specifically to moral value, but the term is used rather in the sense of feeling qualities which may be positive or negative, relatively simple or extremely complicated. It is these affective values, sign-values, so to speak, which give all representations their significance to the ego. (Joffe and Sandler 1967, p. 65)

The line of thought we were pursuing was continued in a paper on the psychoanalytic psychology of adaptation (Joffe and Sandler 1968), in which we commented,

> Although thus far we have spoken of the discrepancy between actual and ideal states of the self representation as being linked with feelings which have a painful component, it should be remembered that from early in the infant's development, the self representation is closely linked with various forms of object representation; we cannot consider any shape of the self representation in isolation. It would probably be more correct to consider (after a certain stage of development has been reached) the actual and ideal shapes of the self representation in terms of self-object representations; for all psychological object relationships are, in representational terms, self-object relationships. In more general terms we can refer to representational discrepancy as being linked with feelings of pain or unpleasure, and lack of representational discrepancy (i.e., states of representational congruity) being associated with feelings of well-being and safety. (P. 450)

We could then put forward what was perhaps the closest we came to an explicit view of motivation.

> From the point of view of the ego's functioning we are now in a position to say that the prime motivators are conscious or unconscious feeling states; and that these are, in turn, associated with various forms of representational congruity or discrepancy. *The aim of all ego functioning is to reduce conscious or unconscious representational discrepancy and through this to attain or maintain a*

*basic feeling state of well-being.* From this point of view we can say that the ego
seeks to maintain a feeling-homeostasis, and this is not to be confused with the
notion of energic homeostasis. (Pp. 450–51)

In 1974, in an attempt to deal with problems in conceptualizing psychic
conflict arising from discrepancies between the structural theory of mental
functioning and clinical psychoanalytic experience, I pointed out that the
understanding of mental conflict was hindered by the common error of
equating the general concept of the unconscious wish with the particular
case of instinctual wishes. But rather than go into the question of the relation
between motivation and mental conflict, I want to return to two papers
published in 1978, one on unconscious wishes and human relationships
(Sandler 1978), and the other on the development of object relationships
and affects (Sandler and Sandler 1978). In both, emphasis was placed on the
role of conscious and unconscious wishes as motives in mental functioning.
"'Instincts' and 'drives' . . . are constructs relating to basic psycho-biological
tendencies of the individual, and to the force and energy implicit in these
tendencies. From a psychological point of view it is sufficient for us to take, as
a basic unit, the *wish*" (Sandler 1978, pp. 5–6). In addition to the emphasis
on the wish, the link between wishes and object relationships can be reinforced. Object relationships were seen as valued role relationships, and those
wishes and wishful fantasies with which psychoanalysts are concerned can be
regarded as containing mental representations of self and object in interaction.

> Thus, for example, the child who has a wish to cling to the mother has, as part of
> this wish, a mental representation of himself clinging to the mother. But he also
> has, in the content of his wish, a representation of the mother or her substitute
> responding to his clinging in a particular way, possibly by bending down and
> embracing him. This formulation is rather different from the idea of a wish
> consisting of a wishful aim being directed towards the object. The idea of an aim
> which seeks gratification has to be supplemented by the idea of a *wished-for
> interaction,* with the wished-for or imagined response of the object being as
> much a part of the wishful fantasy as the activity of the subject in that wish or
> fantasy. (Sandler and Sandler 1978, p. 288)

Again we emphasized that

> there is a substantial part of the mental apparatus which is unconscious in a
> descriptive sense, but which is not id. Many wishes arise within the mind as
> responses to motivating forces which are not instinctual. Perhaps the commonest
> of such motivators are anxiety and other unpleasant affects, but we must equally
> include the effect of disturbances of inner equilibrium created by stimuli from

the outside world (including the subject's own body) as motivators of needs and psychological wishes. The wishes which are aroused may be conscious, but may not be, and very often are not. They may have a drive component, or be developmentally related to the instinctual drives, but this is not a necessary current ingredient of an unconscious wish. Such a wish may, for example, be simply to remove in a particular way whatever is (consciously or unconsciously) identified as a source of discomfort, pain or unpleasure. The wish may be (and often is) motivated by the need to restore feelings of well-being and safety, or may be connected with any one of a whole variety of needs which are very far from those which we normally label as "instinctual." Wishes are aroused by changes in the object world as much as by internal pressures. (P. 286)

It was now possible to speak of the need for "affirmation" by the object world and in this way to link wishes with object relationships. We said,

> If . . . a toddler (who has been playing happily with his mother) . . . notices that his mother has left the room, a need to perceive her and to interact with her, to hold on to her, will immediately become apparent. This will express itself in the form of a very intense wish with a very definite content. Here we can see that this sort of object relationship is certainly very much a continual wish-fulfilment, in which the wish is to obtain reassurance that the mother is nearby (thus fulfilling the need to feel safe). Later in life, the child (and adult) will increasingly be able to make use of an unconscious dialogue with his objects in fantasy in order to gain reassurance. (Pp. 286–87)

We added to this the view that there is a constant need in every individual to externalize his "internal objects," his introjects, in order to anchor his inner world as far as possible in external reality. Externalization of introjects (with all the distortions that have occurred due to past projections of aspects of the self onto these introjects) can, of course, be into the external world or into the world of fantasy. But while all of this is manifestly relevant to the theory of motivation, I need hardly comment that the idea of intense object-related wishes of the sort I have described has not met with universal acceptance.

It is perhaps useful at this point to turn to some of the classical formulations in this area to see where we stand in relation to them. And what can be more appropriate than to turn to Anna Freud herself? Some ten or twelve years ago, a group of us at the Hampstead Clinic (as the Anna Freud Centre was then called) met regularly with Anna Freud in order to discuss her book *The Ego and the Mechanisms of Defence* (1936), and for many of us the reconsideration of what we had read a number of times in the past was extremely enlightening. We were able to see things in the text that we had been blind to before but that were now glaringly obvious (Sandler and Freud 1985). In chapter 5, she describes how the ego's mechanisms of defense are motivated by anxieties of various sorts. The adult neurotic's defenses are prompted, she says, by superego anxiety. The superego, she wrote,

> is the mischief-maker which prevents the ego's coming to a friendly understanding with the instincts. It sets up an ideal standard, according to which sexuality is prohibited and aggression pronounced to be antisocial. It demands a degree of sexual renunciation and restriction of aggression which is incompatible with psychic health. The ego is completely deprived of its independence and reduced to the status of an instrument for the execution of the superego's wishes; the result is that it becomes hostile to instinct and incapable of enjoyment. (1936, p. 59)

Anna Freud goes on to write of objective anxiety, anxiety felt by the child as arising from the outside world. The ego's defenses can be "motivated by dread of the outside world" (p. 61). She then adds, as a source of anxiety and a motivator of defense, the ego's dread of the strength of the instincts, but she points out that the source of the anxiety is not what is important; it is rather the anxiety itself that prompts defense.

In this chapter Anna Freud introduces the idea of defense against affect (as opposed to defense against instinct):

> There is, however, another and more primitive relation between the ego and the affects which has no counterpart in that of the ego to the instincts. . . . If the ego has nothing to object to in a particular instinctual process and so does not ward off an affect on that ground, its attitude toward it will be determined entirely by the pleasure principle: it will welcome pleasurable affects and defend itself against painful ones. . . . It is all the more ready to ward off affects associated with prohibited sexual impulses if these affects happen to be distressing, e.g., pain, longing, mourning. On the other hand it may resist a prohibition somewhat longer in the case of positive affects, simply because they are pleasurable, or may sometimes be persuaded to tolerate them for a short time when they make a sudden irruption into consciousness. (P. 66)

Anna Freud refers to *The Ego and the Id* (S. Freud 1923) and to *Inhibitions, Symptoms and Anxiety* (1926), and quotes Freud in his statement that "what it is that the ego fears from the external [world] and from the libidinal danger cannot be specified; we know that the fear is of being overwhelmed or annihilated, but it cannot be grasped analytically" (S. Freud 1923, p. 57). What is true in regard to the motives for defense must also be true in regard to the motives for adaptation in general, for in a sense everything we do has a defensive aspect, and all defensive activity can be regarded as adaptive.

On looking back it becomes clear that Sigmund Freud's second theory of anxiety, introduced in 1926—in which anxiety was seen as a danger signal to the ego, functioning to warn it of the eventual possibility of being traumatically overwhelmed—was a major stimulus to Anna Freud's formulations. I am in agreement with Ernst Kris, who said in 1947 that he was convinced that Freud's reformulation in 1926 of a considerable set of his previous hypotheses reaches further than anyone, possibly even Freud, realized at the time of publication.

I now return to the point at which this somewhat circuitous journey started. As I mentioned, Anna Freud's criticism of the idea that the patient I described might have become deaf because of the need to recreate the presence of a highly critical internal grandparent figure in her current external world was based, as she put it, on the "world of difference between the mild, all-pervading 'functional' pleasure of perception and a drive, an instinctual urge, such as the one for passive, masochistic experience." She went on to say, "The latter is an id-urge and, as such, can set action in motion; the former is nothing of the kind, i.e., does not belong to the instinct world."

It is interesting that Anna Freud could permit herself to make such a statement, because it testifies to an interesting split that has existed in psychoanalytic thought in the area of the theory of motivation ever since the publication of *Inhibitions, Symptoms and Anxiety* in 1926. On the one hand, it is as if we have to maintain the idea that all driving forces in behavior are motivated by the instinctual drives or by derivatives of the drives. In this connection the first theory of anxiety, in which anxiety was seen as transformed libido, fitted the theory well. On the other hand, the revised theory of anxiety put into the motivation theory a formulation that fitted much better with clinical experience, namely, that anxiety could function as a signal of danger that could initiate intense defensive and adaptive activity. Anna Freud has made abundantly clear that unpleasant affect of any sort can set action in motion, and by no stretch of the imagination can one simply equate unpleasant affect with instinctual drive urges; nor indeed is instinctual drive tension the only source of uncomfortable or painful affect. So there is another set of motives, the motives for defense and defensive adaptation; they have been spelled out by Anna Freud in her book on defense (1936). What has happened in the development of psychoanalytic thought in this area is that the different theories of motivation have been kept quite separate, and psychoanalysts have moved easily from one to another, following the dictates of their particular theoretical and clinical needs at the time. One theory of motivation, which dates back to the end of the last century, equates motives with instinctual drives. Another derives from the radical reformulations in Freud's *Inhibitions, Symptoms and Anxiety* and is based upon the concept that unpleasant affect—anxiety in particular—is a driving force in human behavior. These two theories need to be brought face to face; the differences between them must be reconciled. Let me emphasize that a psychoanalytic psychology of motivation that does not take instinctual drives into account is an impoverished psychology. But so is a drive psychology that does not recognize motives other than the drives.

It could, of course, be argued that Freud's pleasure-unpleasure principle does in fact act as a unifying principle in the area of motivation. But, as Max Schur has effectively shown ( 1966), the pleasure-unpleasure principle has been used differently at different times, essentially either in an economic-energic context or linked with the death instinct and the Nirvana principle. Schur, who proposed that the pleasure and unpleasure principles be divorced rather than brought together, also commented as follows:

> Few analysts . . . who use the concepts pleasure-unpleasure, pleasure-pain principle, spell out precisely which of Freud's formulations they are actually referring to. This is especially confusing in any consideration of the relationship between the regulating principles and the affects pleasure and unpleasure, and in any discussion of those modes of functioning which Freud tried to explain in *Beyond the Pleasure Principle.* (Pp. 126–27)

In all the papers from the Hampstead Index Project referred to earlier, the urge to gain feelings of well-being and safety is regarded as very powerful indeed, even though such feelings lack the excitement associated with instinctual drive gratification. But the need to gain feelings of safety and well-being must at times be stronger than the urge to experience the feelings associated with instinctual satisfaction, because otherwise we would simply be gratifying our instinctual drive wishes as they arose. The whole of the reality principle is, after all, based upon the need to delay instinctual gratification because it is unsafe. What is it then that can make feelings of nonsensual well-being or security more attractive than, say, the direct sexual pleasure associated with sexual drive satisfaction?

Perhaps we can move a little further forward by making use of the concept of "value cathexis" referred to earlier. This is ultimately the feeling state with which a particular mental representation is invested and which is a measure, in a sense, of its positive or negative attractiveness, or of the pressure that motivates one toward it. An object or an activity can have a sexual erotic value cathexis, but it can also have a cathexis of love, which is not quite the same thing. Equally, it can have a cathexis of anger and a cathexis of hate, and here again the two are not identical. But, perhaps most important in the present context, it can have a cathexis of safety or a cathexis of well-being.

It must be apparent by now that the idea of an affective value cathexis is relevant to this discussion of motivation and consistent with the line of thought I described earlier in this chapter. I want to approach the end here by trying to tie a further pair of loose ends together by adding the proposition that the value cathexis—and therefore the attractiveness—of an activity or of an object is a variable quantity; it can even vary from one moment to the next. The value cathexis attached to a particular wished-for state, goal, aim, or object is a function, not only of the intrinsic potential for pleasant feelings associated with that state, goal, aim, or object, but it is also a function of an added investment provided by the need to do away with unpleasant feelings. These unpleasant affects arise from instinctual tensions and also from threats and dangers of the most varied sort. And foremost among these painful affects is anxiety, no matter whether its source be instinctual or otherwise.

Let me formulate this in another way. Imagine the normal child who feels safe when with his or her mother. We can say that the mother is invested with a certain affective value cathexis of safety for the child. Margaret Mahler (Mahler et al. 1975) has vividly described how the toddler "checks back to mother" in order to receive a "refueling"; in this way the child modulates his level of safety feeling and maintains it at an appropriate level. But when the toddler falls and hurts himself, when he suddenly loses sight of mother or is threatened in some other way, her value as a source of safety feeling rises dramatically, for the feeling of safety with which the mother is invested also contains the element of the absence of nonsafety, the absence of danger. The same sort of fluctuation in cathexis of value occurs in relation to the drives. The stronger the sexual urge, the greater the value attached to the sexual object or activity. Here again, the sexual cathexis of value attached to the object at that particular time contains the affective promise of relief from sexual tension. From a clinical point of view, it is extremely common in psychoanalytic work to see impulses of all sorts compounded of the two kinds of elements I have been describing.

The view of motivation put forward here provides a framework for the closer integration of object relations theories with drive aspects of motivation and certainly provides an understanding of object relationships somewhat more satisfactory than the simple formulation that objects are cathected with libido. In every situation of anxiety, for instance, there is a reaching toward the object that can provide safety, and this applies as much to the introjects as to external objects. This was certainly the case with the patient I described earlier. By being deaf she created the illusion of the presence of the object, and the drive to interact with the object in her own particular way was intense. True, she paid a price in pain and suffering in this relationship, but the function of the object as a source of safety and reassurance against threat of abandonment and disintegration outweighed all other factors. Although I also assume that she had a perverse sexual investment in the suffering she endured, the sexual element was not, to my mind, the major motivating factor. This is absolutely in line with the clinical reality that, in masochistic patients, the analysis of guilt-motivated self-damaging behavior often plays a far greater role than the analysis of perverse sexual pleasure—and guilt, as an affect, is a form of anxiety. My answer to Anna Freud's letter, if I were to write it today, would be, "Yes, you are right, when there is no threat, then feelings of safety are mild when compared with instinctual pleasure. But situations of safety, particularly those associated with familiar interaction with the internal or external object, can become even more attractive than instinctual drive satisfaction when danger threatens. No one has demonstrated this more convincingly than you have done in *The Ego and the Mechanisms of Defence.*"

I want to end by emphasizing my belief that psychoanalysts need to develop an approach to motivation that can take into account more satisfactorily than in the past what is known about external and internal object relationships. We know how difficult it is to place a theory of object relations into a drive-reductionist framework, and the answer must surely lie not in a distortion of what we know about object relationships but rather in a modification of our essential theoretical scaffolding.

## References

Freud, A. 1936. *The ego and the mechanisms of defence.* London: Hogarth Press.

Freud, S. 1920. Beyond the pleasure principle. *Standard Edition,* 18. London: Hogarth Press.

———. 1923. The ego and the id. *Standard Edition,* 19. London: Hogarth Press.

———. 1926. Inhibitions, symptoms and anxiety. *Standard Edition,* 20. London: Hogarth Press.

Joffe, W. G., and Sandler, J. 1965. Notes on pain, depression and individuation. *Psychoanalytic Study of the Child* 20:394–424.

———. 1967. Some conceptual problems involved in the consideration of disorders of narcissism. *Journal of Child Psychotherapy* 2:56.

———. 1968. Comments on the psychoanalytic psychology of adaptation, with special reference to the role of affects and the representational world. *International Journal of Psycho-Analysis* 49:445–54.

Kris, E. 1947. Problems in clinical research: Discussion remarks. *American Journal of Orthopsychiatry* 17:210.

Mahler, M., Pine, F., and Bergmann, A. 1975. *The psychological birth of the human infant.* New York: Basic Books.

Sandler, J. 1959. On the repetition of early childhood relationships in later psychosomatic disorder. In *On the Nature of Stress Disorder.* London: Hutchinson.

————. 1960a. The background of safety. *International Journal of Psycho-Analysis* 41:352–56.

————. 1960b. On the concept of the superego. *The Psychoanalytic Study of the Child* 15:128–62.

————. 1962. Psychology and psychoanalysis. *British Journal of Medicine and Psychology* 35:91–100.

————. 1974. Psychological conflict and the structural model: Some clinical and theoretical implications. *International Journal of Psycho-Analysis* 55:53–62.

————. 1978. Unconscious wishes and human relations. Inaugural lecture for Freud Memorial Visiting Professorship. London: University College.

————. 1983. Reflections on some relations between psychoanalytic concepts and psychoanalytic practice. *International Journal of Psycho-Analysis* 64:35–45.

Sandler, J., and Freud, A. 1985. *The analysis of defense.* New York: International Univ. Press.

Sandler, J., Holder, A., and Meers, D. 1963. The ego ideal and the ideal self. *Psychoanalytic Study of the Child* 18:139–58.

Sandler, J., and Joffe, W. G. 1966. On skill and sublimation. *Journal of the American Psychoanalytic Association* 14:335–55.

Sandler, J., and Rosenblatt, B. 1962. The concept of the representational world. *Psychoanalytic Study of the Child* 17:128–45.

Sandler, J., and Sandler, A-M. 1978. On the development of object relationships and affects. *International Journal of Psycho-Analysis* 59:285–96.

Schur, M. 1966. *The id and the regulatory principles of mental functioning.* New York: International Univ. Press.

■
■
■

**Six**            **Personality Change**
■ ■          **through Life**
             **Experience:**
             **The Role of Ego Ideal,**
             **Personality, and Events**
             *Milton Viederman, M.D.*


**P**ersonality change, the discovery or rediscovery of parts of the self that were not before in evidence, may occur at any time during the life cycle. My intent in this chapter is to describe how individuals create and respond to life events and change in the process. The focus is on plasticity rather than fixity of character in some individuals who reveal a motivation for change that resides in the wish to achieve an ego ideal.[1] This motivation is influenced by personality and life experience, the second of which is sometimes created, sometimes adventitious.

The observations and ideas presented here stem from extensive contact with individuals who are either physically ill or normal research subjects. Periodically, one observes individuals who seem to have lived comfortable and engaged lives and who then tolerate the worst of adversities imaginable with courage, reasonable equanimity, and the capacity to enjoy simple things that at times seems to elude us even under the best of circumstances. Although certainly not free of conflict, these people do not designate themselves as neurotic and would not under usual circumstances have consulted a psychiatrist or psychoanalyst. The opportunity to observe the life trajectories of such people convinced me that they not infrequently experienced considerable personality change as adults, an observation that belied the usual

---

1. I will use the terms *ego ideal* and *ideal self-representation* interchangeably for convenience, although I recognize that they are related but different concepts.

psychoanalytic view that personality almost never changes in adulthood without psychoanalysis. What appeared instead in some individuals was an impetus to approximate an ego ideal, to gratify wishes and aspirations either long dormant or new. One patient in particular crystallized my thinking about risk-taking and change and led me to observe that a small group of pregnant, diabetic women experienced considerable personality change under circumstances that included the following: (1) an internal pressure directed toward achievement of an aspect of an ego ideal that previously had eluded them; (2) a decision leading to an action in the world that functioned as a test of their self-representation; (3) the catalytic effect of an important person who affirmed the self-representation modified through action; and (4) on occasion, an identification with that person. These observations led to a broader examination of the circumstances of personality change in the context of life experience. The capacity to experience such change seems to reside in people with certain personality traits related to a tendency toward action, a search for novelty, and the ability to integrate new experiences and to be modified in so doing. To paraphrase Pasteur, chance favors only prepared individuals. Significant life events and people important in the lives of these individuals catalyzed such change.

The personality change I describe does not imply magical rebirth or a total change of personality. Rather, it refers to a significant change in a facet of the self-representation that brings it closer to the ideal self-representation. These internal representations or structures are not fixed but are in constant minor flux as the individual acts in his environment. Nonetheless, in reasonably well-integrated individuals (and particularly in patients with the fixity that resides in character disorder), the fluctuations occur around a defined core that reflects self-perception on many levels in terms of ego capacities, bodily form and function, social roles, and so on. What I am suggesting is that an important shift in an aspect or locus of this core occurs in certain individuals under the circumstance defined below.

## PSYCHOANALYTIC VISIONS OF REALITY AND THEIR IMPLICATIONS FOR CHANGE

Psychoanalysts are understandably wary of the idea that people may change rapidly in the context of life situations. Not only does it run counter to their experience with patients, but there are numerous elements intrinsic to the history and tradition of psychoanalytic theory that argue against this idea. Psychoanalytic theory, though dynamic in a microscopic sense, is, in its broader configuration, a theory of stability rather than of change. Rooted as it was in nineteenth-century positivism and determinism applied to the study of neurotic patients, the natural focus of psychoanalysis was on self-defeating, repetitious patterns of behavior, the product of unconscious intrapsychic conflict of infantile origin. The earliest models were homeostatic and were viewed predominantly as closed systems with channels of discharge utilizing pathways established by regression and fixation. Although I will not attempt to elaborate the modifications and additions that psychoanalytic theory has undergone, particularly with the elaboration of ego psychology by Hartmann (1958) and his followers, a conservative view about change is maintained and embodied in the idea of character structure, which implies organized repetitive patterns of behavior reflective of underlying structural relationships with a slow rate of change. It is indisputable that this point of view remains an essential one for many aspects of psychoanalytic work and the psychoanalytic view of behavior, but it does not adequately encapsulate the radical changes in behavior and character that occur in certain individuals. The concept of object choice, for example—considered to be the most variable aspect of drive—is viewed as inevitably and predominantly determined by unconscious repetition related to the search for early objects and does not explain departures in object choice occasionally observed in the life trajectories of nonpatients.

Of particular interest in this regard is Schafer's (1976) elaboration of four psychoanalytic visions of reality, each with its own perspective and each with special pertinence to aspects of the human experience. Schafer recognizes in the word *vision* a "judgment rooted in subjectivity" and states that the "psychoanalytic process, that special reality about which we know the most," is being used to extrapolate to reality at large, in his words, "for better or worse." The particular visions that he describes so eloquently—the tragic, the ironic, the comic, and the romantic—each shed light on an aspect of experience but are in part contradictory. The tragic and ironic were more central to Freud's thinking and represent the dominant modes of the psychoanalytic Weltanschauung. The tragic is dominated "by the terrible power of fixation, repression, regression, and repetition; the insidious influence of unconscious processes and in particular linearity in time;—what is lost is forever lost." It emphasizes the inevitability of intrapsychic conflict and resultant pain. The ironic, simply stated, maintains the same perspective but focuses on detachment and the observation of these processes. The comic and romantic, though pertinent, are of lesser stature. The first represents hopefulness, the possibility and expectation of change with the view that external obstacles inhibit change and can be eliminated by manipulative action in the world. The romantic focuses on quest and the pursuit of goals with the implication of a "discontinuous leap forward in existence and thereby an emancipation from history."

I elaborate Schafer's view because it has direct pertinence to what I am about to describe. In my work, I have observed behavior that more approximates the comic and romantic visions. These are people—a small number, I emphasize—who seek and experience change hopefully and who, if successful in their endeavor, do seem to make dramatic leaps in the form of changed perceptions of themselves and of others, often with the choice of different objects. They differ in one important respect, however, from Schafer's description of the comic vision. The modification occurs not by overcoming obstacles in the outside world but by using such obstacles in the pursuit of change. Important people in their lives facilitate this process. As these are not psychoanalytic patients or patients in psychotherapy, the data generated by psychoanalysis are not available, but understanding their behavior (used in the widest sense to include intrapsychic data) in psychoanalytic terms does no violence to psychoanalytic theory. If I am changing the structure of the pantheon of psychoanalytic gods, it is not to dethrone the tragic or the ironic visions as the supreme deities but to augment the status of the comic and romantic to the level of significant forces in their own right.

My intent in this section has been to demonstrate the rootedness of psychoanalytic theory in the psychoanalytic situation itself, where it sheds light on and emphasizes stability and repetition. As currently applied, however, it has not addressed important change that occurs outside the psychoanalytic situation.

## CASE ILLUSTRATION

The patient was a forty-three-year-old woman about to donate a kidney to her son, a fourteen-year-old boy born with congenital disease of the urinary tract.[2] The mother was a chronically depressed woman who described indifferent maternal care in her own childhood. Her four pregnancies had been unplanned and unwanted, but she stifled the resentment she felt about the demands of pregnancy and motherhood and attempted as best she could to function in her role as a mother. The only relief came in her work outside the house. Resentment at having the mothering role thrust upon her evoked much guilt, which was accentuated when her oldest child was discovered to have congenital renal disease in the early years of his life.

2. These anecdotes are presented in abbreviated form to illustrate the basic ideas. Fuller descriptions of the cases have been published in Viederman (1986).

Although terrified of surgery, the mother accepted it when it became apparent that she was the best biological donor. Her anxiety heightened during the few days of hospitalization preceding the transplant. She likened the experience to pregnancy itself, emphasizing that it was like a sentence passed upon her from which there was no appeal. It was in this context that she had a visit the night before the operation from a minister who commented to her, "You must really love your son to do so much for him." The patient experienced extreme relief, and the experience had a profound effect upon her. In her own words, "I was astonished to discover that *I wanted* to give him this kidney because I loved him and wanted him to be well. There were no strings attached."

Contact with the patient many years later indicated that the change that this woman underwent in her self-perception as a loving and maternal figure had persisted and led to an increase in self-worth.

This woman had long struggled with the guilty sense of herself as a bad mother pushed into pregnancy by forces beyond her own control. Although she endeavored to nurture her children, it was always with a sense that she was obliged to do so. In this respect she saw herself as like her own mother, who was unhappy as a mother and was even a reluctant grandmother. In the context of the crisis of surgery that she feared greatly, a comment by the minister became an important corrective experience. What before had seemed like an obligation, namely, the pregnancies and the surgery, now became something that she desired to do out of love (an act of choice). In this context she had a major modification of her self-perception as a giving mother with a marked increase in self-esteem.

## THE SUBSTRATE OF CHANGE

Life change is a product of the interaction between the following elements:

1. The ego ideal as a motivating force for change throughout the life cycle. Included here is the concept of a stable ideal self-representation formed through negative identification.

2. Personality attributes that influence the capacity to integrate new experience. This category includes (a) action in the world as movement toward change; (b) attitudes toward new experience presented as a dialectic between the search for novelty and attachment to stability; and (c) meaning and the capacity to develop new belief systems about self and others.

3. The impact of new experience and in particular the catalytic role of new objects as they effect transference distortions.

I wish to examine in the remainder of this chapter the complex interplay between motivations, personality attributes that have motivational elements, and the role of external events in such change. Events lead to structural change only if they are integrated and assimilated; therefore, one must differentiate events from the integration of such events that may be called experience.

## Motivation for Change: The Ego Ideal and Ideal Self-Representation

The impetus to achieve an ego ideal or ideal self-representation acts as a motivational system directed toward change throughout the life cycle. The conceptualization of the representational world (Sandler and Rosenblatt 1962) and its associated concepts of self-representation and ideal self-representation lend themselves readily to the conceptualization of phenomena described below. Although the idea that individuals strive to achieve ideal self-representation is a familiar one, it is commonly utilized in a microscopic way to describe incremental changes in the self-representation and is seen in particular as a type of homeostatic mechanism with constant minor flux but without shift in core except under the circumstance of psychoanalysis. I suggest that the tension between self and ideal self-representations acts as a strong motivational force throughout life and can under certain circumstances be the impetus for marked change in personality. Individuals are motivated toward action in the world to test previously unexperienced but latent aspects of their self-representations in an effort to obtain the normal narcissistic gratification inherent in the approximation of their self-representation with an ideal self-representation. This is closely associated with the implicit desire for mastery that has its origins in earliest infancy.

The concept of development implies change. It is important to note, however, that developmental theory does not imply a motivation for change. Developmental theories have been for the most part descriptive and not dynamic in this respect, at least in a psychological sense. In childhood in particular, a biological substrate, namely, maturation, with special emphasis on the central nervous system, is an important feature of change, although, as Erikson (1959) has elaborated, this maturational change crystallizes in a definable and responsive psychosocial environment. Biological factors, important as maturational forces, continue to play a part throughout the life cycle, but they are less central in adulthood when normative crises more often relate to changes in role expectations (Michels 1980). Only Greenacre (1971) spoke specifically of a "satisfaction of maturational processes" implying a motivation toward change as part of the life cycle. It is to elaborate this theme that I propose the concept of the tension between ideal self-representation and self-representation as a motivational force directed toward change throughout adult life.[3]

The psychoanalytic theory of motivation originated with a concept of instinct closely tied to an energetic hypothesis that involved a pressure toward immediate discharge reflected in the pleasure principle (Freud 1911b). The reality principle and secondary process require the binding of energy and the deflection and modification of drive impulses. The concept of sublimation was closely associated with this modification of drive and was used as an explanatory concept to understand strivings toward long-term goals that could not immediately be achieved and were far removed from their instinctual origins, aims, and objects. These strivings were more syntonic with social demands and expectations. Freud (1930a) dealt extensively with these long-term goals and with the renunciation of instinct, which, in his view, were the basis of both civilization and neurosis.

Hartmann (1958), in his attempt to develop a general psychoanalytic psychology of behavior, was concerned with man's inherent potential for adaptation and developed the concepts of the conflict-free sphere and autonomous ego functions, themselves the product of maturation of the central nervous system. Hartmann attributed a range of behavior to motivations that had their origin in the ego. Hendrick (1942, 1943) took the next step, describing behavior in the infant and young child that he called the "instinct to master" and that he dissociated from libidinal and aggressive drives. "The aim of the instinct to master as I shall use this concept is the . . . *pleasure* . . . in executing a function successfully, regardless of its sensual value" (by sensual Hendrick meant its libidinal quality). Hendrick saw this instinct as having both a reflex phase, by which he meant an automatic maturational potential that was expressed, and a phase of "acquired proficiency and gratification." He emphasized that there is an essential pleasure in ego function separate from drives emanating from the id. "The pleasure was . . . determined by the . . . infant's . . . ability to function successfully, displaying pride like that of a child in its first unassisted walking." This concept was further elaborated by White (1963), who spoke of a "feeling of efficacy" and competence that "is the cumulative effect of the whole history of (positive) transactions with the environment, no matter how they are motivated. . . . Thus it can be said that competence becomes in the course of development a highly important nucleus of motivation. . . . It has a great deal to do with confidence and self-respect" (p. 39). White goes on to underline the well-

3. Since this paper was written, other articles have addressed the issue of developmental change during adulthood. See Settlage et al. (1988) and Emde (1988a, 1988b).

known psychoanalytic proposition that the ego ideal is the repository of narcissistic omnipotence and that the level of self-esteem can be conceived of as a reflection of the difference between the ideal and the actual. This concept of pleasure in mastery can be seen as a theory of motivation for change throughout the life cycle: the persistent influence of unattained aspects of the ego ideal motivates behavior toward change. The motivating force lies in the normal narcissistic gratification attendant upon the achievement of an ego ideal, which, in its most primitive form, presents the infant's wish to regain the blissful state of infantile omnipotence by fusion with parents who have become the repository of delegated omnipotence (Freud 1914c; Murray 1964).

It is important to note that the above authors are particularly interested in the influence of such ego functions on child development. Except for Hendrick, they do not extend this concept in a significant way to the adult experience. Hendrick elaborates the concept of a "work principle," by which he means "the principle that primary pleasure is sought by efficient use of the central nervous system for the performance of well-integrated functions that enable the individual to control or alter his environment" (Hendrick 1943). Only White (1963) focuses on the issue of the ego ideal and narcissistic gratification, but he tends to think of these changes as involving incremental advances toward achievement of the ego ideal. I am suggesting the possibility of more radical, global shifts that occur under special life circumstances.

The sense of effectance, competence, or instinct to mastery is one aspect of the substrate on which an ideal self-representation is built. Yet inhibitions in achieving such ideals occur. A woman seen in a study of pregnant, diabetic women had been troubled by the presence of a negative self-representation since childhood. She had struggled with a painful perception of herself that she wished to change, a perception that was discordant with her ideal self-representation. She had experienced diabetes, which developed when she was seven, as a manifestation of personal defectiveness that was accentuated by her mother's communication that it was shameful and should be hidden. This view was consolidated by the feeling of personal unattractiveness engendered by acne in adolescence. The tension between her self-representation (as defective) and her ideal self-representation (as complete) lay dormant until a particular moment in her life when she decided to test the defective image of herself through pregnancy. That she had approximated an ideal self-representation in one area, professional success, the conflictual substrate of which had been a phallic competition with the brother, permitted available resources (energy, in a metaphorical sense) to be directed toward achieving an ideal self-representation in another area, that of motherhood. When first seen, she had been tormented by fears of having a defective child. These fears were interpreted to her as a product of a fantasy that the child, seen as an extension of herself, would be defective, as she felt herself to be. The interpretation brought on a strong emotional catharsis with total relief of her obsessional ruminations. In a letter one month later, she indicated that the interview had been a turning point in her emotional life. A successful pregnancy led to the repair of her sense of defectiveness through the birth of a "beautiful, intact child," seen as an extension of herself. This phenomenon of a redirection of resources, interests, and attention to an undeveloped aspect of self after achievement in another area is frequently observed in the study of life trajectories.

A similar process may be viewed as part of artistic creation. Gedo (1983), commenting on the creative process of the artist, presents a view consonant with the position presented above:

> Rose [1980] concurs with the critics of Kris's understanding of artistic creation as a regression in the service of the ego, perceptively pointing out that this notion confuses the artist's creative capacities, which must be autonomous and developmentally advanced, with certain personal motivations for understanding the creative task. . . . As an example of such motivations, Rose considers the effort to achieve a form of perfection through creativity, presumably because such perfection was desired but never attained in the course of the artist's first creative endeavor, the organization of his self in early childhood (pages 32–47). Rose calls self-creation "the creativity of everyday life" (pages 114–115). If the artist's motivation for his work is to attain perfection, its reparative function is conceivable only if the work is never completely differentiated from the creator's own person. To this extent, Rose sees artistic activity as the restoration of a state in which the self has expanded through a fantasy of fusion with an external object— an idea similar to Winnicott's concept of "transitional phenomena."

In the creative act, the artist changes. This conceptualization parallels the view presented above of a continual motivation to strive toward perfection throughout the life cycle.

Generally, ideal self-representations crystallize about highly valued attributes of objects, real and imagined, conscious and unconscious, and involve partial identifications with the representations of these objects. Some ideal self-representations, however, are generated by negative or inverse identifications with devalued objects. An example of such a phenomenon was the powerful investment in a maternal role observed in a woman who had experienced profound rejection at the hands of a nonnurturing prostitute mother. Although it seemed clear that her satisfaction in being a mother resided in part in the unconscious vicarious gratification that she experienced through identification with the nurtured child, it was also apparent that her self-esteem had been enhanced by satisfaction in achieving her ego ideal of being a good mother, so different from her own mother. Another woman had been married to a dominant, controlling, and narcissistic man much resembling her father. She was in the process of obtaining a divorce from him when she was hospitalized for severe pain and endometrial bleeding. Her father angrily informed her at that time that she could expect no help from him. This experience consolidated a strong sense of independence and desire to control her life, which contrasted markedly with the stance of her masochistic, humiliated, and dependent mother. This has served her well in her work as a lawyer and in her second marriage to a responsive, supportive man who willingly shares responsibility with her. The impetus to independence and control has not interfered with her capacity to cope with a high-risk pregnancy that requires that she be quiescent and remain at home, where she continues to work, albeit with diminished intensity, as the situation requires. In this she reveals considerable flexibility.

## Personality Characteristics that Influence Availability for Change

In psychoanalytic theory, character has been primarily conceptualized in structural terms, with emphasis on drive derivatives, defensive organization, and superego functioning rather than in terms of the nature and quality of interaction with the outside world, particularly as it relates to susceptibility to new influence. Yet it seems that certain persons are freer to experiment, to test new possibilities, and to change thereby than are others, who are more rigid and fearful. A personality construct called Hardiness (Kobasa 1982), designed to study coping, seems particularly pertinent in this respect. Hardy individuals are defined as having three general characteristics: (1) control—the sense that they have power and control over their lives and their environment; (2) commitment—the sense that their actions and activities are worth engaging in and are valued; and (3) challenge—the tendency to view the experience of a new situation as something to be engaged in with interest and enthusiasm and with the possibility and expectation of change, growth, and mastery rather than as a threat to homeostasis with the danger of ultimate harm. Hardy individuals reveal a wide range of adaptive capacities, not the least of which is the ability to change their self-perceptions in the context of their active engagement in life. The concept of hardiness in the present discussion is extended to examine its relationship to action, the search for novelty, and the capacity to evolve new belief systems that can be translated into new perceptions of self in relationship to the world. The first two may be viewed as personality traits, and the third, an ego function; all three influence the search for new experience and the possibility of change.

*Action and Change* A number of authors have referred to the close relationship between action and psychic structure. It is well established that
insight may follow action as well as proceed it. Radó (1956) relates the
essence of the self to action when he speaks of the action-self. "Of proprioceptive origin, the action-self emerges from the circular response pattern
of self awareness and willed action. It then integrates the contrasting pictures
of total organism and total environment that provides the basis for the selfhood of the conscious organism" (p. 275). Kardiner and Spiegel (1947)
elaborate on this point of view in describing action systems. White (1963)
states that the genesis of reality testing derives from active interaction with
the environment. "Reality testing—finding out about reality and being
guided by it comes about through attempted actions and their consequences.
Reality is not passively received; it does not imprint itself on the mind. It is
slowly constructed through active, varied and persistent exploration, and
what is learned about it is how to deal with it: what actions produce what
effects on what objects" (p. 186). White echoes in psychological terms what
Piaget has described for cognitive development. Action in the world determines the reality that one perceives. It is important to note, however, that not
only is the nature of the reality of the external world being constructed, but,
through action, the nature of the self is being tested and modified. How one
perceives oneself is in part determined by the observations of one's interaction with the environment. This is especially meaningful when an action is
initiated, consciously or unconsciously, to test a self-perception. The diabetic
women described above unconsciously decided to test their views of themselves in a life situation that involved a decision and an action based upon that
decision, though there is no evidence that they were aware initially of what
they were engaging in. Important was the fact that they were characterologically inclined toward action. One may assume that individuals vary in the
degree to which an inclination toward activity is constitutional or belongs to
either the conflictual or the conflict-free sphere. However, even action in the
service of conflict, such as counterphobic behavior designed to defend
against anxiety or activity that defends against depression, may impel an
individual toward commerce with the world which leads to discoveries
about the self that take on secondary autonomy.

## The Search for Novelty versus the Need for Security and Stability

> The first thing that gives pleasure in a narrative is a plentiful variety. Just as with
> food and music novel and extraordinary things delight us for various reasons but
> especially because they are different from the old ones we are used to, so with
> everything the mind takes great pleasure in variety and abundance. . . . I would
> say a picture was richly varied if it contained a properly arranged mixture of old

men, youths, boys, matrons, maidens, children, domestic animals, dogs, birds, horses, sheep, buildings and provinces; and I would praise any great variety provided it is appropriate to what is going on in the picture. (Alberti 1435)

Psychoanalytic theory originally tended to reduce curiosity and the search for novelty to instinctual derivatives of scoptophilia. Hartmann's modification made curiosity an important motivational system related to the ego. The phenomenon is well known to child developmental psychologists who observe in very young infants the curiosity generated by novel stimuli and the infants' general unresponsiveness to repetitive stimuli. Kagan (1984) describes this when he says that "an event that can be assimilated after some effort produces excitement, but one that cannot be assimilated produces uncertainty . . . which though . . . not synonymous with the states of fear or anxiety . . . may precede them. If the infant continues to attempt the assimilation of an event, remains unsuccessful, and, additionally, has no way to deal with the comprehension of failure, a different state is generated. Some psychologists call this subsequent state fear or anxiety." Kagan calls this phenomenon the discrepancy principle. Although Kagan's view resembles Piaget's cognitive model in some respects, unlike Piaget, Kagan emphasizes that the infant's emotional state is affected by his ability or inability to assimilate discrepant events. Kagan further states that "interest, emotion and action typically follow a partial alteration of the usual. Thus the mind grows at the edge where the expected does not occur or is *moderately transformed*" (my italics).[4]

This developmental statement has important implications for the formation of personality attributes as they affect the individual's attitude toward new experience throughout his or her life. If early life experience provides nourishing and measured stimulation in the fullest emotional sense in an atmosphere of comfort and security, the adult is likely to develop an attitude of optimism and interest in a search for new and rich experience that may ultimately lead to personal transformation. Conversely, the frequent experience of helplessness and anxiety in children when confronted with novel situations may lead to the anticipation that new experience is dangerous. Although one would expect that individual life experience and intrapsychic conflict would create different attitudes toward specific categories of experience, each individual is likely to develop his own *window of availability for engagement with the world* in relation to the novel and the new, a window of

4. Interesting new work by Kagen and associates (Rosenbaum et al. 1988) indicates that there are genetically determined traits that lead to behavioral inhibition and shyness in children which are correlated with adult panic attacks and agoraphobia. This would suggest that there is a genetic substrate to a limited window of availability for engagement with the world.

availability that is characteristic of him and becomes an attribute of his personality as it relates to his desire and ability to integrate new experience and be changed by it. The size of the window is determined in general by whether he is threatened or challenged by the new. What evolves is what might be considered a dialectic in the individual between a search for novelty associated with an inclination to risk-taking and the pull of security manifested in an anxious search for the familiar. The inclination to repeat, an attribute of neurotic behavior, not only originates in intrapsychic conflict but, in a complementary fashion, relates to a fear of the new in relationship to reality. In fact, distressing feelings of repetition and stagnation may be the very reason the neurotic is motivated to seek treatment. Obviously, constitutional elements, early life experience, and intrapsychic conflict all play a role in the formation of the window of availability for new experience that led to action and varying forms of commerce with the world and then crystallized in personality change.

Individuals vary in the degree to which they find the repetitious aspect of their lives burdensome, boring, and requiring change, both as a function of personality (trait) and as a function of the context of their lives at a moment in time and, in particular, their stage in the life cycle (state). Rapid changes in childhood, adolescence, and early adult life encourage a search for constancy and stability in the environment, whereas later, stability can become tedious and repetitive and may lead to a search for the novel. By extension, the ability to transform the familiar into something slightly discrepant may lead to satisfaction and continued growth. Moreover, stability in one area, such as marriage, may be a prerequisite for experimentation and risk-taking in another, such as work. These polar opposites have not been presented with the intent of favoring novelty over stability, for it is clear that the exaggeration of either can be a reflection of intrapsychic conflict and lead to maladaption. The search for novelty and associated risk-taking, however, is a personality trait that favors change through experience.

*Meaning, New Belief Systems, and the Capacity for Change*  The framework of the elements of the representational world pertain to conscious and unconscious perceptions of self and of self in relationship to ideals and other objects. Individuals vary greatly in the degree to which they experience an integrated sense of self. Psychoanalysts are constantly confronted with individuals whose rigid self-perceptions dominate their interactions with the world. On the other side of the spectrum are those who appear to be so fluid that they have great difficulty in developing a coherent picture of themselves. In its extreme, this has been described as the as-if personality. One also observes, however, individuals who function quite well in the world but who seem never quite to know what they really feel or what they really want. (I am not referring here simply to obsessional patients.) These individuals present particular problems in the psychoanalytic situation, for they seem to be constantly hypothesizing about their feelings and motivations, and yet none of their verbal productions appear to have meaning. Interpretations made to such patients seem empty and fall flat. In contrast are the "ideal psycho-analytic patients" with a defined core. Their thoughts and feelings have mean-ing, as do the associative connections they establish between these thoughts and feelings and their memories of the past. The capacity to value their mental productions facilitates their ability to develop new perceptions of themselves. For people with this capacity, a thought, feeling, memory, or fantasy that develops in association with a previous constellation is signifi-cant. These are the individuals who develop insight in the context of psycho-analysis, who embrace the new as they feel, think, and elaborate meanings and in this context evolve new self-representations. These meanings are essentially belief systems about themselves that define their relationship to the world. During the process of psychoanalysis, these patients change their present as they change their past, as memories become modified and percep-tions of objects and experiences change. They have the capacity to establish a modified subjective view of self-perceptions and of the world. A modified perception of their life history plays a role in this change. Work in such an analysis is satisfying for both patient and analyst, though it does not occur without pain. Michels (1977) in this regard views myths as being therapeu-tically mutative.

The individuals whom I am describing as capable of radical change fall into this category. These people do not change through a process of self-analysis. Often, as pointed out above, action and new experience lead to change, and insight may be a product of this change, though frequently insight in the sense of conscious awareness may not be present even when change occurs. It is difficult to determine whether this capacity to develop belief systems, have insight, and experience meaning in the sense that I have described is limited to the group of individuals who have the capacity to communicate verbally about themselves. In any case, individuals with this capacity are much more likely to be able to experience the type of change that I have described.

## The Role of Life Events and the Special Importance of a Catalytic Object in Change

It is well established that individuals in a state of crisis are available for considerable change. Crisis might be defined as a life situation that leads to disorganization and disruption of psychic structure, activates regressive infantile transference wishes and fears, and requires the development of a new perspective on oneself in relation to the world as well as an altered perception of one's life trajectory. Crisis thus defined may be provoked by events that disrupt established ways of looking at oneself and demand new perspectives and modes of behavior. They may be imposed by new role requirements such as marriage or pregnancy.

In evaluating the availability of individuals for change in the context of life experience, one must consider the state of the individual at the moment of crisis and the special role that other people may play in the special context of crisis. Janis's work on patients anticipating surgery offers a model to understand the varied responses of individuals to impending surgery (1974). He categorized patients in low, moderate, and high states of anticipatory anxiety about the surgery. The behavior and psychological outcome after surgery of individuals in different categories were clearly distinguished. Individuals with low states of anticipatory anxiety tended characterologically to be minimizers. Characteristically they did little to obtain information about what the experience would be like and had significant difficulty postoperatively. Individuals with moderate anxiety asked pertinent questions about their state, sought reassurance from the people about them, and were able to prepare themselves psychologically for what was to come. This group did best. Individuals with high states of anxiety appeared to be dominated by specific unconscious fears of mutilation, death, disfigurement, and so on. Because of the unrealistic and unconscious nature of their fears, they were unable to reassure themselves and had poor outcomes. This latter group experienced considerable regressive dependency and what Janis called unrepression, by which he meant the availability to consciousness of primitive material previously repressed.

It becomes apparent that in this situation the availability of repressed material and the increased dependency needs offer an opportunity for useful intervention if interventions are addressed to respond to the patient's specific unrealistic fears. The individual who communicates this understanding takes on a special status in the patient's eyes. This intervention may be accomplished by an interpretation of the specific fear or may involve the use of the psychodynamic life narrative (Viederman 1983). Even an intuitive or spontaneous response by some individual that responds to the specific fear or conflict may lead to change, as in the case of the minister who responded to the woman donating a kidney to her son.

The spontaneous response was helpful for a partially blind, diabetic woman in poor control who was advised to have an abortion because the poor diabetic control placed the fetus at great risk of deformity. This woman's view of herself as both damaged and bad was in part a reflection of an identification with a hostile and rejecting mother, who viewed her diabetes as shameful and with whom she had interacted in an angry, rebellious way. She saw herself as "bad, a liar and a cheat," particularly because she stole money to buy forbidden foods. Her mode was to develop a rigid and brittle independence that made her intolerant and hostile toward dependency objects who offered support. In the context of the abortion, which she decided to pursue (her own decision), a female diabetologist, who the patient knew was herself a mother and a diabetic, supported the abortion and stated that she was doing the right thing. The patient was profoundly affected by this supportive response. She developed a changed representation of herself as more worthy, became more tolerant of her dependency needs, assumed excellent diabetic control, and experienced a subsequent pregnancy and motherhood in a positive way with a marked rise in self-esteem. Her previously highly punitive superego function was muted. The patient had experienced a modification of her self-representation with approximation of her ideal self-representation. This special interaction with the diabetologist had catalyzed this changed view by supporting the patient's decision and encouraging a future pregnancy. What might have been viewed as a highly destructive act was now seen as adaptive and in the best interest of herself and the baby she had not yet conceived.

One might view this interaction as a modification of a transference distortion by experience rather than interpretation. Loewald (1980) describes the therapeutic effect of interpretation of the transference in psychoanalysis in a way that readily lends itself to understanding the patient's experience of the diabetologist's comment.

> The re-experience by re-enactment of the past—the unconscious organization of the past implied in repetition—undergoes change during the course of treatment. In part these changes depend upon the current experiences with the analyst that do not fit the anticipatory set the patient brings to his experiencing another, mainly parental, person. In this manner the way of reliving the past is apt to be influenced by novel present experience; certain past experiences are seen in a different light and felt differently. Inasmuch as reenactment is a form of remembering, memories may change under the impact of the present experience . . . with [previously hostile recollections giving way to more positive ones]. . . . It is thus not only true that the present is influenced by the past, but also that the past—as a living force within the patient—is influenced by the present. (P. 360)

One may infer that this patient found a loving, maternal object instead of a hostile, punitive one and was profoundly affected by the experience. In this situation there was no evidence that she changed her perception of her mother, who may well have been aggressively critical and rejecting. What changed was her distorted expectation that all maternal figures have these qualities. With this changed expectation came a change in her view of herself, which was ultimately concretized by the satisfaction generated by a loving relationship with her child. There was a change in her representation of her mother who she now felt could love her for herself and not simply respond to what she had done. A change in representation of the maternal object is a phenomenon not infrequently observed during pregnancy.

How can such brief interactions have such lasting impact when our usual experience suggests that working through such distortions takes years in psychoanalysis? The answer rests in the nature of the disorganization generated by the crisis associated with the actualization of the wish for an ideal loving parent, which allows patients to be available for the integration of new experience.

These experiences can reasonably be called corrective emotional experiences, though they do not conform to Alexander's (1961) definition, which included a contrived stance on the part of the analyst designed to contradict transference expectations. It is unfortunate that the term is associated with this definition, because the corrective emotional experience is a useful concept and certainly occurs in analysis, as pointed out by Loewald (1960).

For these women, the approval implicit in the response of the other person, who had special status in the patient's eyes, consolidated a new self-representation. In each case this person was consciously seen by the patient as central to the change that occurred during the interaction.

Another aspect of the change the last woman experienced resided in her identification with the diabetologist. The patient emphasized that her knowledge that the diabetologist was a diabetic who had successfully given birth to normal children had much to do with the impact of the diabetologist's statement. This patient, previously the "bad girl," was now able to identify with a good and giving mother who had negotiated diabetes and had children. Through this identification, she was reinforced in her ability to become a good and giving mother. The model for this new identification did not reside simply in the reality of the person and behavior of the diabetologist but reflected a wishful, idealizing fantasy. White (1963) comments extensively on the role of identification in development: "identification signifies copying a model whose competence is admired. It is done for the sake of creating the competence in one's self. . . . identification must be conceived of in terms of attempted action, though this does not exclude dreaming about actions beyond the range of present possibility. Through action and its consequences the child finds out which identifications will work and which ones are doomed to fail" (p. 191).

Most important in the interaction and something that is important for change in general is the evocation of a latent self-representation, a latent persona, in a manner of speaking, that may be activated by another person. There are unique qualities in each of our important relationships with others. Occasionally a new and special encounter evokes a latent potential, previously unexperienced and unrecognized. In this way a new self-representation is formed.

An important consideration that arises when examining personality change under the circumstances described is whether the modified self-representation is a new structure or reflects the emergence and integration of a latent representation based on old identifications. There is no reason to assume that both of these phenomena do not occur. In the second instance, latent self-representations that are the product of unconscious identifications may be evoked under special circumstances, or the self-representation may be a composite based on numerous partial identifications with important people over the years. Viederman (1976) has described a patient in psychoanalysis who had a defective feminine self-representation and who identified with a constructed, idealized fantasy of the analyst's wife as a creative artist and maternal figure, based upon inferences about his interests and character and including elements of object representations with which the patient had identified in the past. In identifying with this image, she was able to consolidate a new feminine self-representation.

One may assume that the individual who acts as catalyst activates old benevolent object representations with associated positive self-representations. The idea that important people, long dead, retain their importance in the internalized world of objects and may be re-evoked at moments of need is illustrated by the following case. Over a considerable period of time in analysis, a patient had been working through strong feelings of rejection and disinterest that she experienced from men. She was struggling with her husband's failure to take note of her achievements at work and was examining the roots of this pain as she recovered memories of her father's indifference. Suddenly she remembered with great relief the loving attention and high valuation that she experienced from her grandmother, who had been a pioneer in her own field and had died more than thirty years before. This association should not be viewed uniquely as a defensive avoidance. A nur turing object representation was mobilized at a time of need and utilized as a sustaining influence in the patient's life. In a similar way, one might speculate that the special power of the important figure for the diabetic woman described above who saw herself as bad resided in the activation of transference paradigms of important benevolent figures from the past. Concerning this issue, Michels (1977) notes that psychic changes involve the actualization of a potential, the awareness that one is the creator of the self, and that a person selects and determines the meaning of his life and that myths may be therapeutically mutative.

In the case of the woman who was obsessionally preoccupied with having a defective child, the consultant's intervention defined the nature of the patient's experience of the pregnancy as a test situation. This led to the immediate release from obsessional symptomatology and, in the context of the experience of pregnancy, to changes in self-representation, maternal object representation, fantasy life, and diabetic control. The therapeutic impact of this type of statement has been discussed elsewhere (Viederman 1983).

The outcome in the two situations described above was felicitous, but in either one, a stillbirth or a defective child might have led to another result. In both cases, the crises were experienced unconsciously by these women as a test. In such situations, the disappointment of powerful hopes and expectations may lead to depression and a confirmation of defectiveness or badness. Depressions in crises may reflect unfulfilled, unconscious, wishful expectations for change. A three-month postpartum follow-up visit of a diabetic woman was interesting in this regard. She had a lifelong history of low self-esteem and was inclined to self-denigration. This pregnancy had been preceded by two spontaneous abortions. The third trimester of the pregnancy had been complicated by preeclampsia requiring one month of hospitalization that had prevented her from making the preparations she had wished to make for the baby. A prolonged labor that had almost resulted in a cesarean section had been another source of bitter disappointment. This depressed woman overtly stated that she felt less competent after this experience than she had ever felt before.

It is hardly surprising that observations of change are frequently made in the study of pregnant women. Pregnant women often identify with their mothers in the context of pregnancy. Bibring et al. (1961) were the first to define pregnancy as a normative crisis and to elaborate ideas about personality change and changes in object relationships in a facilitating and supportive environment during pregnancy. Pregnancy has special power as a normative crisis, for it is defined in time and demands radical role change and realistic change in one's life. It touches on the core of the woman's self-

representation and maternal object representations and has regressive reso-
nances with the earliest formative phases of infancy and childhood, thereby
permitting extensive reworking of early psychological structures leading to
altered relationships with primary internalized objects and to modified self-
representations.

## CONCLUSION

I have described a constellation of factors that sometimes leads to radical
change in aspects of personality during the adult life cycle. This chapter,
however, is not intended to encompass the full range of possible conditions
and circumstances in which life experience leads to change. Despair generated by the crisis of physical illness may lead to change when a narcissistic
injury generates such an overwhelming experience of loss that fearful inhibitions are abandoned. At this time, affirmative responses from the environment to new attitudes in behavior can consolidate a new self-representation.
Another area of interest with regard to change is the special circumstances
surrounding object loss.

One might infer that the possibilities for change are as rich as human
experience. What I have attempted to demonstrate here is that a certain
constellation of factors may lead to radical change in aspects of personality.
These include strong forces directed toward change and generated by the
motivation to achieve an ego ideal associated with certain personality factors
that permit an active and meaningful engagement with the environment.
Search for such change—externally induced at times of normative developmental crisis—should shed more light on the dynamics of growth throughout the life cycle.

## References

Alberti, L. B. 1435. *De Pictura.* Trans. C. Grayson. London, 1972.

Alexander, F. 1961. Unexplored areas in psychoanalytic theory and treatment. In *The
scope of psychoanalysis.* Papers of Franz Alexander, 319–35. New York: Basic
Books.

Bibring, G. L., Dwyer, T. F., et al. 1961. A study of the psychological processes in
pregnancy and of the earliest mother-child relationship. *Psychoanalytic Study of
the Child* 16:72.

Emde, R. N. 1988a. Development terminable and interminable I: Innate and motivational factors during infancy. *International Journal of Psychoanalysis* 69:23-
42.

———. 1988b. Development terminable and interminable II: Recent psychoanalytic theory and therapeutic considerations. *International Journal of Psychoanalysis* 68:283–96.

Erikson, E. 1959. *Identity and the life cycle.* Psychological Issues, vol. 1, no. 1. New York: International Univ. Press.

Freud, S. 1911b. Formulations on two principles of mental functioning. *Standard Edition,* 12:215–26. London: Hogarth Press.

_____. 1914c. On narcissism: An introduction. *Standard Edition,* 14:69–102. London: Hogarth Press.

_____. Civilization and its discontents. *Standard Edition,* 14:59–145. London: Hogarth Press.

Gedo, J. E. 1983. *Portraits of the artist: Psychoanalysis of creativity and its vicissitudes.* New York: Guilford Press.

Greenacre, P. 1971. Play in relation to creative imagination. In *Emotional growth: Selected papers of Phyllis Greenacre,* 555–74. New York: International Univ. Press.

Hartmann, H. 1958. *Ego psychology and the problem of adaptation.* New York: International Univ. Press.

Hendrick, I. 1942. Instinct and ego during infancy. *Psychoanalytic Quarterly* 11:33–58.

_____. 1943. Work and the pleasure principle. *Psychoanalytic Quarterly* 12:311–29.

Janis, I. L. 1974. *Psychological stress.* New York: Academic Press.

Kagan, J. 1984. *The nature of the child.* New York: Basic Books.

Kardiner, A., and Spiegel, M. 1947. *War stress and neurotic illness.* New York: Hoeber.

Kobasa, S. 1982. The hardy personality: Toward a social psychology of stress and health. In *Social psychology of health and illness,* ed. G. S. Saunders and J. Suls, 3–32. Hillsdale, N.J.: Erlbaum.

Loewald, H. W. 1980. Psychoanalysis as an art. In *Papers on psychoanalysis.* New Haven: Yale Univ. Press.

Michels, R. 1977. Psychic change in psychoanalysis. Panel report by Allen Compton. *Journal of the American Psychoanalytic Association* 669–78.

_____. 1980. Adulthood in the course of life: Psychoanalytic contributions toward understanding personality development. In *Adulthood and the aging process,* ed. S. I. Greenspan and G. H. Pollack, 3:25–34. Bethesda, Md.: NIMH.

Murray, J. M. 1964. Narcissus and the ego ideal. *Journal of the American Psychoanalytic Association* 12:466–511.

Radó, S. 1956. Dynamics and classification of disorder behavior. In *Psychoanalysis of behavior.* New York: Grune and Stratton.

Rose, G. J. 1980. *The power of form: A psychoanalytic approach to aesthetic form.* New York: International Univ. Press.

Rosenbaum, J. F., et al. 1988. Behavioral inhibition in children of parents with panic disorder and agoraphobia. *Archives of General Psychiatry* 45:463.

Sandler, J., and Rosenblatt, B. 1962. The concept of the representational world. *Psychoanalytic Study of the Child* 17:128–45.

Schafer, R. 1976. *A new language for psychoanalysis.* New Haven: Yale Univ. Press.

Settlage, C. F., et al. 1988. Conceptualizing adult behavior. *Journal of the American Psychoanalytic Association* 36:347–70.

Viederman, M. 1976. The influence of the person of the analyst on structural change. *Psychoanalytic Quarterly* 45:231–50.

———. 1983. The psychodynamic life narrative: A psychotherapeutic intervention useful in crisis situations. *Psychiatry* 46:236–46.

———. 1986. Personality change through life experience I: A model. *Psychiatry* 49:204–17.

White, R. W. 1963. *Ego and reality in psychoanalytic theory.* Psychological Issues vol. 3, no. 3. New York: International Univ. Press.

**PART 3**

# THE EGO AND
# THE SELF

# Introduction
*Helen Meyers, M.D.*

ándor Radó was one of the early ego psychologists who gave the ego a central position in the psyche, assigning it authority, motivation, and adaptational purpose. In 1939, he proposed "that all dynamics be de-cribed in terms of integrative ego functioning," what he called *egology* Radó 1945–55). By 1945, Radó had replaced the term *ego* with the term *action-self.* He felt this was closer to ordinary language, less mechanistic, and lso more meaningful in its descriptive aspects. He defined the action-self as ›oth the organism's central organizer and its systematic picture of itself, lerived from information about its activities by the sensory system:

> Of proprioceptive origin, the action-self is the pivotal integrative system of the whole organism. It integrates the organism into an intentionally acting and self-aware whole; it separates the organism's awareness of itself from its awareness of the world about it, and builds up the unitary entity of total organism in contrast to the total environment. Selfhood of the organism depends on this contrast as well as awareness of its unbroken historical continuity.

The action-self processes comments from the human environment" and ›cuses on equipment to control the environment and adapt the organism adaptation); it responds to inner needs and tensions and the dictates of the ›onscience, and "reacts to dangers with emergency emotions, with fight or ight." It arises out of a body self in contact with reality, is influenced by genetics, and is nourished by past pleasurable experiences of successful action," with special emphasis on the infant's sucking activity (Radó 1945–55).

Compare this with Freud's well-known final summation about the ego in the "Outline" (1938):

> Here are the principal characteristics of the ego: In consequence of the pre established connection between sense perception and muscular action, the ego has voluntary movement at its command. It has the task of self-preservation. As regards *external* events, it performs that task by becoming aware of stimuli, by storing up experiences about them (in the memory), by avoiding excessively strong stimuli (through flight), by dealing with moderate stimuli (through adaptation) and, finally, by learning to bring about expedient changes in the external world to its own advantage (through activity). As regards *internal* events, in relation to the id, it performs that task by gaining control over the demands of the instincts, by deciding whether they are to be allowed satisfaction, by postponing that satisfaction to times and circumstances favourable in the external world or by suppressing their excitations entirely. (Freud's italics)

As for the superego, as far as it "is opposed to the ego, it constitutes a third power which the ego must take into account." He goes on to discuss the ego's need to avoid unpleasure and danger, and the use of the anxiety signal. Thus he concludes, "an action by the ego is as it should be if it satisfies simultaneously the demands of the id, of the superego and of reality."

The similarities in the two concepts are clear: the body origin by way of perception and consciousness in contact with reality, the relationship to needs and conscience and reality, the function of dealing with danger (defensive function) by flight or fight or adaptation (compromise), and so on. Of interest, however, are the differences. Radó stressed the centrality, authority and power of this set of functions and their adaptive purpose—hallmarks of ego psychology as we now know it. He stressed, though in a rudimentary fashion, self-other differentiation, formation of a concept of self and other and self-awareness—such important ingredients now in separation individuation and current object-relation theory. He posited the importance of early oral experience with mother—essential in current preoedipal considerations. The self as agent foreshadows current self theories, and his stress on action finds echoes, but only echoes, in Schafer's (1976) action language concepts. "The essence of the self is action. Try to think in terms of self initiating processes of thought, of feelings, of activity" (Radó 1945–55).

The term *action-self* has been discarded and *ego* continues to be in use. But the centrality of this set of functions, the very concept of self, self-other differentiation, and relation are central in current thinking. The self as person or as supraordinate concept and a stress on action are still the subject of current discourse.

Of course, Freud's own term in German, *das Ich,* translated by Strachey as the more abstract "ego," connotes both the person and the agency within; it suggests both subjective self experience and a system. Further, at one time, Freud (1930) explicitly equated *Ich* ("I") and *Selbst* ("Self"); at other times, he used the term *Individuum* ("individual") (1914) for the whole person. Freud's terminology was purposely ambiguous, human and humanistic. Even what has been translated as "mind," he called *Psyche* (really translatable as "soul") or *Seele* ("soul"). He meant by this not the religious concept but the essence of a person. Had he used the German word for "mind," he might have been in even more mystical waters, as the word is *Geist,* which literally means "ghost." Whatever our question about errors in translation, however, Freud did approve the translation and the definition of *ego* in the narrow sense implied in that translation—so we must accept it as his judgment as well.

Of course, analytic terms, such as *ego* or *self,* are only labels or names for concepts. As such, they are as we define them and assign them meaning, these particular terms having been defined and determined by historical usage—a kind of shorthand for the concepts they represent. If we wish to change them, we must redefine them. But terms are necessary for communication. The concepts also are only constructs arrived at by convention and culturally limited and must not be reified or deified as truth. Concepts, however, are indispensable in structuring our thoughts. They are to be retained as long as they are useful for explaining, understanding, or exploring further ideas, but they must be changed or discarded when no longer so.

Now what has happened to the concepts of ego and self? In 1950, Hart-mann divided the ego into a system ego and self-representations—the content or view of itself—which formed by identification with internalized object representations. At the same time, he also mentioned the Self as the whole person, which he did not pursue but which was to resurface later. Some applauded this division as a clarification and have integrated this concept of self-representation into their thinking. Others deplored it as creating an artifact in the ego concept, an artificial split, preferring Freud's more inclusive concept (Kernberg 1982); some wished to dispense with the term *self* altogether (Spruiell 1981).

For myself, I find most meaningful the following conceptualization, which I believe, to a large extent, corresponds to current usage. Obviously, these concepts have become a great deal more complex since the days of Freud and Radó.

Conceptualized as a set of functions, more or less stable over time, the ego contains both experiential and nonexperiential aspects (Sandler and Rosen-blatt 1962). In addition to the adaptive and defensive functions, we now concern ourselves with the maturation of autonomous functions of the ego (Hartmann 1939), such as perception and motility, synthetic and integrative functions, and particularly cognition—from sensory-motor through symbolic to operational intelligence (Piaget 1936). The view of defenses themselves has become more sophisticated. Seen developmentally as arising not only in the context of danger and reality and in identification with parental functions but also in relation to the maturation of some of these autonomous functions, a hierarchy of defensive maneuvers over time has been concep-tualized—from prototype through precursor through infantile defensive acts to intrapsychic defenses proper—from the primitive, such as splitting, to the more mature, such as reaction formation. Defensive symbolization or true repression, for example, cannot be utilized until certain cognitive stages are achieved. The adaptive and defensive functions continue, of course, to be seen in the service of safety and self-preservation as well as of need satisfac-tion, adapting the individual to his environment and the environment to the individual's needs. Defending against internal and external danger, they me-diate unconscious conflict, leading to compromise functions, and establish habitual modes of meeting the demands of the inner and outer world by way of character. The mechanisms in themselves are nonexperiential, inferred only by their results such as symptoms, acts, or character traits.

On the experiential side, we now further view the ego as it evolves not just out of contact with reality, its character determined by "precipitates of abandoned object cathexis" (Freud 1923), but out of internalized object relations, as self differentiates from and relates to object by way of maturing perception and cognition, frustration and gratification, and cohesive self and constant object representations coalesce out of temporary partial and oppos-ing images within the ego (Mahler 1972a; Jacobson 1954). The self, the integration of various self-representations, in affective relation to various internal objects essentially becomes the content of the ego (Kernberg 1976).

In this model, then, the self is conceived of as content, as experiential and subjective, as an object of reflection. And there are many different compo-nent selves, depending on the context of the encounter—the analyst, the friend, the wife. Yet they are experienced as part of a whole related to identity—that is, the way one sees oneself and perceives others as seeing one constant over time, as defined by Erikson. These selves, though perhaps best conceptualized as fantasies or stories about oneself, are also, it appears to me more than that. Developing out of experience, something is laid down psy chically that is experienced and, though not directly knowable, is expressed as a sense of self. In addition, the way we perceive ourselves influences the way we function, or must function, and thus our self-perception becomes motivation or a partial center for initiative.

These are, of course, some of the areas of current controversy, or matters of different emphasis, around the concept of self. Looking at it developmentally, at the child that is, both Stern (1985) and Mahler (1967) describe an emerging sense of self separate from narration: Mahler ascribes formation of the sense of self by way of separation-individuation processes out of an original symbiotic phase, whereas Stern postulates the building up of separate self and object images from the beginning—describing a developmental sequence of the emergence of five senses of self, which then continue to coexist: emergent sense of self, core sense of self, subjective sense of self, verbal sense of self, and finally a narrative sense of self, possible only after language and storytelling capacity have developed. Schafer (chapter 8 in this volume), on the other hand, looking at the self genetically as communicated in analysis, looking back, as it were, at the reconstructed child, finds the objective "thing in itself" (Kant's *Ding an sich*) as unknowable and as such almost irrelevant for our purpose, and suggests that the many different selves presented by a patient (such as Winnicott's true and false selves, or Schafer's own second work self) can best be viewed as different narratives about himself. Related to this view, Grossman (1982) is willing to accept the notion of self provided that we are clear that it represents a fantasy about oneself, a personal myth—and that there are many such fantasies within one individual. Almost as if to illustrate this point, one whole genre of contemporary fiction (for example, John Barth) portrays characters with so many alternative selves that it has been referred to as "literature of exhaustion" (Haase 1985).

This brings me to the last view of the self (implied but not developed by Hartmann): the supraordinate self, the self as agent, as initiator of action, the self as a whole. The idea of a supraordinate something called the mind or soul or person is, of course, hardly new. Freud, in his well-known delineations of ego, id, and superego (1923, 1933), surely showed them to be parts of one larger whole that contains these three parts (tripartite model). This further is the I or self, as Ticho (1982) has suggested, of the early alternative schools of Alfred Adler, Carl Jung, and Karen Horney. Clearly, there is a person who is the center of initiative and identity, who is the source of needs and desires, the one who feels and thinks and acts, the defender and executor. This person can, of course, be called the I or self. The question is whether there is an advantage in conceptualizing it as the self rather than the person. Both are holistic concepts which, though philosophically valuable and aesthetically elegant, are, it seems to me, limited in their analytic usefulness and need to be broken down into narrower concepts for further exploration of psychic functioning (see also Michels, chapter 7 in this volume). This self as supraordinate is, of course, the concept of the bipolar self of Kohut's self psychology (1977). This self is subjective, experiential, positive; it has power, purpose, and needs of its own—needs for cohesion, continuity, and self-esteem—and psychic structure is subsumed within it. This, then, is the most controversial concept of the self, with its emphasis on self structure as opposed to conflict and its correlated self-psychologic treatment approach, stressing empathy and transmuting internalization. It would eliminate the component concepts of structural theory, but substitute two poles of ambition and ideals with a facilitating arch of capacities between them, the last essentially replacing the ego concept. It brings us back in a partial circle, in that it bears some resemblance to Radó's action-self in its conceptualization of the self as core agent and initiator of action, but, of course, it differs fundamentally in that it discards conflict.

In summary, I have reviewed various aspects and views of the concepts of ego and self and their relationship since the days when the Columbia Institute was founded. I have discussed questions about the self as subjective or objective, unitary or multiple, as content or supraordinate agent, as structure or fantasy or as a story told about oneself. I find both concepts—ego and self—alive and well and mutually complementary. Both, I believe, are useful in psychoanalytic theory and clinical practice and in furthering new knowledge. It was, after all, exploration of the ego concept, as it was in use then, that led to both further clarification of the ego and to the newer conceptualizations of the self.

In terms of analytic theory, the current conceptualization of the ego enriches and maintains a structuring of the mind along conflict lines and, by its definition, is designated as a center of initiative for action in the service of mastery, self-preservation, and internal balance. Clinically, the ego concept is most helpful for understanding and dealing with conflict, defense and resistance, character and compromise, assessing and working with the patient's strength and weakness, his capacity to analyze and observe himself, his ability to adapt and change.

The self, as content of the ego, enriches psychoanalytic theory in two directions. As the subjective face of the ego it relates to such issues as identity, ego ideal, and narcissism and provides the motivational impetus for self-esteem regulations. As the experiential component, as laid down by early infantile experience, it illuminates the whole area of development of psychic structure, with understanding of self-other differentiation and internal and external object relations. Clinically, the self concept is essential in understanding and dealing with primitive pathology, early defenses such as projective identification and splitting. And as an experience-near concept, it helps to understand and relate to the self-experience of all patients.

## References

Freud, S. 1914. Zur Einfuehrung des Narzissmus. In *Gesammelte Werke* 10:138–70. Frankfurt: Fischer Verlag, 1946.

———. 1923. The ego and the id. *Standard Edition* 19:3–68. London: Hogarth Press, 1961.

———. 1929. Das Unbehagen in der Kultur. *Gesammelte Werke* 14:421–506. Frankfurt: Fischer Verlag, 1948.

———. 1930. Civilization and its discontents. *Standard Edition* 21:64–145. London: Hogarth Press, 1964.

———. 1933. New introductory lectures. *Standard Edition* 21:57–80. London: Hogarth Press, 1964.

———. 1938. An outline of psychoanalysis. *Standard Edition* 23:141–206. London: Hogarth Press, 1964.

Grossman, W. 1982. The self as fantasy: Fantasy as theory. *Journal of the American Psychoanalytic Association* 30 (4):919–39.

Haase, E. 1985. An old cow steals the butcher's knife: A study and application of psychoanalytic thought in the work of D. Barthelme, J. Hawkes and T. Pynchon. Senior thesis in Princeton University Archives.

Hartmann, H. 1939. *Ego psychology and the problem of adaptation.* New York: International Univ. Press, 1958.

———. 1950. Comments on the psychoanalytic theory of the ego. In *Essays on ego psychology: Selected problems in psychoanalytic theory,* 113–41. New York: International Univ. Press, 1964.

Jacobson, E. 1954. The self and the object world. *Psychoanalytic Study of the Child* 9:75–127.

Kernberg, O. 1976. *Object relations theory and clinical psychoanalysis.* New York: Aronson.

———. 1982. Self, ego, affects and drives. *Journal of the American Psychoanalytic Association* 30 (4):893–918.

Kohut, H. 1977. *The restoration of the self.* New York: International Univ. Press.

Mahler, M. 1967. On human symbiosis and the vicissitudes of individuation. *Journal of the American Psychoanalytic Association* 5:740–63.

———. 1972a. On the first three subphases of the separation-individuation process. *International Journal of Psychoanalysis* 53:333–38.

———. 1972b. Rapprochement subphase of the separation-individuation process. *Psychoanalytic Quarterly* 41:487–506.

Piaget, J. 1936. *Origin of intelligence in children.* New York: International Univ. Press, 1952.

Radó, S. 1945–55. *Adaptational psychodynamics.* New York: Science House, 1969.

Sandler, J., and Rosenblatt, B. 1962. The concept of the representational world. *Psychoanalytic Study of the Child* 17:128–145.

Schafer, R. 1976. *A new language for psychoanalysis.* New Haven: Yale Univ. Press.

Spruiell, V. 1981. The self and the ego. *Psychoanalytic Quarterly* 50:319–44.

Stern, D. 1985. *The development of the infant's sense of self.* New York: Basic Books.

Ticho, E. 1982. The alternate schools and the self. *Journal of the American Psychoanalytic Association* 30 (4):849–62.

# Seven
■ ■

■
■
■

# The Mind and
# Its Occupants
*Robert Michels, M.D.*

t is characteristic of mental life that we experience our subjective world as structured, patterned, and organized. This is, of course, highly adaptive; the world is itself organized, and by organizing our experience we create what may be a more valid and effective internal model of that world, one that can better guide our plans and actions. Furthermore, organizing information is efficient; patterns and regularities are easier to encode, store, and retrieve. We also know, however, that as we organize our inner experience, we not only perceive and reflect the organization of the world but also create and project patterns that originate from within ourselves. Some of these may be "preadapted" to the outer world, programmed in our constitutional endowment, and selected by evolution for their adaptive value; others may have little or no relationship to the external world. Indeed, recognition of the importance of our tendency to project our inner mental life into our experience of the world is a central discovery of psychoanalysis. We observe aspects of this process as primitive man studies the stars and describes constellations, as mysterious events are explained by omens or superstitions, as scientists select among alternative explanatory hypotheses, or as psychoanalytic theorists construct theories of the mind. In fact, whenever we structure our experience in the form of symbols or language, we are structuring it in categories of understanding that have been generated by culture. Although they may also be related to the nature of reality "out there," they inevitably reflect social and personal structures that are among the inner determinants of experience. The experiences encompassed by our concepts of the mind are sufficiently ambiguous and unstructured that they provide a projective test for theorists of the mind.

There are two traditions in thinking reflectively, directing our attention to our own mental life. Each of these can be traced back at least as far as Aristotle. One conceives of the mind as analogous to the body. It is apparent that the body has several distinct parts, differing from one another in form and function, and some of the most interesting are quite invisible from the outside. Careful study of this seemingly unitary outside, however, does provide clues to what lies underneath. By analogy, the relatively seamless surface of mental life might also conceal deep internal structures, structures that are vital in creating the surface and maintaining its functioning. Freud may have believed that psychoanalysis provided us with methods of dissection that could allow us to describe and identity those hidden structures, that the royal road to the unconscious was analogous to the dissection of the body. He formulated this idea in the words of his "Impartial Person" in *The Question of Lay Analysis*, calling the recently described structural theory "a strange anatomy of the soul" (*S.E.* 20:194). Psychoanalysts have described a variety of mental organs, linking them with biological, social, developmental, and other aspects of behavior.

The second tradition in considering mental life thinks of the mind as basically different from the body and has usually called it the soul. It emphasizes the unitary nature of mental life rather than its divisibility into components. In fact, for Aristotle, this unity was a defining characteristic of the soul:

> Some hold that the soul is divisible, and that one part thinks, another desires. If, then, its nature admits of its being divided, what can it be that holds the parts together? Surely not the body; on the contrary it seems rather to be the soul that holds the body together; at any rate when the soul departs the body disintegrates and decays. If, then, there is something else which makes the soul one, this unifying agency would have the best right to the name of soul, and we shall have to repeat for it the question: Is it one or multipartite? If it is one, why not at once admit that "the soul" is one? If it has parts, once more the question must be put. What holds its parts together, and so *ad infinitum?* (*On the Soul*, Book 1, Chap. 5, trans. J. A. Smith)

In this tradition, mind has no parts because mind is that which integrates and unifies, which transforms components or precursors that are not yet mental or personal into a unitary entity that is. Components are by definition impossible, and adverbs are used to describe aspects of mental functioning—

thinking, feeling, acting—rather than nouns to describe components of the mind. The myth of a person acting replaces the myth of a mind existing.

Both of these traditions in thinking about mental life are alive and vigorous in contemporary psychoanalysis. Each has been interesting and productive, and of course each has been the object of criticism. I believe that there has been a pattern of misunderstanding in this criticism stemming from the failure to differentiate the several meanings of psychoanalysis and the several functions of concepts, models, and theories that relate to these different meanings. Freud, in his 1923 encyclopedia article, says that psychoanalysis is the name of three things: (1) "a procedure for the investigation of mental process," (2) "a method . . . for the treatment of neurotic disorders," and (3) "a collection of psychological information" (*S.E.* 18:235)—that is, first, a scientific method, second, a treatment, and third, an array of facts. Each of these needs models, theories, and concepts, but, although many seem to have assumed otherwise, they might not be best served by the same models, theories, and concepts, and, perhaps even more important, the criteria for evaluating a particular model, theory, or concept will be quite different from one to the other. I believe that some of the arguments concerning competing models can be explained by different attitudes toward the relative importance of these three psychoanalyses and therefore different emphases among the various criteria and different conclusions about the various concepts.

Freud's first psychoanalysis is a scientific method. Scientific methods use concepts as tools, with the goal of new knowledge. Valuable concepts enrich the process of inquiry, point to areas of investigation, suggest relationships, and generate hypotheses. Their meanings should be clear enough to promote communication among members of the profession, and they should encourage recognition of the relationships between psychoanalysis and other areas of inquiry—studies of brain, behavior, development, communication, and social relationships.

Viewed from the perspective of scientific method, a concept cannot be criticized for being untrue or even untestable. It can be criticized for being sterile or uninteresting. Integrative, overarching, perhaps superordinate concepts are often criticized in these terms. Most scientists do not find the notion of soul very helpful. Some psychoanalysts have criticized unitary or holistic conceptions of self for similar reasons. I am here referring to the term *self* as used in what Kohut calls "the psychology of the self in the broad sense" (Kohut 1977, p. 311). In fact, the relative sterility of unifying, integrating, or "soullike" conceptions of the mind might explain why, after a time, proponents of these views either lose interest in them or begin to dissect them into a new system of organs and components, an anatomy of the new soul, with poles or tension arcs that are as conjectural, untestable, and distant from the surface of subjective experience as were the older organs. When one wants to study a subject scientifically, one dissects it into components.

Freud's second psychoanalysis is a method of treatment, a psychotherapy. Concepts and theories have quite different functions in therapies than in methods of inquiry. We have much less interest in whether our therapeutic concepts are logically coherent, whether they point to new areas of knowledge, or even whether their meanings are consistent from person to person. We do want them to be close enough to the patient's experience and the analyst's thoughts to be therapeutically valuable. They should enrich the experience of the analyst with the patient, suggest relationships, patterns, or meanings in the clinical material, and be helpful in formulating interpretations.

Patients as well as analysts bring concepts and theories of the mind with them to psychoanalysis. One of the goals of psychoanalysis is to work with the patient in examining and understanding his original theory, in the process using psychoanalytic theories to suggest and explore possible new theories, theories that will respect where the patient started but will exploit the insights and understanding of psychoanalysis so that the patient's new way of experiencing himself might be less defended and more open, both to what the patient brought to the treatment but may have kept out of his theory and to what the analyst brought. In order to facilitate this process, the theories the analyst brings to the therapeutic situation must be close enough to the patient's theories that he will be able to resonate with them—but not too close, or they will offer nothing new. If the patient insists that his behavior is integrated, cohesive, a whole, theories that help to identify the conflictual or hidden themes will be valuable. If the patient disavows the role of his integrated personal identity, feels himself the object of impulses or fears or fragments of relationships that control and determine his existence, then theories that emphasize the concealed or disavowed cohesive, purposive central tendency will be helpful. Theories also must be comfortable for the analyst, for they must become his spontaneous way of thinking rather than a foreign body that he brings to the treatment from his supervisor, institute, or journal article.

They must be simple enough and sufficiently elegant that they can have effect at a preconscious level. Analysts analyzing are not supposed to be focusing their thoughts on complex theoretical systems; they are supposed to be listening with "free-floating attention," open to their experience of the patient and also open to contributions from within themselves. These latter include the forms and structures of psychoanalytic theory, but only the theory that emerges in the analyst's thoughts during the therapeutic process, not the theory that he might be able to reconstruct if he turns his attention from the therapeutic experience and attempts to "think theoretically." In some ways the theory that informs the therapeutic process has the same relationship to the theory written by theorists as the dream has to the day residue.

Some criticisms of metapsychology and of aspects of ego psychology may have come from analysts who perhaps, unlike Freud, saw this therapeutic meaning of psychoanalysis as primary. Freud was happy deriving the concepts of his clinical theory from the neurobiology or evolutionary biology of his time, but these analysts felt that psychoanalytic theory should be derived from clinical experience, that it had come to be too distant from the patient, too complex and abstract to be remembered, let alone to emerge in response to clinical stimuli. Further, when metapsychological concepts were applied to clinical data, they often seemed to lead away from meanings that were therapeutically valuable, to suggest relationships that were more interesting to theorists than to patients. Other critiques have focused on the scientific status of metapsychology rather than its therapeutic value, but these should be kept distinct, as they relate to a different meaning of psychoanalysis. A theory might be richly rewarding clinically, suggesting meanings and relationships that facilitate therapeutic work, while at the same time it suffers from major defects when considered as a scientific hypothesis: undefinable operationally, untestable, and unfalsifiable. Libido theory might fit each of these descriptions. However, this inconsistency between scientific and clinical judgments of theory should not surprise us. There is no a priori reason our therapeutic models should be good scientific theories or our scientific theories should be helpful without translation in our clinical work. It is only important that we recognize the distinction and understand how they are related to one another.

The third meaning of psychoanalysis is a collection of psychological information. This is psychoanalysis as a set of data, a body of facts. The ultimate criterion for evaluating a concept here is that it is consistent with the data, that it does no violence to observations, but organizes and abstracts from them. Concepts don't have to be "true" (indeed, it isn't clear what it would mean to claim that a concept was "true"), but they should not be false. In contrast, concepts may be false and yet be useful therapeutically. Incorrect concepts, like inexact interpretations, can have a valuable influence on the psychoanalytic process. Concepts may even be false and yet valuable to the process of inquiry; wrong ideas can suggest interesting questions or point to new domains of knowledge. Early models of trauma suggested exploration of the experiences of early childhood and helped to collect the data that challenged those models. However, when we evaluate a concept in terms of its ability to organize and encode what we know, rather than to guide us in our search, we place greater emphasis on its compatibility with our observations.

The three psychoanalyses are really three aspects of one psychoanalysis; our models of inquiry, therapy, and organizing our scientific data are largely the same, and our criteria for evaluating them overlap extensively. Nevertheless, I hope that I have made a point. Concepts or models, or at least those in common use, are rarely good or bad; they are better for some purposes, worse for others, and irrelevant if we have no purpose in mind. Furthermore, it is quite likely at this stage in the history of psychoanalysis that some concepts will be better for one purpose, others for another, and this should not surprise us. An emphasis on the purpose, whether science or therapy, rather than on the concepts will lead to much greater flexibility in shifting from one concept to another with shifts in goals.

With these considerations in mind, I turn to the mind—and the various candidates for its occupants. Freud's first dissection of mental organs focused on the difference between conscious and unconscious mental life. It served as an excellent guide to inquiry and helped in collecting and describing his discoveries regarding the different characteristics of these two types of mental activity. However, he found it less valuable in his therapeutic work. It did not provide the focus he wanted on unconscious forces that were counter to drives or on the central role of conflict. Freud's structural theory, his new anatomy of the mind, was at first a richer guide for the practicing analyst. It also provided suggestions regarding the role of early object relations in the formation of psychic structure, opening avenues to genetic considerations that had not been suggested by the topographic model. More important, it provided a framework for discussing the themes and transformations of childhood fantasies and psychic conflicts. However, although the new anatomy was closer to the clinician's understanding, it was also more difficult for the student or scientist to discern. Academic psychology may have had trouble with the notion of unconscious mental life, but in time it was able to generate operational definitions and even experimental tests. Ego and id, however, were too much; they were more like metaphors than scientific concepts and were less likely to support bridges between psychoanalysis and other disciplines. They were also more abstract, less obviously linked to the words and events of the consultation room. The new anatomy provided a clearer rationale for the treatment, but it was further removed from what was immediately apparent upon meeting the patient. This anatomy was later criticized for being just that—too scientific, too biologic, too reductionistic, too mechanical, for treating the mind as though it were part of the body rather than recognizing that, like its precursor, the soul, it was made of different and special stuff.

The most recent arrival claiming residence in the mind of psychoanalysis is the "self," a term that is much older than psychoanalysis and that has several different meanings in the psychoanalytic literature. Perhaps the oldest is the informal use of self as equivalent to person, a concept that became essential after the scientific connotations of "ego" left the mind of psychoanalysis without a person in sight. Hartmann, writing twenty-seven years after Freud introduced the term *ego,* said, "A clear distinction between the terms ego, self, and personality is not always made. . . . in using the term narcissism, two different sets of opposites often seem to be fused into one. The one refers to the self (one's own person) in contradistinction to the object, the second to the ego (as a psychic system) in contradistinction to other substructures of personality" (Hartmann 1950, p. 127). It is clear that ego is no longer the person, and self must be introduced if we are going to talk about people as well as structures of the mind.

Self has also been used as equivalent to self-representation—not the person, but the person's mental image of the person. This is an essential part of any concept of an inner or representational world, and, considered in its narrowest sense, it offers no special conceptual problems other than those associated with any other representation. However, our image of ourselves has special importance, and conceptual problems begin to emerge as the concept of self-representation is expanded with such notions as identity, the investment of the self-representation with dynamic force or authority, and any other implication that it is more than an image or a representation—that it is in effect a structure within the mind.

The view of self as a structure within the mind can be a step toward self as virtually a synonym for mind, or at least the unifying, integrative, holistic aspect of mind—Aristotle's soul returned. This transition has occurred in Kohut's "self psychology." In 1977 he wrote, "The self, whether concerned within the framework of the psychology of the self in the narrow sense of the term, as a specific structure in the mental apparatus, or, within the framework of the psychology of the self in the broad sense of the term, as the center of the individual's psychological universe is . . . not knowable in its essence" (Kohut 1977, pp. 310–11).

As I described earlier, the next step in the evolution of the self concept is the dissection of the holistic self into components, the discovery of new organs and a new anatomy of the mind-soul. This brings us full circle, and of course the coexistence of these contradictory conceptions of the mind and its components over the centuries should have led us to suspect that each of these views would generate problems that would suggest the alternate view as a solution.

How are we to select between self and ego, or should we select at all? Can we identify the purpose or situation in which one or the other would be more helpful?

First, let us notice that there are alternatives. A second theory may or may not tell us about the world, but it almost always tells us something about the first theory. It is similar to the way that learning a second language teaches us something about the hitherto unrecognized idiosyncrasies of our first language. Freud compared himself to Copernicus, who revolutionized our Ptolemaic thinking about the heavens with a second theory that said that the sun was the center of the universe. Copernicus, of course, was wrong; the sun is no more or less the center of the universe than is the earth. However, he did help to remove the earth from its inappropriate central role, and thus his second theory, though fundamentally no truer than the first, helped to de-idealize the first from the status of an absolute truth to that of a troubled hypothesis.

Whatever the value of the self concept, it has helped to remind us that ego and structural theory are a concept and a strategy, not a discovery and a law of nature. There are other possible strategies, and one must select among them depending upon one's purposes. Freud's topographic theory taught us that all behavior is not consciously controlled, his structural theory taught us that forces other than drives are at work in mental life, and the self concept reminds us that there are emergent properties of integrated mental life that are lost when we break it down to its components.

The self concept emphasizes the early development and the genetic origins of psychic structures rather than later mental functioning and the development of childhood conflicts. It calls attention to the unresolved issues of infancy, while the ego concept focuses on the themes of childhood. This raises the question of whether persisting infantile needs are related to the methods of psychoanalysis, or whether analysis is only relevant if these infantile themes have been transformed and restructured in the course of development so that they are better conceptualized in ego terms. One answer would be to link self-conceptualizations to psychotherapy but not to the exploratory and interpretive methods of psychoanalysis; another would be to see ego and structural theory as a special developmental case of the more general concept of self; a third, to tie ego to later and more differentiated psychopathology and to link self to earlier and more general disturbances. All of these, of course, are strategies related to psychoanalysis as a therapy. Perhaps the most important thing to remember in thinking about therapeutic concepts is that, like everything else that has to do with psychoanalysis as a therapy, if a single concept or single mode becomes too important, it may become a barrier to rather than a facilitator of the treatment.

What of the choice between ego and self when we shift from the therapeutic to the scientific aspects of psychoanalysis? Here the problems are great, but the choice is easy: we need not choose. There is no need to be conservative in scientific work and no concern if competing conceptions abound. An analyst should be loath to experiment with patients but eager to experiment with ideas. If anything, the science of psychoanalysis has been troubled by too few original and interesting alternatives, not too many. There is a challenge provided by the opportunity to compare, contrast, and evaluate two ways of regarding the mind.

Psychoanalysts do several things. As therapists they are conservative. New ideas have impact only as they are assimilated into a way of proceeding and responding that has already been crystallized and that operates automatically and preconsciously rather than with conscious attention and effort. As scientists, they should search out and play with new ideas. When the ego concept was new, it was greeted with considerable resistance by psychoanalytic clinicians. For most, it has now become second nature. The self concept points to some of the problems with the ego model, but even in this early stage we can already discern problems with the self, for it is not only old wine but also an ancient bottle. However, the availability of multiple conceptual systems enriches scientific dialogue, keeps this century-old science youthful, and even has the potential to enrich clinical work.

## References

Aristotle 1984. *The complete works of Aristotle.* Ed. Jonathan Barnes. Trans. J. A. Smith. Princeton, N.J.: Princeton University Press.

Freud, S. 1923. *Two encyclopaedia articles. Standard Edition,* 18.

———. 1926. *The question of lay analysis. Standard Edition,* 20.

Hartmann, H. 1950. Comments on the psychoanalytic theory of instinctual drives. In *Essays on ego psychology: Selected problems in psychoanalytic theory.* New York: International Univ. Press, 1964.

Kohut, H. 1977. *The restoration of the self.* New York: International Univ. Press.

**Eight**
■ ■

# Narratives of the Self
*Roy Schafer, Ph.D.*

T he concept of the self can be approached in two ways: as posing a
significant problem for theory construction in psychoanalysis and as a
significant feature of the self psychology of everyday life. The terms and
the results of these two approaches need not be as different as one might
expect. That is to say, the self psychology of theory may be shown to have a
good deal in common with everyday self psychology as it appears in the
ordinary language that analysts hear from the couch. In particular, both
approaches may be characterized as the construction of narratives. Grossman
(1982) has already taken up some of these problems under the aspects of
individual *fantasy* of a self and individual *theory* of a self, and he related both
of these aspects to the theories of the self that analysts put forward.

## THE SELF IN CONTEMPORARY ANALYTIC THOUGHT

The self has become the most popular figure in modern, innovative psychoanalytic accounts of human development and action. Usually, the self is
presented in these accounts as an active agency: it is the source of motivation
and initiative; it is a self-starter, the originator of action; it is the first person
singular indicative subject—that is, the "I" of "I come," "I go," "I will," "I
won't," "I know," "I wonder," and "I do declare!" This is the self that exhibits
itself and hides itself and can love or loathe its own reflection.

There is still more to the usual presentation of this active self. The self

**153**

appears in these accounts as the subject of experience: it constructs and participates in an experiential world; it is the self of taste, value, impression, and emotional direction; it is the sexual self, the private self, the fragile self, and the bodily self.

Furthermore, this active self is the central organized and organizing constituent of the person considered as a structured psychological entity. In this aspect of self, it is the unity, the essence, the existential core, the gestalt, and the mastermind of one's life.

Consequently, in modern times this self, or some selective version of it, has been called the self and the self-system by Sullivan (1940), the action-self by Radó (1956), the true self by Winnicott (1958), and the cohesive or nuclear self by Kohut (1977). Additionally, it is the superordinate self of Kernberg (1982) and the self as agent of the philosopher Macmurray (1957).

This self is not, however, always and only active. It has often been presented as being the object rather than the subject of action and experience. And often, as in reflexive locutions, this self appears as the object of its own action and experience, as when we speak of self-observation and self-esteem. Moreover, the self as object is not just a reactive agency or an observed agency; it is also the ensemble of self-representations. That is to say, it is the core content of all of one's ideas about oneself—the self-concept or self-image. In this mixing together of agency and content, there is some serious overloading of the conceptualization of self and possibly some theoretical incoherence as well (Schafer 1976, 1978). Be that as it may, modern theory has it that the object self is impinged upon by internal and external stimulation, and, as a result, both the functional self and the represented self may be fragmented, shriveled, inflated, chilled, and so on.

Even in a brief and incomplete introductory survey of the self in contemporary analytic thought, which is all that may be claimed for the first section of this chapter, it is mandatory to mention that this self has also been presented, at least implicitly, as a force. In one respect this force is very like an instinctual drive, the aim of which is full selfhood or self-realization; in another respect this force is very like a growth principle that vies with or replaces Freud's (1911) pleasure principle. On my reading of Kohut (1977), this obviously teleological self principle or self drive is at the center of his self psychology, where it plays just as essential a part in explanations of psychopathology and cure as it does in explanations of normal development and personality organization. I discern a similar teleological thrust in Erik Erikson's (1950, 1956) "ground plan" of development and its particular manifestation in a close relative of the self, namely, identity formation.

To continue establishing the terms for a narrative account of the self, I must discuss, first, the self as active agent and, second, the experiential self.

# THE SELF AS AGENT

It is intrinsic to any psychological theory to view the human being as an agent or actor in certain essential ways and to some significant extent (Schafer 1976, 1978, 1983). Even an extreme tabula rasa theory must include an account of how the person who has been written on by the surrounding world and by bodily processes becomes in turn an author of existence. Although the person may be a repetitive and largely preprogrammed author, he or she cannot be that entirely, for there is no one program to be applied to everything identically. The person must select and organize in order to construe reality in one adaptive or maladaptive way or another. Certainly the theorist advancing a new set of ideas about human psychology must be viewed as a selective and organizing agent.

An author of existence is someone who constructs experience. Experience is made or fashioned; it is not encountered, discovered, or observed, except upon secondary reflection. Even the idea of experience as that which is turned up by the introspecting subject introduces an actively introspecting subject, an agent engaging in a particular set of actions, and thus someone who may introspect in different ways and for different reasons (Grossman 1967). The introspecting subject extracts from the plenitude of potential experience what is wanted, which in one case may be sense data and in another case a self, or, as is more usual, an array of selves. With the exception of what is remembered, introspection does not encounter ready-made material. For these reasons, developmental theories cannot avoid giving accounts of the different ways in which experience is constructed as advances take place in the child's and adult's cognitive and psychosexual functioning; in this connection, analysts refer to phase-specificity.

All of which has to do with the self, for in necessarily presupposing an agent, psychological theories of the self usually equate agency with selfhood. These theories then speak of what the self does. This is a permissible move in the game of theory construction. Once agency and selfhood have been equated, however, it must become evident that at least two new problems will have to be dealt with.

## Self or Person?

The first problem is explaining what advantage is gained by saying that a self engages in actions rather than saying that the person does. Why speak of activity at one remove from the person—from him or her or, for that matter, from you or me? Might there be some misguided need on the therapist's part to add an air of detachment to the discussion, an air that spuriously gives the discussion an appearance of scientific legitimacy or clinical objectivity? Is it demonstrably more plausible or heuristic to say that a self can be organized and organizing than to say that a person can be?

But perhaps it is not an image of scientific detachment and of clinical objectivity that is at stake. Perhaps it is a culturally reinforced need to retain in our psychologies some extrapersonal source of agency and thereby some implicit passive stance toward life. Although the self that is set apart from the person is not quite a soul or a god, it may be viewed as an idea that is not quite free of the kind of disclaiming of personal agency that most of us associate with souls and divine visitations. This is so because the person is retained alongside the self as a necessary figure in adequate accounts of human actions.

The person is retained in self psychologies in this way. These psychologies tend to exempt the "I," the first-person singular indicative pronoun, from the self, and it is this exception that is used to make the theories work, for it will be the "I" that will be the informative witness to its own self and the source of the theorists' data. Comparably, when Freud talked psychic structure, he still found it necessary to refer to the person or subject, for the structural theory couldn't do all the work; it needed a psychological being to stand behind it and to contain it, and it is that being that I call the person. In "The Ego and the Id" (1923), for example, Freud introduced the person through blatant personification of the ego (see, for example, p. 58).

### Doubling and Multiplying the Self

The second problem encountered by psychological theories that attribute agency to the self rather than to the person follows on the heels of the first. If the theorist tries to deal with the first problem by making every effort to include the "I" within the self, then he or she is required to speak of that self as being self-constructing, self-maintaining, self-containing, and self-evaluating. That is to say, the theory is committed both to self as mental mover and to self as mental content or as subject and object simultaneously and thus to a self that includes itself. There occurs at the least a doubling of the self. This doubling of the self is a feature of Kohut's self psychology, for example, in that the Kohutian self is not only an experiential self; it is also a center of initiative that establishes and repairs self-experience in general and self-esteem in particular. Additionally, in order to account for the profusion of diverse tendencies that characterizes each person's life, the self psychologist must sooner or later, and more or less officially, propose the existence of various subselves (such as the grandiose self, the true and false self). Each of these subselves is supposed to be viewed as acting as a more or less independent agent, even while it is still to be regarded as part of one basic self.

What is the result of this doubling and multiplying of selves? It seems that one ends up with a mind that is located both within and outside its boundaries and that contains numerous little minds that are *within* itself and at the same time *are* itself. This odd turn in the theory is a sign that it is in deep trouble. The self theory has become fluid if not weakened. In contrast, it is less artificially detached and perhaps theoretically and scientifically less pretentious to think more plainly in terms of persons constructing and revising their various experiential selves of everyday life and ordinary language. Then each person is taken to be a narrator of selves rather than a non-Euclidean container of self-entities. Some further consideration of the experiential self may strengthen the case for a narrative approach to the self.

## THE EXPERIENTIAL SELF

I begin with a puzzle and my solution to it. The puzzle is analogous to the one where one looks for hidden faces in a sketch of a landscape. Here is the puzzle: How many selves and how many types of self are stated or implied in the following account? An analysand says to his analyst, "I told my friend that whenever I catch myself exaggerating, I bombard myself with reproaches that I never tell the truth about myself, so that I end up feeling rotten inside, and even though I tell myself to cut it out, that there is more to me than that, that it is important for me to be truthful, I keep dumping on myself."

I count eight selves of five types. The first self is the analysand self talking to his analyst, and the second is the social self who had been talking to a friend. These two selves are similar but not identical, in that self-organization and self-presentation are known to vary to some extent with the situation one is in, and in many ways the analytic situation is unlike any other in life. The third self I count is the bombarding self; the fourth, the derogated self that exaggerates; and the fifth, the exaggerated self itself. The sixth is the truthful self one aspires to be; the seventh, the conciliatory adviser of the bombarding self, the self that advises cutting out the reproaches; and the eighth is the defended self, the one with redeeming features. As to type, there is what is presented as the actual self (whether exaggerated, reproached, or defended), the ideal self (truthful), the self as place (the one with the rotten inside and the one that can be dumped on), the self as agent or subject (the teller, the bombardier, the aspirant, and the adviser), and the self as object (the self observed, evaluated, reproached, and defended).

My answer to the puzzle introduces once again my thesis that there is value in viewing the self in narrative terms. I suggest that the experiential self in this analysand's statement may be seen as a set of varied narratives that seem to be told *by* a cast of varied selves *to* and *about* a cast of varied selves. And yet, like the dream, which has one dreamer, the entire tale is told by one narrator. There is nothing here to support the common illusion that there is a single self-entity that each person has and experiences, a self-entity that is, so to speak, out there in nature where it can be objectively (introspectively) observed, clinically analyzed, and then summarized and bound in a technical definition—as if Humpty-Dumpty could be put back together again. Whether our material is rhymed, brief, and cute like Humpty-Dumpty, or prosy, long, and difficult like most analytic material, we may be said to be constantly dealing with self narratives, which is to say with all the story lines that keep cropping up in clinical work, such as story lines of the empty self, the false self, the secret self, and so on. Let us move on then to consider self narratives more closely than we have so far.

## SELF NARRATIVES

I must first point out that it is consistent with ordinary language to speak of self narratives. In ordinary language, one refers to one's self or to the self of another person in a variety of ways that derive from different vantage points that one occupies at different times and in different emotional contexts. Implicitly, it is accepted that, except for certain rhetorical purposes, there is no one way of telling it "like it is." For example, in my puzzle, it comes across as perfectly in order to produce what appears to be one narrative that includes a self that never tells the truth and another self possessed of other and more estimable tendencies within which is situated the self that exaggerates. It is taken for granted, and it is common practice to converse on the understanding that, whether in the role of observer or observed, one can only *tell* a self or encounter it as something *told* (Schafer 1983), or, as the case may be, tell more than one self. The so-called self exists in versions, only in versions, and commonly in multiple simultaneous versions.

For example, to say, "I told myself to get going," is to tell a self story with two characters, an admonishing self and an admonished self, or perhaps with three characters, if one includes the implied author who is telling about the admonishing. To say, "Deep inside him there is a grandiose self," is also to tell a story about two selves, this time about one self contained within another. And smacking one's head after making a mistake is to make a show of punishing a dumb self. This last example also makes it plain that some of these versions of self are nonverbal. They are versions that are shown in expressive moments or life-style rather than told verbally; however, showing may be regarded as a form of telling, so that it is warranted to treat nonverbal manifestations as self narratives presented in another form of our common language, say, as charades of self narratives.

To debunk thus the ideas that personal experience discloses a single self-entity and that theory must include that overall self is not to maintain that all self narratives are inherently unstable and inconsistent; nor is it to maintain that all these narratives are on the same level; nor yet that the content of these narratives concerns only chronic flux or chaos. Many of our actions may be presented noncontroversially as differentiated, integrated, and stable, and these presentations themselves may share these organized and enduring qualities. In many instances, certain self narratives are so impressively stable in organization and content and so clearly superordinate to others that it seems a matter of simple observation to say that there must be, or we must be seeing, psychic structure. There must be nuts and bolts somewhere, we feel, or good strong glue to make it possible. But in reacting thus, we are following the old story line of primal chaos: this chaos is the baby with only an id with which to start life; it is the seething cauldron of instinctual drives that must be curbed and contained by psychic structures. This is not the account of the preadapted baby in a world of prepared objects that today seems by far the most adequate to express the way we make sense of humanness and its development.

At the same time, however, it must be said that in daily life we seem to have acquired an exaggerated impression of single and unvarying self-entities from our unreflective attitude toward the heavy use we all make in our ordinary language of first person singular pronouns and of such reflexive terms as self-esteem and self-control. Also, having available to us self as agent as a culturally or linguistically well-established narrative possibility, we gain an apparently experiential conviction that we possess a unitary and enduring self that may be experienced directly, unmediated by language and story. Locutions such as "be yourself" and "divided self" are instances of what I mean. Our common language authorizes us to think and speak in terms of single, stable self-entities. And so we want to protest that the self is not a matter of language, theory, and narrative mediation at all: the self is something we know first-hand; it is (in that marvelously vague phrase) the sense of self, a self we feel in our bones. To which it is, correct to reply that "to feel it in your bones" is to resort to yet another old story line of the knowing body or the body as mind; the "sense of self" does not escape the web of narration.

Add to this the further consideration that, from the psychoanalyst's point of view, there are still more and differently told experiential selves to take into account than was suggested by my first answer to my puzzle. In that answer I referred only to selves that appear to be consciously or preconsciously available at the moment. Unconsciously, the analysand in my puzzle may also be regarded as transferentially experiencing and presenting to the analyst a helpless self, that is, a child self that can't run its own affairs and so must appeal to a parental figure for help. Additionally, the puzzle statement may be indicating to the analyst that, unconsciously, the speaker is maintaining, among other experiential selves, a cruel and totalistic moral self, a grandiose self without blemishes, and an anal self that defiantly makes messes by lying.

I have named only a few of the narrative retellings of the troubled analysand's self stories that the analyst may have to develop in the form of interpretations. Even what I called his actual self may have to be retold. For example, it may turn out that, for the analysand of my puzzle and by conventional standards, his actual self is given very little to exaggerating; he produces no impressive evidence that he does exaggerate to any notable degree; and the significant problem may be that, fearing the envy of others, he has suppressed the presentation of a justifiably proud actual self and has substituted for it an unconvincing defensive account of an outrageous braggart. The self that is claimed to be felt in one's bones cannot possibly encompass all of these experiential selves, even if it could think; neither could the "sense of self" encompass all of them.

At this point, one might ask whether, in the interest of our own mental safety, we should not avoid this milling crowd of narrated selves in which we could easily get lost or trampled. Shouldn't we instead mingle with only a few well-behaved self categories? My answer is, first, we do have available for use of that sort superordinate self categories, such as the actual self and the ideal self (Schafer 1967), and, second, we should be careful not to lose sight of the proliferation of selves in each person's construction of experience lest we begin to mistake our superordinate categories for entities discovered and observed in nature without narrative mediation. In principle, no limit can be set on the number of experiential self constructions that it may be profitable to discuss in one or another context of inquiry. It is no good saying that we already have enough concepts to do the job of interpretation, for to do so is to close the book on new approaches and the new phenomena made available by these approaches. As I have argued in connection with prisoner fantasies (1983), each proposal in this realm should be assessed on its merits.

## STORY LINES

Although I have alluded to the story lines of self narratives, I have neither attempted to define them nor provided examples of them. One may ask, "What *is* a story line?" and "What is the relation of story line to self-representation, fantasy, and metaphor?" for these are three apparently germane concepts that clearly occupy more or less established or at least familiar places in analytic thought.

First, then, what is a story line? By story line I refer to whatever it is that can be used to establish a set of guidelines and constraints for telling a story that conveys what convention would certify as having a certain general kind of content. These guidelines and constraints may be derived from one or more symbols, metaphors, similes, images, themes, or dramatic scenes, or some combination of these. This story line serves as a tool for working out ways to retell other stories in its terms and so makes it possible for narrators both to generate many versions of what is conventionally regarded as the same basic story and, through reduction, to create faithful repetitions of these versions out of apparently diverse narrative materials. For example, the story lines of imprisonment, rebirth, and odyssey are commonly developed in the course of analytic work. To take just one instance: when using rebirth as the story line, the analyst may take an analysand's references to new growth, new beginnings, glowing embers among the ashes, emergence from water, revival, and so on, as references to rebirth. Similarly, analysts develop stories of oedipal victory and defeat, separation-individuation, and masochism. And to take one more example: when using the oedipal story line, the analyst may interpret a negative therapeutic reaction in part as a frightened retreat from oedipal victory and in part as a switch to the negative oedipal position. In contrast, when using the masochism story line, the analyst may interpret a negative therapeutic reaction in part as a sign of powerful reluctance to give up preferred forms of compromised and painful gratification and in part as a bid for the analyst's pain-inducing, preferably sadistic response to the dashing of his or her therapeutic hopes.

With this sketchy account of story line and its uses in analytic interpretation, let us now compare and contrast story line with self-representation, unconscious fantasy, and metaphor.

### Self-Representation

Self-representation is a concept with a complex history and present status in psychoanalysis. I single out one of its most relevant features. Use of the concept of self-representation is intended to announce one's assumption or realization that the self, like the object, is knowable only through more or less individual, partial, or whole versions of it. These are the versions the analyst encounters or defines in the analysand's psychic reality, and they may have little to do with conventional or putative versions of the self.

There is nothing mutually exclusive about the concepts of story line and self-representation. Story line may, however, be regarded as the more inclusive of the two because, in clinical practice, single representations are not identified and analyzed as static and isolated mental contents. Rather they are dealt with thematically, that is, as being significant insofar as they actually or potentially play parts in basic stories of the self. For example, the prisoner story line includes a large array of not necessarily glaring representations of one's self as deprived, confined, or punished; at the same time, it includes a large array of more or less subtle representations of others as judges, jailers, or fellow prisoners. The job of interpretation is to show that those are the representations that must be defined more sharply and related to one another in a thematically unified rendition of the analysand's diverse associations. Seen in this light, story line pulls together and develops important aspects of the conceptualization of self-representations.

## Unconscious Fantasy

Unconscious fantasy, too, is a concept with a complex psychoanalytic history and present status. Arlow (1969a, 1969b), in two discussions that seem to have become the standard references to unconscious fantasy in modern Freudian literature, came close to the idea of basic story line that is being developed here. He took note of the aspect of unconscious fantasies that he called "plot line." However, Arlow was not concerned with working out a narrative approach to psychoanalytic topics; he referred to these plot lines in a way that was conceptually subordinate to fantasy, and he mentioned plot line only in a footnote (1969a, p. 47); obviously, he was engaged in making another kind of contribution.

From the standpoint of narration, one must go beyond the idea that to speak of a fantasy is to imply that one is referring to mental content organized by a story line; one must also note that story line has a more obvious generative connotation than plotted fantasy does, for it is forward-looking or anticipatory. On this basis, story line can more readily encompass the many variations of basic stories we conventionally recognize in daily life and analytic work. Fairy tales, too, have many versions; indeed, they have so many that it becomes unclear at what point one may no longer speak persuasively or confidently of a specific story's being an unusual version of the same basic story (Smith 1980). The same is true of any of the story lines I mentioned earlier: odyssey, for example, which can encompass a lot of variations, has the generative advantage and at the same time the disadvantage of unclear outer limits. In practice, it can become unclear when the analyst is forcing the same story line on material that is extremely varied.

## Metaphor

Have I been talking of metaphor all the while, and, along with metaphor, of metaphoric entailment (Lakoff and Johnson 1980)? Metaphoric entailment is exemplified by the basic spatial metaphor, "good is up." This metaphor entails that, among other attributes, intelligence, good taste, and wealth are up, while stupidity, vulgarity, and poverty are down. For example, very intelligent is "highly" intelligent. These are entailments insofar as consistency and coherence of discourse are the goals, which they usually are. These few remarks on metaphor and entailment seem to suggest that metaphor says the same as story line.

Again, however, story line seems to be the more inclusive term of the two. As I noted earlier, metaphor may establish a story line, and what is called "unpacking a metaphor" is in certain respects much like laying out the kind of story that is entailed by the metaphor. For example, "analysis is hell" entails the analyst being experienced as the devil; the analyst's attention to departures from the fundamental rule is experienced as the heat being put on; perhaps in analogy with "war is hell," the analyst's discipline is likened to Sherman marching to the sea; the stress of the analytic process becomes punishment for past sins; and so on. The example shows that it is understood that the manifestly metaphoric "analysis is hell" is to be used as a set of latent instructions or rules for telling a certain kind of story about being analyzed. Analysts who can work through an analysand's core conflict show that they understand the narrative regulations of metaphor; they show it by their steady sense of relevance as they listen to apparently diverse communications.

Perhaps these brief remarks comparing and contrasting story line with representation, fantasy, and metaphor will have begun to bring home what I mean when I speak of the story lines of self narratives and why I give story line the central position that I do.

## A CLINICAL EXAMPLE

There are many ways in which children are provided with story lines for the construction of self narratives and narratives concerning others. The dynamic content involved in these transactions is well known to analysts, but because that content has not usually been conceptualized in narrative terms, I present a clinical example of consequential story lines to bring it into relation with the topic of childhood memories.

The example concerns a successful, hard-driving, loveless career woman in her forties, once-divorced, who had never managed to establish a lasting, intimate, and gratifying relationship with an adequate and assertive man. From her early years on, she had been warned emphatically by her mother never to let herself be dependent on a man. That warning conveyed to her a number of interrelated story lines, some of which follow below.

She received the message that, as a girl and woman, she was fated to be vulnerable to helplessness in relation to any man with whom she became deeply involved; further, that the only way to develop and maintain significant strength and dignity was to cut herself off from heterosexual love; thus, that a heterosexual female self is a weak and degraded self; and that to love her father was to make herself vulnerable to this fate. In the broadest terms, she was fated to live in a world of powerful, dangerous, and certainly untrustworthy men. Although this woman had by no means renounced her heterosexuality altogether, she had repetitively developed and played out many versions of this set of story lines in her relationships, and ultimately she did so in her transference to her male analyst. Penis awe and envy, fantasies of castration and of a hidden penis, and primal scene themes were woven into the grim stories that she both elaborated and followed.

Before going any further, I should clarify that it is not being suggested that her parents and others around her were the only conveyors of story lines. Analysts assume that the child is a storyteller from the onset of subjective experience. For example, there is the child's own story line, "I once had a penis and lost it." As was indicated earlier, the usual analytic term for childhood constructions of this sort is fantasy. I have been saying that fantasy is a story and that children manufacture stories that interweave what they are told and what they imagine. The only new aspect of this point is the emphasis on narration.

To return to the analysand: An additional and congruent burden had been imposed on her explicitly during her adolescence and early adult years by her father's admonishing her never to have children. In this way, he authorized and reinforced her own guilty, anxious, and defeated account of her childhood oedipal romance. This romance included the usual wish to bear her father's child. Thus, from her father's side, too, she was being pressed to renounce her heterosexual femininity, for now in large part she was to construct stories of marriage as offering extremely limited prospects of satisfaction and fulfillment; there was little to hope for even in the ordinary marital form of displaced and matured forms of oedipal love. Furthermore, her father's admonishment could not fail to add weight to the account of herself as an unwanted and burdensome child who somehow was responsible for her parents' unhappiness and lack of fulfillment.

As was to be expected, she repetitively applied and elaborated this self story in her transference. For example, the repetition began with her earliest appointments when she insisted on paying for each visit at its conclusion; it turned out that she did so in order not to be a financial burden on the analyst, and in addition, in the terms of the story line of dangerous dependence on men, she was not to be indebted to the analyst in any way. The embittered story line she was acting on was this: The only good woman is a good man— more exactly, a tough, utterly self-reliant man in drag. In effect, by paying as she did, she was saying, "This is the story of my life." There were, of course, other major story lines touching on anality, concerns with social status, and so on.

I hope it is clear from the way I summarized these few aspects of this analysis that what is intended by this presentation is primarily theoretical clarification rather than revision of the dynamic variables that analysts customarily invoke to understand clinical phenomena. My theoretical point is that so-called self-concepts, self-images, self-representations, or, more generally, the so-called self may be considered to be a set of narrative strategies or story lines to be observed in developing an emotionally coherent account of one's life among people. We organize our past and present experience narratively. There is no alternative.

On my reading, this perspective on experience as a narrative construction is implied in Freud's final comments in his 1899 essay, "Screen Memories." After commenting on the "peculiarity of the childhood scenes," where the child is portrayed as an outside observer of the scene in which he or she is an involved participant, and therefore taking this peculiarity as "evidence that the original impression has been worked over," Freud concluded,

> The recognition of this fact must diminish the distinction we have drawn between screen memories and other memories derived from our childhood. It may indeed be questioned whether we have any memories at all *from* our childhood: memories *relating to* our childhood may be all that we possess. Our childhood memories show us our earliest years not as they were but as they appeared at the later periods when the memories were aroused. In these periods of arousal, the childhood memories did not, as people are accustomed to say, *emerge;* they were *formed* at that time. And a number of motives, with no concern for historical accuracy, had a part in forming them, as well as in the selection of memories themselves. (P. 322; Freud's italics)

I believe that Freud was indicating the view, subsequently developed in ego-psychological terms by Ernst Kris (1956) and now by me in narrative terms, that theoretical clarification of this sort does make a difference in practice. It encourages analysts to be aware that the clinical material being worked with may be usefully approached as a series of tellings and retellings constructed over the course of development and indeed over the course of the analysis itself. In this light, what we call free association may be retold as the production of bits and pieces, or even larger segments, of life stories being constructed and related in the here and now of the analytic relationship.

Speaking in terms of memory, Freud said, "the raw material of memory-traces out of which it [the screen memory] was forged remains unknown to us in its original form" (p. 322). I am adding the point that analysts do best to think of the raw material itself as having become *psychic* material in narrative form, however rudimentary the narrative. In other words, the clinical questions to be put to whatever the analyst hears are these: Of which story is this now a part or a version? For which further stories has it served or is it now serving as a story line? With regard to the self specifically, the questions become these: Which self stories are now being hinted at or disclosed, or are now in the process of being constructed or revised, and for which purposes?

## References

Arlow, J. 1969a. Unconscious fantasy and disturbances of conscious experience. *Psychoanalytic Quarterly* 38:1–27.

———. 1969b. Fantasy, memory and reality testing. *Psychoanalytic Quarterly* 38:28–51.

Erikson, E. 1950. *Childhood and society.* New York: Norton.

———. 1956. The problem of ego identity. *Journal of the American Psychoanalytic Association* 4:56–121.

Freud, S. 1899. Screen memories. *Standard Edition,* 3:299–322. London: Hogarth Press, 1962.

———. 1911. Formulations on the two principles of mental functioning. *Standard Edition,* 12:218–26. London: Hogarth Press, 1958.

———. 1923. The ego and the id. *Standard Edition,* 19:3–66. London: Hogarth Press, 1961.

Grossman, W. I. 1967. Reflections on the relationships of introspection and psychoanalysis. *International Journal of Psycho-Analysis* 48:16–31.

———. 1982. The self as fantasy: Fantasy as theory. *Journal of the American Psychoanalytic Association* 30:919–38.

Kernberg, O. 1982. Self, ego, affects, and drives. *Journal of the American Psychoanalytic Association* 30:893–918.

Kohut, H. 1977. *The restoration of the self.* New York: International Univ. Press.

Kris, E. 1956. The recovery of childhood memories in psychoanalysis. *Psychoanalytic Study of the Child* 11:54–88.

Lakoff, G., and Johnson, M. 1980. *Metaphors we live by.* Chicago: Univ. Chicago Press.

Macmurray, J. 1957. *The self as agent.* London: Faber and Faber.

Radó, S. 1956. *The psychoanalysis of behavior.* Vol. 1, *Collected papers 1922–1956.* New York: Grune and Stratton.

Schafer, R. 1967. Ideals, the ego ideal and the ideal self. In *Contributions to a psycho-analytic theory of behavior: Essays in honor of David Rapaport,* ed. R. R. Holt, 129–74. New York: International Univ. Press.

———. 1976. *A new language for psychoanalysis.* New Haven: Yale Univ. Press.

———. 1978. *Language and insight: The Sigmund Freud memorial lectures 1975–1976, University College London.* New Haven: Yale Univ. Press.

———. 1983. *The analytic attitude.* New York: Basic Books.

Smith, B. H. 1980. Narrative versions, narrative theories. *Critical Inquiry* 7 (no. 2):213–36.

Sullivan, H. S. 1940. *Conceptions of modern psychiatry.* New York: Norton.

Winnicott, D. W. 1958. *Collected papers: Through pediatrics to psychoanalysis.* New York: Basic Books.

# Nine
■ ■

■
■
■

## Developmental Prerequisites for the Sense of a Narrated Self
*Daniel N. Stern, M.D.*

What is needed developmentally for someone to tell a self story or a narrative? In the spirit of what Robert Michels has written, I will here view the self in terms of the various senses of the self that emerge developmentally. Let me take the *narrated self* as a starting point

When we speak of an adult's narration of self, we assume at least two things that there is an array of past and present lived experiences that the person can weave into a coherent narrative; and that there is such a thing as a narrative form, a way of thinking about an experience and talking about it to someone else. Narratives are recountings of things that have happened. They usually (but not always) involve agents who have feeling states, motives, and goals and who execute actions to achieve goals that have consequences. This narrated story usually unfolds in a temporal and causal sequence. It also has a point of view.

In adults, we assume that the narrative form exists, but from the developmental perspective we cannot do that. There exists a time prior to perhaps the third year when the infant has a rich array of experiences from the past as well as from the present but lacks the capacity to plot it verbally—that is, to make a narrative out of it. The capacity to narrate emerges developmentally later than the sense of a self who is the central figure of a narration. This lag is the focus of the present discussion. When the infant finally does acquire the narrative capacity, what has happened? A new and different sense of self has emerged—one that can be added onto and at times can embrace the already existing senses of self.

There is an epistemological and methodological issue here: is there a privileged position for defining what the self is and when it comes into existence? For instance, from a strict methodological point of view, psychoanalysis must say that the self is knowable—in fact, exists—only when one is capable of narrating about it. Whatever may have been experienced as the self before that is not knowable. Most psychological positions hold that there is no such thing as the self until one can show self-awareness or be self-reflective, as demonstrated by words or actions. On the other hand, what is it that one becomes self-reflective about when the capacity for self-awareness first emerges? There is a regress here, and the criterion for how we define self is not arbitrary but reflects a theoretical position.

What, then, do I mean by a sense of self? I agree with Schafer that the "sense of self" is a vague concept, and I think we do well to leave it purposefully vague at this point. I mean a subjective organizing perspective that attempts to make order out of lived experience at whatever level such experience is registered and organized. Infants begin to make subjective order of their experiences with persons as well as with objects from the moment they are born, in a very active way, on every level of which they are capable, to reach the highest level of organization attainable at that time.

Five different senses of self emerge developmentally over the period from birth to three or four years. The arrival of the fifth sense of self, that is, the narrated self, is especially important from the developmental viewpoint because the narrated self is the one encountered in psychoanalytic retellings of an analysand's life story.

The five senses of self and their approximate time of emergence are, in brief, as follows (for greater detail, see Stern 1985). An *emergent sense of self* begins to act between birth and two months; a *core sense of self* emerges between two and six months; a *subjective sense of self* emerges beginning around nine months; a *verbal or categorical sense of self* begins at about eighteen months; and finally (for our purposes), a *narrative sense of self* begins sometime between the third and fourth years (Stern 1985). It is important to stress at the outset that these different domains of self experience are not stages or phases each of which has a limited sensitive period in which it flourishes to be eclipsed by the succeeding phase. Rather, each sense of self encompasses a different domain of experience. And each domain, once formed, remains for the span of life and operates in concert with all the coexisting senses of self already present. These senses of self are like the lines of development described by Anna Freud.

The notion of these domains is conceived in large part from my reading of the developmental, experimental, and observational literature. I will skip the first sense of self so as to move quickly to the fifth, or narrated, self. I begin with the core sense of self, which emerges between the second and sixth months of life. The core sense of self involves experiences of self that are ultimately tacitly assumed or openly recounted in narrating about the self. They are some of the experiences of self that predate any retellings.

In thinking about what one would need in order to begin to talk about some sense of self that would have any meaning, there are at least four essential things that one would want: agency, coherence, affectivity, and continuity or historicity, so that the self "goes on being," in Winnicott's term. I will not be able to detail the infant experiments that permit one to talk about these, but the evidence is extremely suggestive that the infant is capable of experiencing each of them.

Let us start with agency. As infants can perform voluntary, nonreflexive, purposeful actions, they must be able to elaborate motor programs that are executed as planned. That ability is probably at the core of a sense of volition. In addition, these actions always produce sensory feedback in the form of proprioception, which provides another of the phenomena at the heart of a sense of agency. But how may the infant learn not to confuse his own actions with feedback reactions from another? Almost everything the infant does is constantly reinforced. When he closes his eyes, the world goes dark. Whenever he moves his arm, he gets proprioceptive feedback. If an infant could differentiate schedules of reinforcement, the task of discriminating self-caused from other-caused events would be simpler. By three months of age, infants are able to distinguish different schedules of reinforcement. This should make it much easier for them to know that when they have done something, the action occurs in an invariant organization of mental plans, sensations, and consequences. Agency, at a primitive level, should not be hard for a baby after the first three months or so.

Coherence is the second phenomenon of interest for a core sense of self. By coherence, I mean a sense of being a bounded, unitary, physical entity. The infant, partly through innate design and partly through learning, recognizes that certain disparate things belong together as a whole. For instance, things that move coherently or together against a background are perceived as belonging together and constitute coherent unities. Mother walking across the room is going to be moving as a unit against the background. She is already perceived by then as a coherent entity. The situation may be different, however, when mother and baby are very close to each other. For instance, if mother's arm is moving across her chest, the infant might perceive the arm as different from the chest. But the infant can use other invariants to identify units. In addition to coherence of locus and motion there is also coherence of temporal patterning. Infants automatically expect anything that moves and makes sounds in the same beat or rhythm to belong to a single unity. When we talk, we move our mouth, head, and body in synchrony and thus end up orchestrating our own speech. Infants have the capacity, beginning, at least, by the third month, to recognize that things that move and make sound synchronously constitute single entities. This capacity is a great help in sensing coherence of self versus other.

Infants can detect coherence of intensity level and contour. By intensity level, I mean that infants expect that something of a certain intensity in one modality (such as audition) should match something of a certain intensity in another modality (such as vision). Similarly, for intensity contour, when the baby is crying and the cry accelerates, the intensity of the cry that is experienced in the vocal cords is matched by the intensity of the feelings in the chest and by the intensity of the kinetic movements of the arms; all three are coherent from the point of view of shifts in intensity. That, too, helps establish what constitutes coherence.

The third element of a core sense of self is affectivity. From the Darwinian point of view, affects are seen as discrete behavioral expressions as well as qualities of feeling that have evolved into species-specific social signals. Considered as such, affects probably change less than all other human behaviors from the age of two weeks until the time of death. Facial expressions of the discrete affects do not change at all over development. This means that whenever the infant is having a certain affect state, he is also experiencing invariant patterns of feedback from the face, perhaps from the autonomic nervous system, and probably certain invariant qualities of feeling. So affectivity constitutes a certain core that helps in the recognition of a sense of the self.

The last element contributing to a core sense of self is continuity. A sense of continuity in time is based upon the memory capacities of the infant, which are extraordinary. We know that babies have recognition memory across the birth gap, that they can remember things for long periods of time, and, most important, that they have evocative or recall memory. This can be demonstrated for motor acts by three months and for emotional events by nine months. The infant is presumably forming a representational world of many specific memories that are organized and reorganized. The basic building blocks in representations of self and others most probably consist of repeated, lived, interpersonal experiences that include the invariants of agency, coherence, affectivity, and continuity. Representational constellations form by way of memory. Such memories of lived experiences are generalized (see Stern, 1989, for speculations on how this generalization occurs).

This account differs from Margaret Mahler's account in that, here, the infant is *first* designed to have other-self differentiation. Furthermore, the sense of being with another person (in a symbiotic or other state of union) follows. Primary states of union are thus no longer assumed. All wishes and fears of union are secondary. Other persons certainly are regulators of self experience in a profound fashion. But, once again, it is the interaction of a self with the other that gives the sense of being with the other, and notions of symbiotic merger are probably only the product of a more mature mind. In my view, a sense of merging with or being with somebody is the product of a successful integration of events and the laying-down of representations about being with somebody; it does not result from the failure of differentiation.

What do we have so far of a narrative self? We have the beginning of agents; we have certain distinct objects in the world. The infant has a sense of causality and some sense of continuity over time. The infant may even have the beginning of sequence recognition and memory. But the infant can't make a narrative yet because he or she lacks many other things: the notion of motives, of intentions, of affect states that makes things happen, of intersubjectivity between people, of objectifying and symbolizing the self, of symbolizing verbally, and of having a narrative form.

Of all of these missing ingredients for a narrative, the next to be acquired is the sense of motives, intentions, and intersubjectivity, that is, the ability and need to share inner subjective states. The next step emerges at about nine months, with the acquisition of a new sense of self. We will call it the subjective sense of self. At about nine months, babies make a remarkable discovery that philosophers have long discussed: they discover "a theory of separate minds." The baby gets the notion (via cognitive maturational leaps) that he or she has a mind that has contents, that others have minds that have contents, and that the contents of two minds can be in alignment. Overt behavior becomes only the sign of underlying subjective states. The evidence for this kind of intersubjectivity between infants and adults is inferential. For example, at about this point babies begin to point, and they point in a particular fashion. They look down their arms at the target, look back at mother's face, and then look back and forth until she looks at the target, that is, until there exists a joint focus of attention. This requires the assumption on the infant's part that it is possible for the mother and him or her to share or not share joint attention. Sharing a focus of attention is interattentionality, a different form of intersubjectivity that is now possible. The same is true with regard to intentions. For instance, if the baby wants a cookie (well before nine or ten months), he will stretch, reach out toward the cookie, and make a grasping movement with his hand, once again referencing his hand, the cookie, and mother's face, going back and forth until the mother brings a complementary intention into play that the infant already assumes is present. One can now speak about interintentionality. Feelings are yet a third internal state or mental content that is potentially part of subjectivity and not embraced by an understanding of overt behavior alone. Here we know from a variety of experiments that the infant seems to get the notion that somebody can feel something that may be the same or similar to what he is feeling. Mothers struggle with this in trying to get in touch with the baby's subjectivity. The issue is, how does a parent let the infant know that he or she knows what the infant has experienced subjectively, but without using language? This is one of the major tasks of being the parent of a preverbal baby. One might think that an easy way for a parent to do this would be to imitate the infant. But if a parent just imitates the baby, he might think the parent only knows what he did and not what it felt like. How does the parent get around the overt behavior and directly reference the subjective state? Mothers often selectively imitate what the baby does and then recast it back to the infant as an analog of what he did. For instance, if the baby has done something fun and is surprised and delighted, he may look up at the mother with a surprised facial expression that has a crescendo/decrescendo form—that is, the infant's face opens up to a full expression and then gradually falls back. The mother is very likely to respond to that by saying something like "yeaahh," where the pitch and volume of the word rises and then falls. She is taking the prosodic melodic line of her voice and creating an analogous match to the kinetic crescendo/decrescendo of the baby's facial expression. In that way she can reference the baby's subjective state and say, "I know what it felt like to have that contouring of intensity that you felt." Furthermore, she is referencing what it felt like inside and not what it was like overtly to perform (the latter requires only a faithful imitation). Such analogic recastings are common at this age. They are called *affect attunements.*

The question the baby is exploring is: What constitutes the shareable universe? What can be shared with regard to what's going on in one's mind? Besides having agency, some causality, and what not, infants now have several more things: intentions, feeling states, and foci of attention. Most important, they know that others have similar contents of mind and that these are shareable, that is, they have a sense of intersubjectivity. All of these are crucial features for the ultimate making of a narrative structure.

Still, the infant does not yet have a sense of self that is objectifiable, self-aware, or self-reflective. This brings us to the next domain, the verbal or categorical sense of self. This begins at about eighteen months and represents another quantum leap in maturation. Infants become self-aware at this point. This can be shown with mirror experiments in which rouge is put on the baby's forehead when he is not looking. Before eighteen months, the infant will point to the mirror, if he does anything. After eighteen months, he will point to himself or to the spot on his real self, indicating he understands that he can be objectified in some representational form outside himself. This representation of self can also now be seen in fantasy play and is perhaps most importantly and dramatically evident in the emergence of speech, which permits babies to refer to themselves with pronouns—me, my, mine, I—and also with proper names. A major step has been taken in which the infant, beginning at around eighteen months, has the capacity to represent himself and his lived experience in verbal form, albeit primitively. What he still does not have is the narrative mode.

This brings us to the next domain, the narrated self. Nobody knows yet exactly when this begins. It is an active area now in child development research. Infants appear to be able to make narratives that include agents, intentions, goals, consequences, and sequences with beginnings, middles, and ends starting at about three or four years of age. Much current thinking on the matter suggests that the capacity for narrative—the narrative form—may, in fact, be an emergent property of mind like language itself. It may be a universal feature of the organization of human experience and, as such, may greatly influence how humans perceive and comprehend self experience once they have the capacity to think in the narrative mode.

I turn now to some special issues and problems in moving developmentally from the core and subjective senses of self to the verbal and narrative senses of self. The problems are similar, in a way, to some of those of narration in general and of the correspondence between narrative truth and historical truth. I mention just a few of the problems of representing lived experience in verbal and narrative form.

One problem has to do with how verbal meaning is established, and it is instructive to consider the matter from the baby's point of view. One current view suggests that verbal meanings are jointly constructed. A meaning belongs neither to the infant alone, nor to the parent alone, nor to the culture, but has an existence of its own. Most meanings are coconstructed "we" meanings. This can be seen even with such easily agreed upon categories as "dogs," where it would seem that the meaning is simply given to the child via the parent by the culture rather than mutually agreed upon. However, most parents who are willing to work in the child's zone of proximal development will, in the beginning, permit "dog" to mean anything with four legs from the size of a horse to a chihuahua. Any such creature is a legitimate "dog" as ratified and agreed upon between mother and baby for a period of time. (The definition narrows gradually.) Internal states—states of consciousness, feeling states, or states of appetite—which, unlike dogs, can't be seen, the difficulty of establishing the boundaries of meanings increases, and almost all meanings are established as we-meanings. Let me give a quick clinical example. Two girls, eleven months old, were equally exuberant. When one of them had a bout of exuberance, the mother usually made an attunement at the point when the girl's enthusiasm was at its peak or still rising. The mother's responses were filled with many "oh wows"s and so on. With the same kind of behavior from an equally enthusiastic little girl, the other mother seemed to make most of her attunements after the bubble of enthusiasm had burst, when the girl's exuberance was on the descent. Her attunements were more along the lines of "oh, that's okay honey," "it'll come around again," "so it goes," and so on. The interesting thing was that the mothers were referencing (in the subjective domain) different parts of the girls' experience of exuberance, and, later, both came to label them differently. The first mother, who made an attunement with rising or cresting enthusiasm, called the state "delight." The second mother, who was making the attunement with *ex* thusiasm, so to speak, called the state "excitement," but with a slightly negative connotation. The label for what they could agree upon as the felt experience started to be different, even though the experience the girls originally had or continued to have was the same. The relationship between the linguistic version and the felt experience is fluid and unknown. The linguistic version, however, usually becomes the official version. It becomes the version for which one is accountable. It is the version one cannot deny without confronting someone, whereas one is far more readily allowed to deny things that occur in nonverbal domains, such as tone of voice. And the nondeniable, accountable, verbal version presumably becomes the initial version for a narration.

The problem of verbal labeling and then telling is equally or perhaps more complicated for moral or value statements. For instance, when father says "good girl" and mother says "good girl," the child knows perfectly well that the words are saying the same thing, but both of them may be referring to quite different attributes of herself. Meanings are coconstructed between people. This is what L. S. Vygotsky (1962) emphasized. Speech, in the beginning, is akin to a transitional phenomenon, as John Dore (1985) has noted. The child is in a peculiar position, because she already understands some concept and discovers that a word exists that matches the concept. On the other hand, although the word was given to her from the outside, it couldn't have been given and accepted unless there was something inside her experience to match. It was both discovered by her and given to her at the same time (see D. W. Winnicott 1971).

There may be an even more profound problem of putting things into words, at least from the point of view of the developing infant. Language can fracture the way the world is experienced by an infant. Infants are in the position, most of the time, of experiencing things amodally. They experience in the terms described by Heing Werner and Bernard Kaplan (1963), T. G. R. Bower (1978), and others who emphasize the abstract, global feeling perception in which infants engage. For instance, a baby looking at a chandelier would be experiencing some level of intensity with a certain kind of diffuseness to it: it would be happy, and it would certainly have some warmth. Then the baby's mother would walk into the room and say "Oh! Look at that pretty light." She would specify what it is the baby is doing: looking, having a visual experience, seeing an object with a name. She would thus fracture the experience that was going on in the global feeling perceptive mode. This is what happens when infants start to put global and feeling experiences into the verbal domain and then begin to try to narrate them. In some ways the acts of verbalization and narration themselves create a split between experience as lived and as told or as retold, and yet that's what we have to work with.

One of the things that happens in making narrations of self experience is that we work very hard to try to tell about experiences in these prenarrative domains, which is in a good part what makes these story lines or narratives so complicated and multiple.

One of the potentially interesting features of this view of developing senses of the self that culminate in the narrated self is that each newly emerging sense of the self corresponds to a major shift, a discontinuous quantum leap, in maturation. Children acquire a different social "feel," almost a different presence, as each new sense of self emerges. I suggest that these senses of self are what the shifts are all about and not the more traditional life issues or phases such as orality, anality, attachment, autonomy, and so on. Margaret Mahler and Melanie Klein's developmental sequences are closer to what I am talking about, because they address shifts in sense of self and other. However, such phenomena as attachment, trust, security, independence, autonomy, and merging are not sensitive phases of early development but are issues for the life span and are in fact closer to developmental lines. Most of these major clinical issues, such as attachment and security, go on for the entire life span and don't have phase specificity. What seems to have more phase specificity is the developmental emergence of different senses of the self.

This view of the development of the different senses of the self has two potential clinical values. It is partially informed by experimental findings from developmental psychology and, to that end, it offers an independent source of data to validate, challenge, or enrich psychoanalytic theories. Such information acts to alter ideas on theories. The therapist starts with a theory, which is a narrative about development, and in coconstruction with the patient, they work out what will be the felt experience of the patient's past. The issue of what constitutes the repertoire of conceivable and likely clinical self-stories or narratives about developmental history is very much informed by what makes common sense from experiments coming from outside psychoanalysis. A final point about this issue: If psychoanalysis confines itself strictly to a study of narratives, all events prior to about age three and a half (including the anal phase) are relegated to nonprivileged information that exists adjacent to the work of the analysis.

A second possible clinical value of this viewpoint lies in the manner of therapeutic exploration. Clinical psychoanalytic inquiry contains an implicit ever-backward search for an actual point of origin of psychopathology, a point that our theory has determined should exist. The theories dictate roughly where and when the actual point of origin ought to be, and analysts look for it, or at least are supposed to, in a sense, by moving the search ever backward in time. By making clinical issues and developmental tasks such as security, attachment, and independence into developmental lines (life issues and not phases of development) and by supplanting them with sense of self, at least in defining the quantum leaps in development, the therapeutic search to find the historical and narrative point of origin of pathology becomes freer. The answer is less known in advance. Analysts can listen without relatively specific theories indicating what constitutes salience and what historical events should be attended to with particular vigilance on the part of the therapist (to the exclusion of other matters). This increased freedom may be derivable from viewing early development in the manner that, I have suggested, may finally contribute to the coconstruction of better therapeutic narratives.

## References

Bower, T. G. R. 1978. The infant's discovery of objects and mother. In *Origins of the infant's social responsiveness,* ed. E. Homan. Hillsdale, N.J.: Erlbaum.

Dore, J. 1985. Holophrases revisited dialogically. In *Children's single-word speech,* ed. M. M. Barrett. London: Wiley.

Stern, D. N. 1985. The interpersonal world of the infant: A view from psychoanalysis and developmental psychology. New York: Basic Books.

———. 1989. The representation of relational patterns: Some developmental considerations. In *Relational disorders in early childhood: Developmental approach,* ed. A. Sameroff and R. N. Emde. New York: Basic Books.

Vygotsky, L. S. 1962. *Thought and language.* Cambridge: MIT Press.

Werner, H., and Kaplan, B. 1963. *Symbol formation: An organismic-developmental approach to language and expression of thought.* New York: Wiley.

Winnicott, D. W. 1971. *Playing and reality.* New York: Basic Books.

■ ■ ■

**PART 4**          **PSYCHOANALYSIS,
PSYCHOLOGY, AND
NEUROBIOLOGY**

■
■
■

# Ten
■ ■

# The Crucial Role of Mentalism in an Era of Neurobiology
*Ethel Spector Person, M.D.*

"What's matter?"
  Never mind.
"What's mind?"
  No matter!

The dream of a fruitful collaboration between psychoanalysis and the neurosciences is not a new one.[1] At the start of his clinical investigations, Freud had hoped that the obscurities of mental life could eventually be understood in terms of the brain sciences, and he outlined those hopes in his "Project for a Scientific Psychology." But Freud ultimately abandoned the Project,[2] because he had become increasingly aware of the importance of intention, wishes, motives, and meaning in clinical work and realized that the contemporary model of brain function was limited in its ability to illuminate those aspects of mental life. Given the burst in his creative output

1. I am not a historian of science, and in this chapter I rely heavily on many secondary sources, among them Daniel Robinson's account of the birth of modern psychology, Philip Rieff's account of Freud's gradual abandonment of a materialistic position, and Jonathan Miller's survey of some current thinking in the field of psychology. See Robinson's *Toward a Science of Human Nature,* Rieff's *Freud: The Mind of the Moralist,* and Miller's *States of Mind.* I would like to thank Arnold Cooper, M.D., Richard Druss, M.D., Sandy Kadet, Ph.D., and Ellen Rowntree, M.D., for their helpful comments in response to an earlier draft of this chapter.

2. Freud, "Project for a Scientific Psychology." Sándor Radó continued in Freud's original hope long after most theorists had turned their attention to primarily metapsychological concerns. In the interest of promoting a fruitful exchange with the life sciences, he proposed a psycho-analytical curriculum that would include courses in the psychodynamics of growth and development, comparative analysis of cultures, experimental analysis of animal behavior, psycho-physiobiology, and related findings from neurophysiology and neuropathology. His commitment to an innovative, interdisciplinary approach proved fruitful for work done at the Columbia Psychoanalytic Center. Abram Kardiner, David Levy, and George Daniels were pioneers in the studies of, respectively, culture, early development, and psychosomatic medicine.

following that strategic reversal, one can hardly doubt the wisdom of his choice. And over the years the distance between psychoanalysis and the other life sciences has continued to widen. There has been an increasing trend in psychoanalysis toward understanding the phenomena of psychic life in exclusively psychical or mentalist terms and a growing belief that the psychical and the physical might remain two separate domains.

Although such intellectual compartmentalization may have been necessary for psychoanalysis to consolidate and validate its own methods, theory, and techniques of treatment, there are those who feel that the continued isolation of psychoanalysis from neurobiology may now prove detrimental. Therefore the timely question for members of the profession (and others) is whether psychoanalysis ought to renew a dialogue with the neurosciences.

This issue has become pressing as the result of dramatic new findings in brain function and neurochemistry. Both the proven efficacy of certain drug therapies and the relatively recent discovery of chemical neurotransmitters suggest the importance to clinical work of an understanding not just of brain anatomy but of neurochemistry as well. Psychiatry today is riding a wave of enthusiasm revealed in the excitement over the promise of research and neurobiology and in the belief that we are on the threshold of still more revolutionary insights into the nature of mental life.

New research has already had an immense impact on the way psychiatrists formulate clinical problems. Recently, listening to a presentation on the New Diagnostic and Statistical Manual (DSM III) of the American Psychiatric Association, a distinguished colleague and friend of mine quipped that while DSM II was brainless, DSM III was mindless. Being somewhat witless myself, I did not immediately understand his joke. But I finally grasped that he was referring to a literal change in the emphasis of psychiatry—from the mind and a focus on psychogenic etiologies of mental illness to the brain and a focus on organic etiologies. This shift of focus in psychiatry from the mind to the brain is an attempt to remedicalize psychiatry. The concept of the brain as organic matter, heir to all the frailties of the flesh, presents us with new insights into the mechanisms of mental illness and new therapeutic strategies for some long-standing unsolved clinical problems.

Psychoanalysts cannot ignore the biological revolution that has occurred in academic psychiatry. Thus it is that a rapprochement between psychoanalysis and the neurosciences—the study of the mind in relationship to its brain—appears urgent to many analysts, particularly those who participate in both psychoanalytic and psychiatric education.[3] What we know, hope to

3. The phrase "the mind and its brain" is adapted from Popper and Eccles's *The Self and Its Brain: An Argument for Interactionism.*

know, and may someday actually know about this relationship has immense implications for psychoanalysis and must inevitably influence our therapy judgments, institute curricula, research priorities, and basic theories.

However, the hoped-for integration may be more easily wished for than accomplished. While not ignoring the implications of the biological revolution in psychiatry, psychoanalysts must also acknowledge the ongoing limits to the dialogue between psychoanalysis and the neurosciences. The task of conceptualizing the mind in relationship to the brain continues to pose immense problems, which have to do not only with the very wide chasm that separates our understanding of intentionality and wishes from brain chemistry, but more fundamentally with large questions about the nature of consciousness. The question of the relationship or interaction between consciousness (conscious mind) and matter (or brain), which has long haunted philosophy, has now insinuated itself into psychology. At first glance, the revival of a materialistic focus (on brain as matter) that has yielded so much new information may seem to promise the resolution of that long-standing philosophical problem, but the mind-body problem has remained problematic for cause and cannot be so easily disposed of as some proponents of brain research seem to hope. To study the relationship between conscious mind and brain is to come up against "that most mysterious of barriers, utterly impenetrable to the human understanding, that runs through the middle of what is the undeniable oneness of our personality—the barrier that divides our subjective experience from the objective, verifiable physiological events that occur in our body" (Konrad Lorenz, quoted in Eccles and Robinson 1984, p. 26).

In order to assess the inherent problems and potential benefits to psychoanalysis of any interdisciplinary effort with neurobiology, it is useful to put the development of psychoanalysis in a historical context and to explore those scientific considerations that have led to its present isolation. Part of what I want to touch on, though I can do so only incompletely and in very abbreviated form, is the story of changing conceptualizations of mind and the different strategies utilized in attempting to understand it. This requires a brief description of the development of psychoanalysis against the background of nineteenth-century philosophy and psychology and an explanation of why Freud's achievement could have come about only through his intellectual liberation from the constraints of both materialism and "psychological associationism"—the reigning psychologies in the scientific world to which he was heir.[4] It is probably no accident that the continued success of psychoanalysis in the world of ideas coincided with its intellectual and in-

---

4. Philip Rieff makes this point powerfully, and I find myself persuaded by his arguments.

stitutional isolation from twentieth-century psychology and neuroscience, for these disciplines explore different phenomena, ask different questions, use different methodologies, and make different assumptions. Nonetheless, these disciplines may now once more find some common ground, if not a common language.

I would like to take advantage of the rekindling psychoanalytic interest in neurobiology to urge the initiation of a dialogue with cognitive psychology as well. I suspect that the greater medical (and media) attention given to break-throughs in the neurosciences may obscure the equally important strides in cognitive psychology and may predispose psychoanalysts to an exclusive consideration of the interface with the neurosciences, to the neglect of the somewhat simpler task of working out the boundaries and areas for collaboration between psychoanalysis and cognitive psychology.

Though the presentation that follows is necessarily schematic, due not just to the immensity of the subject but also to my limited knowledge of the history of science, I hope that my bias will seem justified. My bias is as follows: although I believe in the importance of interdisciplinary study, I believe with equal strength that our enthusiasm for the recent breakthroughs in the neurosciences should not dull our appreciation of the mentalist approach. The complexities of the mind-body problem have not magically disappeared and will not do so in the future. They are part of the human condition. Nonetheless, new information from the neurosciences, and particularly from cognitive psychology, will inevitably have a profound impact on psychoanalytic models of the mind.

## THE MIND-BODY PROBLEM: PSYCHOLOGY
## AS PART OF PHILOSOPHY

Despite its intellectual distance from both the physical sciences and the broad field of psychology, psychoanalysis has been immensely influential in changing the way most educated people think about human beings, the mind, and behavior. The complexity of the mind first became obvious with Freud's formulation of the concept of an unconscious mind in interplay with the conscious one. Psychoanalysis has not only shown the sources of human motivation and conflicts, but, as D. O. Hebb points out, through its focus on the *unconscious,* it has for the first time apprised us of the "enormity of the problem of mind" (Hebb 1948). (That Hebb—a man not known for being a great friend of the psychoanalytic point of view—should acknowledge Freud's contribution in this regard is remarkable.)

Beginning with Descartes and Locke, concepts of mind have been based on man's awareness of *conscious* mental processes (Robinson 1982). In their attempts to understand the mind, only introspection was seen as necessary, and mind was equated with consciousness. This left Locke and others with the problem of how to explain many everyday phenomena of mental life, for example, the preservation of memories when they were not present to consciousness, as evidenced by the simple phenomenon of recall. Freud met this dilemma head on with his conceptualization of unconscious mental processes. Although we are familiar with the shocked reaction to the sexual part of Freud's theory, we may be less aware that his radical reconceptualization of mind—with its focus on the unconscious and preconscious—initially seemed just as strange. The idea of an unconscious mind was met with disbelief (Freud 1925). Only gradually did the various professions and the educated public accept such a fundamental reformulation, and then largely because it offered logical explanations of many diverse phenomena, including memory storage and retrieval, the ability to perform instant arithmetic calculations, and the occurrence of otherwise inexplicable forms of psychopathology.

Although estranged at the outset from much of what constitutes psychology, now, many years later, psychoanalysis can be seen to have had enormous impact on the field of cognitive psychology, particularly in its formulation of the unconscious—ironically so, because that concept was in large part responsible for the early estrangement between psychoanalysis and psychology (particularly during those years when behaviorism was psychology's dominant ideology). According to the philosopher of science Daniel Dennett, Freud's discovery of the unconscious not only served to revitalize clinical work; it "also paved the way for the more recent developments of 'cognitive' experimental psychology" (Hofstadter and Dennett 1981, p. 12). He refers here to the dramatic shift in psychology away from the narrow focus on "behaviorism" and toward a study of the brain's capacity for information processing, much of which is now known to be carried out unconsciously.

The acceptance of the concept of the unconscious mind, however, leads to another irony. A hundred years ago no one believed in the unconscious mind, whereas today we find ourselves uncertain how to comprehend consciousness. To some degree, Freud is responsible for this startling reversal in the conceptualization of the mind and for the different philosophical questions that this entails. Although there may have been a tacit understanding to keep the mind-body problem restricted to philosophy and out of psychology, it has become dramatically revitalized as a central concern today, as arguments about the relationship between consciousness and the brain resurface.

Historically, there have been three major philosophical theories about the relationship between the mind and the brain (or body): the dualist, the monist, and the third, which is often called interactionist.[5]

Dualists maintain that the brain and the mind are two distinct entities, that is, that the mental and physical represent two different realms of existence; the main question is how the two are related. The dualist position was definitively formulated by Descartes and has remained a major theme in Western thought ever since. (For a brief account of Descartes's formulation of dualism, see Robinson 1982, pp. 5–8.) Trying to achieve for the biological sciences a parity with the physical sciences, Descartes turned his attention to sensation, emotion, action, and intellect. Although he established to his own satisfaction that many biological and psychological phenomena could indeed be understood in mechanistic terms, there remained certain mental processes—in particular, the capacity for abstract thought—that could not. Descartes was unable to derive the ability to reason abstractly from experience (sensory input) alone. He disclaimed the concept of "innate ideas"; nonetheless, he believed that there were elements of cognition that could not be explained in terms of sensation, memory, or experience. He felt it was therefore necessary to postulate irreducible mental attributes. In so doing, Descartes may be said to have forged the archetypal dualist position. He viewed matter as substance that had extension in space but did not think, whereas mind was substance that thought but had no spatial dimension. This formulation of the mind-body duality places mind outside the strictly biological realm and thus establishes the necessity for a mentalist approach. As for the interaction between the mental soul and the material body (as, for example, when the mind comprehends a visual image), Descartes believed the interaction took place in the pineal gland. Mentalism, then, begins with Descartes. It posits that the workings of the mind cannot be understood by reduction to mechanist terms but must be understood within the laws of mental life.

In contrast to the dualists, monists claim that brain and mind are but one entity seen from two different perspectives. By and large, monists subscribe to materialism (though some few may posit idealism instead), itself part of a larger naturalism that seeks to uncover those fundamental laws by which all phenomena can be both described and predicted. In other words, materialism is quite literally reductionistic, its goal being to reduce each science

---

5. I have, of course, simplified the metaphysical problems for purposes of this paper. For an excellent overview of all the metaphysical possibilities—monism, idealism, materialism, identity materialism, dualism, parallelism, epiphenomenalism, and so on—see Edelson, "The Convergence of Psychoanalysis and Neuroscience."

to a more fundamental level. In this scheme of things, biology would be reduced to chemistry and chemistry to physics, the most basic of the sciences. From the perspective of radical materialism, conscious experience is simply a reflection of brain activity. Although a less radical materialism views the mind as distinct from brain activity, it nonetheless evaluates the mind as a mere epiphenomenon.

By the eighteenth century, the Enlightenment had decreed an extremely strict naturalism and physicalism, and dualism was no longer intellectually respectable. Instead, there was a new faith, rationalist and materialist, that eventually all phenomena would prove comprehensible under the reign of the same encompassing laws, laws that would also establish the connection between mind and body. As Voltaire put it in his attack on the notion of free will, "It would be very strange that all the planets should obey fixed and eternal laws, and that a little creature, five feet tall, should act as he pleased, solely according to his own caprice" (quoted in Robinson 1982, p. 7). However, it was not until the nineteenth century that the methodological recommendations of the previous century crystallized into a rigorous philosophy of science. This philosophy entailed a materialism so stringent it almost destroyed the belief that anything could be or should be studied without recourse to chemistry and physics. The scientific credo of this period was positivist, determinist, and monist, and it sharply distinguished between science and metaphysics. A mechanistic, materialist approach to knowledge of the mind was propagated, and in this spiritual climate the so-called human sciences were born, bringing logical and rationalist assumptions to the study of passion, desire, and irrationality.

Even so, the limitations of materialism have always been self-evident, at least to some, and have elicited strong criticism from many quarters. As Carlyle wrote in 1829, "Truly may we say with the Philosopher, the deep meaning of the Laws of Mechanism lie heavy on us; and in the closet, in the Market place, in the temple, by the social hearth, encumbers the whole movement of our mind and over our noblest faculties is spreading a nightmare sleep" (quoted in Robinson 1982, p. 2). Such widespread criticisms of materialism and reductionism resulted in a widening breach between science and art. Science was viewed by its critics as hopelessly mired in the limitations of the empirical method, while the hope of transcending these limitations was vested in intuition and imagination. What science failed to arrive at by observation, art might still realize through intuition or imagination. (The conversion of faith in the power of science to a belief in intuition also describes the significant revolution in regard to Freud's thinking. Freud came to believe that his debt was more to the creative insights of art than to philosophy or science, hard as he had tried to become a "biologist of the mind" [in Sulloway's phrase, 1979].)

Even so, despite its vocal nineteenth-century critics, radical materialism (monism) continues to have many proponents and may be growing in influence in our own "scientifically" imbued era. Gilbert Ryle, in his influential book *The Concept of Mind* (1949), deplores the legacy of Descartes, who propounded the belief that "mental happenings occur in insulated fields known as 'minds' and there is . . . no direct causal connection between what happens in one mind and what happens in another" (Ryle 1949, p. 13). Ryle decries the mystical "Ghost in the machine" that is thereby invoked.

The still unresolved question for psychology is whether mental life can be defined and understood in materialistic terms, or whether, by its nature, its understanding requires a different approach, one that is best called "mentalist." Is mind more than an aggregation of atoms governed by the laws of physics? If one answers yes to that question, one surely must value an ongoing mentalist approach to the study of mind, though one hardly need eschew the materialist approach. In interactionism—or causal interactionism, as it is often called—there is recognition and acknowledgment of the reciprocal influences of mental processes and physical processes. It is this latter proposition that is most congenial to me in conceptualizing mental life—and that provides some conceptual bridge for thinking about the relationship of psychoanalysis to its contiguous disciplines without renouncing a mentalist approach.

## THE BIRTH OF PSYCHOLOGY

Launched in the nineteenth century as a separate discipline, psychology of necessity inherited conflicting philosophical formulations of the mind-body relationship. Many nineteenth-century biologists promulgated a radical materialist approach to mental phenomena (Hermann von Helmholtz, for example, measured the time it took a nerve impulse to travel in a severed frog's leg), but those psychologists whom we regard as the real founders of modern psychology favored a mentalist approach. Their task was to develop a science of human nature that would explain what is specific and exceptional to the subject: those characteristics that differentiate the human from the animal. Those psychologists thereby restored the pre-nineteenth-century credo that knowledge about the world was divided into three separate domains: the material or inanimate world, the biological or living world, and the mental world.

Wilhelm Wundt, credited with establishing psychology as a separate scientific discipline, defined psychology as "the science of immediate experience," by which he meant the conscious inner experience of human beings (quoted in Miller 1983, p. 16). The first attempts at a systematic study of mental life were based on introspection. By this methodology, the subject observes his own sensations and records them as objectively as he can. The introspectionists' focus on consciousness and mental data makes clear that many of the early proponents of scientific psychology were to some degree recoiling from the positivist, materialist, and monist dogmas of their time. They recognized a discrepancy: what was known of physical processes could not adequately explain what was known of mental processes. Their essential problem was to observe the different components of the mind and to establish the law by which these different components grouped or associated themselves—hence the appellation "Associationists."

Differentiating themselves from the radical materialists, the mentalists took as their subject matter those mental phenomena previously regarded as irreducible and then dared to appropriate science's empirical methods of observation in the service of that which had been considered alien to science. But they made one profoundly limiting—and ultimately fatal—assumption: they equated the mind with consciousness and were apparently unaware of unconscious mental processes, even though such awareness was a prominent part of nineteenth-century Romanticism and had been intuitively known beginning in antiquity.

## FREUD'S ACHIEVEMENT

When Freud began his investigations, then, there were essentially two approaches to the question of the mind: the materialist and the introspectionist. The materialists depicted the mind by analogy with a machine or an electrical circuit. Mental sickness was believed to occur when parts of the machine or electrical circuit fell into disrepair or out of synchrony with one another. Mental illness resulted from the breakdown of a physical process of which the patient was completely unaware. By contrast, the empiricist British Associationists understood mind as precisely that of which one *could* be aware through the act of introspection, restricting their concept of mind almost exclusively to the content of consciousness, believed to be formed from sensory input. Although this psychology paved the way for scientific studies of perception, it was, finally, as William James complained in 1890 in his book *Principles of Psychology,* sterile.

Freud's training was in "the school of Helmholtz," which was committed to the materialist doctrine of physiology (Holt 1965, pp. 94–95). Freud began his clinical studies with the express hope of correlating neurophysiologic hypotheses with physical concepts. He told Fliess that he was completely obsessed with his proposed "Psychology for Neurologists"; his ambition was clearly to be part of the materialist, reductionist tradition. In the draft of his ultimately abandoned treatise, what we know as the "Project for a Scientific Psychology," he states that his "intention is to furnish a psychology that shall be a natural science: that is, to represent psychical processes as quantitatively determinate states of specifiable material particles" (Freud 1895, p. 295). He proposed that "The neurones are to be taken as the material particles" (p. 295). Later, of course, he came to base psychoanalytic theory on mental rather than physical laws, concluding that "every attempt to discover a localization of mental processes, every endeavor to think of ideas as stored up in nerve-cells and of excitations as passing along nerve-fibers has miscarried completely" (Freud 1915, p. 174). Yet at the same time he held on to the earlier faith, stating his belief that "for the present" the psychical topography had nothing to do with anatomy while still hoping that psychological phenomena might eventually be explained physiologically (p. 175). Even in 1920, Freud stated his belief that "The deficiencies in our description would probably vanish if we were already in a position to replace the psychological terms by physiologic or chemical ones (Freud 1920, p. 60).

Despite these oft-repeated hopes and dreams, Freud's triumph ultimately was in his ability to break with the stagnant assumptions of both the materialists and the empirical psychologists and so to undermine the foundations of turn-of-the century psychology. It took what Philip Rieff has referred to as creative daring for Freud to disengage from his materialist bias. In this he was no doubt aided by his practice as a physician, which did not allow him to exclude subjective experiences, unseemly behavior, or apparently irrelevant facts from his field of observation, for he recognized them as part of the totality of the emotionally disturbed person even if he could not account for them by anything he had been taught. His courage lay in his commitment to thinking seriously about those phenomena which others considered marginal or even disreputable and beyond the pale, including such symptomatology as hysteria and such apparent medical quackery as hypnosis; his creativity lay in seeing such phenomena as possible clues to an enlarged understanding of the mind.

Perhaps another aspect of Freud's genius lay in his ability to hold, in a kind of enlivening, fertile solution, two mental constructs fundamentally at odds with one another. Freud seemed to remain a materialist while taking as his main subject the study of the unconscious. It was as though he simply put his materialistic assumptions on hold and, while waiting for twentieth-century science to create the tools to validate those assumptions, moved ahead with that work which another existing set of tools—his intuition, sensitivity, insights, in short, his art—made possible in the present. That the assumptions of the one conflicted with the conclusions of the other seems not to have deterred him—and in that multiple suspension of disbeliefs may lie the real key to both his creativity and his courage.

Though Freud continued through much of his life to invoke neurophysiology as the ultimate bedrock of psychological understanding, he nonetheless radically reconstituted his basic assumptions. As early as 1900, in *The Interpretation of Dreams,* he had turned away from a physiological, materialistic approach, insisting that the dream was a psychological event and had a symbolic or wish-fulfilling function, even when its trigger was physiological. (Holt has pointed out that it was *when* Freud turned his back on the anatomical-physiological model that he wrote the ground-breaking *Interpretation of Dreams.* )[6] In this formulation, the unconscious, as it expresses itself through the dream, is not (as the materialists would have it) illusory but is as real as consciousness and is causally of great importance.[7]

But it seemed to take Freud a long time to see how dramatic a break with the materialists he had effected. Only late in his career, when the success of the psychoanalytic enterprise was ensured, did Freud make explicit his intellectual distance from the reigning materialism of his day. In 1925 he said, "the direction taken by this enquiry [psychoanalysis] was not to the liking of the contemporary generation of physicians. They had been brought up to respect only anatomical, physical and chemical factors. They were not prepared for taking psychical ones into account and therefore met them with indifference or antipathy. . . . they regarded such abstractions as those with which psychology is obliged to work as nebulous, fantastic and mystical" (Freud 1925, p. 215).

I do not mean to imply that Freud entirely reversed his belief in a materialist, deterministic universe.[8] But for the purpose of his work, he drew up a

6. For a full discussion of this reversal in Freud's thinking, see Rieff, *Freud.*

7. Holt, "Review of Some of Freud's Biological Assumptions." Holt also notes that this was a major turning point in Freud's life—one involving professional identity, friendship, the nature of his research, and other aspects of his life as well.

8. Nor can I conclude that Freud's immersion in the neurological assumptions of his day was completely detrimental to his theory-making; those assumptions gave him a skeleton around which to theorize. And there persists some legitimate doubt as to whether he ever relinquished his original frame of reference, the traditional rendering of his intellectual metamorphosis notwithstanding. (See Holt for a discussion of how Freud held onto his biological assumptions, though in an entirely inconsistent fashion. See also Sulloway.) In a sense, Freud's achievement lay in his ability to cut through the impasse of the mind-body problem. He took a mentalist approach while maintaining a monist point of view.

causal series as it applied to mental life. In other words, he proposed that there was nothing arbitrary or unmotivated in mental life. Although he maintained a biological framework, for all practical purposes he constructed biological and psychological phenomena as two different causal series. But he postulated the intersection between psyche and soma through the agency of instinct. (Similarly, Descartes had earlier speculated that the pineal body was the point of intersection between mind and brain.)

Though Freud was less interested in the work of the introspectionists than in that of the materialists, his work had profound consequences for the way associationism came to be regarded. As a result of his work, the inadequacies of the empirical tradition became clearly apparent. By giving us our first insight into the significance of the unconscious, he showed that introspection was not enough for the study of the mind, that the mind was not transparent, as had been assumed by all mentalists since Descartes. Because behavior was predominantly governed by motives of which the individual was unaware, psychology as the study of conscious mind was too limited, and Freud proposed that unconsciousness rather than consciousness ought to be the primary area of study for psychologists. Freud's abstract theories of mind—his concept of the unconscious, of active repression, of mental mechanisms such as condensation and displacement—may prove to be his most significant contribution to the large field of psychology.

Even if we were to grant that eventually we will be able to understand the mind strictly in terms of matter (and we shall grant it only for the moment and argue the case shortly), we can see that in Freud's day such an approach could only be what we would now be obliged to call "premature reductionism."

## THE ISOLATION OF PSYCHOANALYSIS

Psychoanalysis, isolated in its inception from neurophysiology by virtue of Freud's break with the dominant materialist ethos of his period, has remained separate from psychology as well.

As already suggested, psychoanalysis is commonly believed to have been repudiated and isolated because of its sexual content. But the grounds for its isolation are much broader, having primarily to do not with content, but with methodology. The scientific psychology of the mentalists, by virtue of its focus on introspection, was initially seen as an alternative to absolute materialism. This psychology was still committed to direct observation (albeit through introspection), the only approach by which psychology might be accepted as scientific. Psychoanalysis, on the other hand, took as its subject of study that which could not be observed, either in the outside world or by introspection; from this very crucial distinction flowed many others. Associationism (the empirical psychology of its day) focused on sensation and images, psychoanalysis on desires and dreams. Associationism emphasized the conscious, psychoanalysis the unconscious. Associationism was largely an academic pursuit, while psychoanalysis was a therapeutic method. They shared only their common interest in a mentalist approach.

Because of its divergent assumptions and by virtue of its being as much a clinical treatment as a theoretical discipline, psychoanalysis in the United States found its natural home in academic departments of psychiatry rather than in psychology. Yet even in its intellectual heyday, though it was preeminent in academic departments of psychiatry, psychoanalysis was a stepchild of medicine, too, precisely because it dealt with the mind, not with the body. But the deepest rift between psychoanalysis and psychology was yet to come, a consequence of the forty-year preeminence of behaviorism in psychology and of the almost diametrically opposite assumptions held by psychoanalysts, on the one hand, and behaviorists, on the other.

## PSYCHOANALYSIS AND TWENTIETH-CENTURY PSYCHOLOGY

Psychoanalysis must be considered as a branch of psychology if psychology is defined as the science of the mind, but the definition of psychology has been in flux over the past fifty years. Choosing a psychology textbook at random, dated 1963, I found the following definition of psychology: "Psychology has usually been defined in terms of its subject matter. Fifty years ago, the most common definitions described psychology as the science of the mind, consciousness, or experience. Today, we usually define psychology as the *science of behavior.* The newer definition is preferable because behavior is objective in a way that *mind, consciousness,* and *experience* are not" (Kimble and Garmezy 1963, p. 15). This reflects the behaviorist redefinition of psychology that was promulgated in the 1920s. Such an approach dealt with the relationship between stimulus and behavioral variables by direct measurements, and the resulting descriptive statements were verifiable and testable. It also had the advantage of being applicable to the study of infants, the extremely mentally disturbed, and animals—subjects unable to report on their thoughts, who therefore could not be successfully studied by introspective methods. These changes in focus and method were considered necessary reforms if psychology was to be considered scientific. The mind was relegated to the "black box," and that box was not to be opened. The textbook just cited also declared psychoanalysis to be a part of psychiatry, not psychology.

Behaviorism presents an extreme case of radical materialism. Behaviorists considered any interest in mentalism to be suspect, even viewing it as a covert way of reintroducing dualism, with its baggage of soul or spirit—the "ghost in the machine"—into the "scientific" study of psychology. John Watson and the other early behaviorists hoped to avoid the traps of mentalism by concentrating instead on the study of the conditioned reflex—a subject highly amenable to direct observation and therefore subject to verification. This was the exact opposite of the risky course Freud had set for himself, in which the most important phenomena were those not visible and verification was not possible.

As has often been pointed out, behaviorism was successful not so much for its ideology—obviously its subjects as well as all its major exponents lived their lives as though desire, intention, and consciousness were real enough—but for its laboratory research approach; it appeared pragmatic, and it side-stepped issues that smacked of mentalism and, therefore, of dualism. It was a method as much as it was a theory. By restricting the range of inquiry to the observable and verifiable, it guaranteed itself a certain degree of success on its own terms. Thus the behaviorists opted for "objectivity" over psychic reality.

It is strange to think how psychoanalysis and behaviorism coexisted for so many years, both flourishing in separate spheres while cut off from one another by their radically different philosophical assumptions. Yet both were vital new approaches that served to rescue psychology from the dead end of introspectionism.

Today, however, behaviorism has fallen on hard times. Analysts may be so preoccupied with their own place in the world of ideas that they tend to overlook the fate of their colleagues in psychology. During the past half century we have witnessed the wide dissemination of psychoanalytic theory, though its preeminence in psychiatry has diminished in the past twenty years. At the same time, those who were looking witnessed the rise and somewhat dramatic fall of behaviorism (Taylor 1979, p. 12).

Although behaviorism yielded verifiable results, it was ultimately beset by two fatal flaws. First, and perhaps most important, it was found that the effect of a stimulus varied according to a subject's range of expectations. (Today we know very well that perception and the responses to it depend on many different variables).[9] The simple reflex turned out to be not so simple! The second major limitation was that those results which were verifiable revealed little of interest about human behavior or motivation, issues that were of vital concern to people other than behaviorists. As a result, the decline of behav-

9. See Jerome Bruner's discussion of cognitive psychology in Miller's *States of Mind.*

iorism was inevitable, and it reflected a growing conviction that subjective experience could not be ruled out as a legitimate and necessary focus of psychology. It was not possible to exclude memory, feelings, intention, anticipation, and dreams from psychology indefinitely. Further, it has been suggested that, as our concept of machines was enlarged, psychologists became willing to talk about new metaphors of the mind. In speaking of the restoration of a mentalist focus in psychology, one observer remarked that "the mind came in on the back of a machine," meaning that, as machines were developed that incorporated the concept of feedback mechanisms and servomechanisms, psychologists could talk about "purposeful" behavior in physical terms.[10] Intentionality became legitimized. What could be conceptualized in machines must surely be allowed as part of the human mental apparatus.

By the 1960s, the immense prestige of behaviorism had begun to erode, replaced by the burgeoning success of cognitive psychology.[11] Cognitive psychology has reinstated a primary interest in such subjective areas as perception, memory, and thinking and in the question of how goals and intention influence behavior. Information-processing and artificial intelligence have emerged as new models or metaphors for the mind. And, as I have already suggested, it is partially as a result of Freud's understanding of unconscious mental processes that the unconscious (albeit in different terms) has become a focus for psychologists interested in cognition and linguistics.

Maria Callas's notorious lament was that first she lost weight, then she lost her voice, and, finally, she lost Onassis. According to the *Encyclopaedia Britannica* (1971), psychology has experienced a similar divestiture: "'Pity poor psychology,' it has been said. 'First, it lost its soul, then its mind, then consciousness, and now it's having trouble with behavior." However, I would describe psychology today as being fragmented rather than diminished. Modern psychology is enormously diverse, encompassing many different areas of study and many different methods and techniques of investigation. Although in a broad way psychology is once more defined as the science of mental life, it is so multifaceted that one group of psychologists is often unaware of the framing questions and methodologies of others.

Psychoanalysts are certainly guilty of this kind of isolation and—at this stage of the development of psychoanalysis—to their detriment. Many commentators, prominent among them Philip Rieff, have indicated the se-

---

10. Jonathan Miller, *States of Mind*, 26. George Miller gives the examples of the thermostat and of the military developing a system to point a gun at a target.

11. For an overview of the cognitive revolution, see Gardner, *The Mind's New Science.*

riousness of the charge that "psychoanalysis ignores basic functions of mind in its ordinary activities" (Reiff 1961, p. 12). Freud's great sin of omission was not his retreat from a study of the brain—the limits of the tools then available made that retreat advisable—but rather the incompleteness of his study of the mind. Because his focus was on drive, important mental operations such as perception, memory, and cognition received short shrift.

Unlike their scientific observers, however, "the mind and its brain" do not respect the separation implied by the array of separate psychologies. Some rapprochement or communication among them is clearly in order. The scientific achievements made in recent years by these different disciplines make it both plausible and advisable to restore a dialogue today.

## TOWARD A RAPPROCHEMENT

Thus far I have tried to describe—albeit schematically—how psychoanalysis became isolated from those contiguous disciplines with which it might have been expected to have a fruitful dialogue. Though it was essential to Freud's creative insights that he discard the assumptions of a "sterile" psychology and a simplistic materialism, he did so at the price of a certain intellectual isolation. This isolation has in time proven unfortunate because it has denied psychoanalysis some basic tools that might prove useful in working out problematic areas of our theory. (Take, for example, the question of how intense affect influences memory encoding.)

To some degree, the resumption of a dialogue between psychoanalysis and psychology and neurobiology has already resumed. Though this may not yet be reflected in our classrooms and curricula, the dialogue has been extremely productive, as is demonstrated by the recent work on the relationship between cognitive and affective development in infancy and its implications for theories of self and object discrimination, a field in which the psychoanalyst Daniel Stern, for one, has distinguished himself. I refer also to new research on sleep and dreaming. Best known, of course, is the reconceptualization of clinical anxiety and depression based on new research that throws light on their basis in biology.

Unfortunately, some analysts may regard these efforts as a threat to the integrity of their own science, believing that they restrict the purview of psychoanalysis. I believe they may be confusing the impact on therapy with the impact on theory. No doubt research has established treatment modalities other than psychoanalysis as more efficacious in the treatment of certain mental illnesses. But Freud and all subsequent generations of analysts have been only too aware of the limitations of a psychoanalytic intervention in some patients, and we must gratefully welcome these additional treatment modalities. From the perspective of theory, too, it seems clear that input from academic psychology is indispensable. I am thinking here of basic conceptual work on symbolism or dream work, for example. Thus far, it appears to me that the major contribution of research may be the light it throws on perception, memory, and affect, but I do not wish to minimize the importance of other findings, for example, what we have learned about the exposure of the prenatal brain to hormones, or the implications of the research done on split-brain patients. In short, it seems to me the potential benefits to psychoanalysis are enormous.

But the exchange should go—and to a great extent has gone—both ways. Analysts tend to be more aware of the impact other disciplines have had on psychoanalysis while losing sight of the irreplaceable value psychoanalysis has had, and continues to have, in framing questions and formulating hypotheses that inform other disciplines. I have already spoken of the impact of Freud's elucidation of the unconscious. To cite a few smaller but still cogent examples, I point to such framing questions as those regarding the origins of the psychological sex difference or the structure of the perversions.

The neuroscientist Jonathan Winson is one of the strong proponents of an interdisciplinary effort who reiterates the current view that now is the appropriate time to link psychoanalytic observation with brain function. As he points out, though such attempts were made periodically in the past, earlier endeavors were foiled by our limited knowledge of the physical workings of the brain.

Winson's optimism leads me to essential differences of opinion and expectations, and, regarding these, I would like to strike several cautionary notes. Some investigators look forward to a resolution of mind-brain dualism as more and more information about the brain is garnered. I take a different point of view. The first caution refers to the incompleteness of our present state of knowledge about the brain and how it functions. Like Freud, we must continue to wage the battle for knowledge with whatever tools are at hand, and today's tools for organic investigation, although much more sophisticated than those of Freud's time, are still very limited.

Neuroscientists, despite their revolutionary breakthroughs, are nowhere near the point where they can map the entire "wiring" of the brain. John Eccles has noted that neuroscientists obviously find the identity or monist theory attractive because it gives the future to them (Popper and Eccles 1977). They argue that, although our present understanding of the brain is inadequate, as we learn more, these problems will simply disappear. Karl Popper has labeled this belief or theory "promissory materialism" (pp. 96–

98). According to promissory materialism, future scientific advances will render currently inexplicable mental phenomena amenable to materialist analysis. Promissory materialism suggests that the victory of materialism over mentalism will eventually be complete, but at the same time it explicitly acknowledges that, at least at the current time, we cannot account for most mental phenomena by materialistic explorations.

Whether or not reductionism or radical materialism ultimately proves to be viable, premature adherence to such a philosophy would be self-limiting. Freud was able to achieve his extraordinary insights into mind—insights that changed the whole psychological enterprise—only by overcoming his predilection for materialism and gambling on mentalism. As evidence for the negative impact of premature reductionism, I quote from the strange defense that Hebb makes of Watson's limited direction:

> Outrageous Watson may have been in treating mind as a myth and images and ideas as mere misleading verbal habits, but he had solid scientific basis for that view—the neurophysiology of the day denied the possibility of any activity of the brain other than sensory motor transmissions. There was no holding or reworking of sensory input, no interaction between inputs, no output originating in the brain itself, according to existing anatomical and physiologic knowledge. One would think that any philosopher of science who respects logic would also respect Watson for basing theory on the facts at his disposal and not on tradition and personal preference. Unfortunately for Watson, the facts were wrong—at least incomplete. (Hebb 1980, p. 9).

This strikes me as an utterly perverse evaluation and a demonstration of precisely those dangers that threaten were psychoanalysis to limit its investigation and theory of mental phenomena to what is known of the nervous system. My caution, then, is based on the knowledge that premature closure may blind us to what we can know and may cut off critical avenues of investigation.

My second caution is more fundamental, insofar as it is based in philosophy, not pragmatism. It is my conviction that consciousness, by definition, cannot ultimately be grasped by a materialist approach. This caution is prompted by a reaction to the current reassertion of a radical materialism by some biologists and to the concrete identity theory they propound. According to Morowitz, "biologists, who once postulated a privileged role for the human mind in nature's hierarchy, have been moving relentlessly toward the hard-core materialism characterized by nineteenth-century physics" (Morowitz 1981, p. 34). (He also notes the enormous irony of the fact that physicists, by contrast, are currently moving toward a view that posits the observing mind as an effective agent in physical events.)

Radical materialism proposes the identity of mind with brain.[12] Materialists do not deny the existence of the mind or consciousness but relegate it to a passive role. They see mental experience as an epiphenomenon accompanying some types of brain activity but incapable of effecting change in its own right. This belief, echoing the old philosophy of extreme materialism, considers a mentalist approach as outdated or unscientific. It is Eccles who, to my mind, has raised the critical limitations of such a theory:

> all materialists of the mind are in conflict with biological evolution. Since they all . . . assert the causal ineffectiveness of consciousness per se . . . , they fail completely to account for the evolutionary expansion of consciousness, which is an undeniable fact. There is first its emergence and its progressive development with the growing complexity of the brain. Evolutionary theory holds that only those structures and processes that significantly aid in survival are developed in natural selection. If consciousness is causally impotent, its development cannot be accounted for by evolutionary theory. According to biological evolution, mental states and consciousness could have evolved and developed only if they were causally effective in bringing about neural happenings in the brain with the consequent changes in behavior. That can occur only if the neural machinery of the brain is open to influences from the mental events of the world of conscious experiences, which is the basic postulate of dualist-interactionist theory. (Eccles in Eccles and Robinson 1984, p. 37)

Eccles's is the classic statement of the interactionist theory, which seems to me the most persuasive of the three theories that purport to explain the connection between mind and brain. In the renewed debate on the question of whether mental life can finally be understood in chemical and physical processes, I have been persuaded by those who answer with an unqualified *no*. It appears to me simplistic to believe that we will one day be able totally to understand psychological phenomena through neuroanatomy and chemistry. In fact, the reverse may be true. As Julian Jaynes points out, "We can only know in the nervous system what we have known in behavior first" (Jaynes 1976, p. 18). The point has been made that, even if we were so fortunate as to have a complete blueprint of the brain, including knowledge of the contents of each neuron, we would still be left with the great mysteries of consciousness and subjective experience. The introspectionists may have been right, at least to some degree, in their insistence that we must start with consciousness, with introspection, for how else do we identify the very phenomena we are trying to explain?

The ultimate irony—considering the checkered career that unconscious-

12. In the following argument, I follow closely those arguments proposed by Popper and Eccles in *The Self and Its Brain*.

ness has had in psychological thinking—may be, as Thomas Nagel has said, that "Consciousness is what makes the mind-body problem really intractable" (Nagel 1981, p. 391). Freud appears to be saying the same thing when he declares, "The starting point for this investigation is provided by a fact without parallel, which defies all explanation or description—the fact of consciousness" (Freud 1938, p. 157). We may be faced with an unsolvable existential dilemma, in that mentalist phenomena and physical, chemical phenomena may ultimately constitute unbridgeable, separate domains—this despite their interactive, interdependent nature. Perhaps the reason William James has so much appeal to some of us is our intuition that, for all practical purposes, we may have to take the position of philosophical pragmatism.

Despite my cautions, I believe that psychoanalysts must rethink the relevance to their own science of current formulations not only of neuroscience but, even more particularly, of cognitive psychology. Unfortunately, given the current structure of psychoanalysis, psychiatrists and psychoanalysts have more access to the "hard" neurosciences, so many neurobiological research labs being located in medical centers, whereas there is no such ease of access to the findings of cognitive psychology, which is centered in psychology departments. (Psychoanalysts of course have access to journals, but there are fewer personal on-the-job interactions, which so often provide the real stimulus for dialogue.)

Research paths for future psychoanalytic researchers cannot be legislated, but educators of psychoanalysts can make sure that their students have access to knowledge about these contiguous disciplines. New knowledge from these fields has direct impact on our thinking; examination of the questions they address, their assumptions, methodologies, and goals helps us to reexamine our own underlying philosophy assumptions and may paradoxically lead us to appreciate even more the necessity of the mentalist perspective and the uniqueness of the psychoanalytic mode of inquiry.

## References

Eccles, J. and Robinson, D. N. 1984. *The wonder of being human: Our brain and our mind.* New York: Free Press.

Edelson, M. 1986. The convergence of psychoanalysis and neuroscience: Illusion and reality. *Contemporary Psychoanalysis* 22 (no. 4):479–519.

Freud, S. 1895. Project for a scientific psychology. *Standard Edition,* 1:283–317. London: Hogarth Press, 1966.

————. 1900. The interpretation of dreams. *S.E.,* 4–5. London: Hogarth, 1953.

————. 1915. The unconscious. *S.E.,* 14:159–215. London: Hogarth, 1957.

————. 1920. Beyond the pleasure principle. *S.E.,* 18:1–64. London: Hogarth, 1955.

————. 1925 [1924]. The resistances to psychoanalysis. *S.E.,* 19:213–22. London: Hogarth, 1961.

————. 1940 [1938]. An outline of psychoanalysis. *S.E.,* 23:139. London: Hogarth, 1964.

Gardner, H. 1985. *The mind's new science: A history of the cognitive revolution.* New York: Basic Books.

Hebb, D. O. 1948. *Organization of behavior.* New York: Wiley.

————. 1980. *Essay on mind.* Hillsdale, N.J.: Erlbaum.

Hofstadter, D. R. and Dennett, D. C., eds. 1981. *The mind's I: Fantasies and reflections of self and soul.* New York: Basic Books.

Holt, R. R. 1965. A review of some of Freud's biological assumptions and their influence on his theories. In *Psychoanalysis and current biological thought,* ed. N. S. Greenfield and W. C. Lewis. Madison and Milwaukee: Univ. of Milwaukee Press.

James, W. 1891. The principles of psychology. In *The great books.* Chicago: Encyclopaedia Britannica.

Jaynes, J. 1976. *The origin of consciousness and the breakdown of the bicameral mind.* Boston: Houghton Mifflin.

Kimble, G. A., and Garmezy, N. 1963. *Principles of general psychology.* 2nd ed. New York: Ronald Press.

Miller, J. 1983. *States of mind.* New York: Pantheon.

Morowitz, H. J. 1981. Rediscovering the mind. In *The mind's I: Fantasies and reflections of self and soul,* ed. D. R. Hofstadter and D. C. Dennett. New York: Basic Books.

Nagel, T. 1981. What is it like to be a bat? In *The mind's I: Fantasies and reflections of self and soul,* ed. D. R. Hofstadter and D. C. Dennett. New York: Basic Books.

Popper, K. and Eccles, J. 1977. *The self and its brain: An argument for interactionism.* New York: Springer-International.

Rieff, P. 1961. *Freud: The mind of the moralist.* Garden City, N.Y.: Anchor Books/ Doubleday.

Robinson, D. N. 1982. *Toward a science of human nature: Essays on the psychology of Mill, Haggel, Wundt, and James.* New York: Columbia Univ. Press.

Ryle, G. 1949. *The concept of mind.* London: Hutchinson.

Sulloway, F. J. 1979. *Freud: Biologist of the mind: Beyond the psychoanalytic legend.* New York: Basic Books.

Taylor, G. R. 1979. *The natural history of the mind.* New York: E. P. Dutton.

Winson, J. 1985. *Brain and psyche: The biology of the unconscious.* Garden City, N.Y.: Anchor Press/Doubleday.

# Eleven
■ ■

# Will Neurobiology Influence Psychoanalysis?
*Arnold M. Cooper, M.D.*

P sychoanalysis may be characterized as an attempt to decode, that is interpret, a patient's communications according to a loosely drawn set of transformational rules concerning underlying meanings, motivations, and unities of thought. The analyst does his best to understand the patient's communications as the patient intends them to be, but both patient and analyst are heavily influenced by a theory, or a group of theories, used by both parties. For example, patients have theories about the nature of responsibility and the causal agents of behavior; these theories may range from extremes of conviction that "everything is my fault" to "nothing is my fault" or from "I intended to do that" to "something made me do that." Patients have theories about the nature of their motivation; some are convinced that all their actions are altruistic, while others believe that their most innocent thoughts are evidence of their murderous intent. Patients have theories about the sources of their behavior; some are firmly convinced that all their actions are explained by the nature of their nurturance, and others are convinced that only a bad fate could explain their lives.

We take for granted that these theories, no matter how firmly held, reflect defensive needs and are to be regarded as an entry to different—we usually

This chapter is a slightly revised version of a paper that appeared originally in the *American Journal of Psychiatry* 142, no. 1 (1985): 1395–1402. Reprinted with permission of the *American Journal of Psychiatry.*

imply deeper—aspects of the patient's personality. We also assume that all human beings weave their experience and their capacities into a holistic way of understanding themselves and their world and create a theory that provides some degree of comfort. At high levels, these theories may be philosophies, religions, and life attitudes.

Analysts also have a range of available theories with which we are all familiar. While we share many things in common, it makes a difference whether we see the world through Freud's lens, or Schafer's, Kohut's, Kernberg's, or our own variation of how to view analytic data. The theory will determine how the analyst shapes the patient's material so that he will have the benefit of theory that the patient has; that is, he too will be able to have a holistic, seemingly rational, view that will explain the entirety of his patient's behavior and provide the analyst with a bit of needed comfort and confidence in his professional world. Theories also lead us, no matter how we may try to be merely the recipient of the patient's story, to collaborate with the patient in creating a new personal myth, a life narrative more acceptable to analyst and patient. If we believe that the Oedipus complex is central in neurosis, any patient will provide ample opportunity for demonstrating the existence, vitality, and significance of oedipal fantasies. If we believe that preoedipal arrests or fixations are determinants, again it is a rare patient who does not provide adequate opportunity to construct the life story so that preoedipal issues will occupy a central place.

I am not nihilistic about the role of theory. I do not think that theories do not matter; rather, I think they matter crucially. But until we have better ways of testing our theories, different theories will coexist, and we will go on, consciously or unconsciously, intentionally or unwittingly, educating our patients to see the world as our theory has already told us the world is. This is inevitable. Because there is a paucity of validating strategies in psychoanalysis, it is important that analytic theories not be out of touch with developing new knowledge in areas adjoining our own area of interest, lest they become idiosyncratic and isolated from the mainstreams of science and the humanities. Information from other disciplines may provide a check on our own findings and theories.

The question posed by the title of this chapter could be phrased another way: "What does it take to change an analyst's theory?" More precisely, "What are the possibilities that anything found in neurobiology will change the way an analyst hears his patient talking?" It may be instructive to examine, as an example, the relationship of direct child observation to psychoanalysis. There has always been and still is a significant group of analysts who have maintained that child research is interesting and even worth knowing for its own sake or for some yet unforeseen purpose but has no relevance to the analytic situation, in which we are interested solely in the psychic reality verbally conveyed by the patient rather than infantile reality observed by the investigator. That is, psychoanalysis in its working mode accepts as data of infancy only the patient's construction of it or our interpretive understanding of the patient's construction of it and not the so-called objective data.

Despite this claim, however, most of us have seen a quiet revolution in analytic theory and practice secondary to the work of investigators as different as Mahler and Bowlby. Whether or not one subscribes to all their views, the data on the central role in development of attachment behaviors and their consequences in separation-individuation have led most analysts to give far more emphasis to these aspects of development in their reconstruction of patient's lives, to give greater weight to the interpersonal and object-relational portions of the developmental narrative, and to look more closely at preoedipal issues than was the case when libidinal and aggressive drives were seen as more simply derived. Furthermore, the recent and ongoing discoveries of the spectacular range of cognitive and affective capacities of the very young infant, with evidence for very early development of capacities for control and for distinguishing self from other, give rise now to new questions concerning the nature of the infant's early tie to the mother. These findings also are leading to suggestions for new theories of the self and different ideas about the so-called symbiotic phase. We do not yet know how these newer findings and formulations will affect the ways in which we listen to our patients' stories, but it is, I think, unlikely that they will leave us unchanged. Similarly, the work of Harry Harlow and the movies of his socially deprived baby monkeys have subtly, but profoundly, altered the way we construct meaningful life narratives when we encounter chronically depressed and anxious and solitary individuals.

Any data or theories on development may fade in significance when we encounter seemingly contradictory evidence from the patient, but we know that the evidence from the patient is always the stuff of our interpretation, not the bedrock, and our interpretations will be, and ought to be, in accord with what is objectively known about development. Our confidence in our interpretations will be strengthened by the knowledge that they are in accord with scientific data. Freud, for example, was significantly handicapped in not eventually knowing the data on infant sexual seduction. While his discovery of his error in believing that all neurosis was caused by seduction led to the development of the core of psychoanalysis, the world of psychic reality, it is possible that better information later would have led him to modify the overemphasis he had given to instinct and to alter his theory to find a role for the environment and for the more interpersonal and object-relational modes that were available to him in his practice but were not included in his metapsychology at that time.

Because it is my thesis that neurobiology ought to, probably already does, and surely will influence psychoanalysis, I want first to emphasize the primacy of our effort to listen, as Freud urged, with freely hovering attention, or, as Bion said, without memory or desire, or, as Kohut said, empathically seeing the world as our patients see it. We should be equally aware, however, of the inherent and inevitable limits to achieving these goals that result from the necessity for an organizing analytic theory. All outside knowledge potentially biases the observer not to hear his patient but to confirm his own a priori knowledge and avoid cognitive dissonance—that great source of anxiety. Knowing that we cannot succeed in achieving "unbiased" listening does not relieve us of the obligation to attempt it.

Many psychoanalysts believe that psychoanalysis can derive useful data only from its own activities, that the scientific development of psychoanalysis depends solely on findings derived from the psychoanalytic situation. It helps if one realizes that what many accept as the standard psychoanalytic points of view—whether the stages of libidinal development, the nuclear role of the Oedipus complex, or the nature of transference—are not simply derivatives of analytic experience but are amalgams of varieties of analytic experience and other kinds of knowledge. Neurobiologic concepts are built into the core of psychoanalysis. Think for a moment of a few of our core concepts. The pleasure-unpleasure principle is a biologic as well as a psychological concept, whether phrased in Freud's early energic terms—that the individual acts to reduce neural excitation to the lowest level and to maintain homeostasis—or in psychological language—that the individual acts to maximize pleasure and safety and to avoid pain and danger. Those are different ways of phrasing the principle of adaptation, which is at the heart of every consideration of organismic functioning. Much of the modern neurobiology can be seen as an effort at the level of the molecule and the cell receptor to understand the ways in which homeostasis, pleasure, and safety are maintained at levels appropriate to the effective functioning of the organism. Even if one chooses to abandon Freud's concept of drive and to accept the psychological concept of wish, as Holt and others have recommended, I think that most of us would agree that psychoanalysis would benefit from a better understanding of the biologic substrate of wishes, their categories, their mixtures, and the regulators that turn them on or off.

Freud did not hesitate to go outside psychoanalysis for aid in obtaining information useful in forming his concepts. Not only did he model his thinking on the scientific mode of his era, but he looked for specific data. He used the work of the Hungarian pediatrician, Lindner, to support his libido theory that the sexual drive must be an important part of infantile oral activity even if no overt sexuality, as then conceived, could be demonstrated (Freud 1905). Lindner's description of the infant's evident sensuality while sucking strengthened Freud's conviction about his new theory. He used the data of Sophocles, as described in drama, to support his view that the Oedipus complex was itself a central drama. Freud used his vivid phenomenologic description of the baby's relationship to the mother to support his view of the core constancy of drive aspects of object relations and the nature of transference regression. Although Freud gave up his Project, which aimed at making psychoanalysis a branch of, or at least entirely compatible with, neurobiology, he never gave up the desire that psychoanalytic findings accord with and be affirmed by findings in other sciences and the humanities. In a footnote to his paper "The Dynamics of Transference" (1912) Freud said,

> I take this opportunity of defending myself against the mistaken charge of having denied the importance of innate (constitutional) factors because I have stressed that of infantile impressions. A charge such as this arises from the restricted nature of what men look for in the field of causation: in contrast to what ordinarily holds good in the real world, people prefer to be satisfied with a single causative factor. Psychoanalysis has talked a lot about the accidental factors in aetiology and little about the constitutional ones; but that is only because it was able to contribute something fresh to the former, while, to begin with, it knew no more than was commonly known about the latter. We refuse to posit any contrast in principle between the two sets of aetiological factors; on the contrary, we assume that the two sets regularly act jointly in bringing about the observed result. Endowment and Chance determine a man's fate—rarely or never one of these powers alone. The amount of aetiological effectiveness to be attributed to each of them can only be arrived at in every individual case separately. These cases may be arranged in a series according to the varying proportion in which the two factors are present, and this series will no doubt have its extreme cases. We shall estimate the share taken by constitution or experience differently in individual cases according to the stage reached by our knowledge; and we shall retain the right to modify our judgement along with changes in our understanding.

It is in this spirit that we should look at neurobiology today. It may now merit a larger share.

I have suggested a number of ways in which findings of infant observation and ethology already have changed the way we work. Neurobiology, in the broad sense, will almost surely further change some of the ways in which we understand development, affect, learning, sexuality, and the meaning of symptoms. I will mention a few areas of current study in which growing neurobiologic knowledge may require that we reexamine and perhaps alter aspects of the theories with which we listen to our patients and the ways we teach them.

## RESEARCH IN ANXIETY

We know that Freud had an early theory of anxiety that he did not entirely abandon when he developed his later one. According to his original view, anxiety represented psychologically contentless overflow of neuronal excitation, an overflow of blocked and transformed libidinal energy. In this early view, anxiety was not in itself a psychological phenomenon but signaled homeostatic disturbances elsewhere, either in psychological systems or in neuronal function. Freud's second theory of anxiety treated anxiety as part of an evolutionarily evolved biologic warning system, with a signal form of anxiety serving as a mild stimulus for the institution of defense mechanisms in order to ward off more powerful forms of anxiety. Anxiety is part of a biologic fight-flight alerting system, preparing for action to avert dangers either from unconscious impulses or from the environment. It is also assumed that the experience of anxiety is disorganizing and unbearably painful and that it is a major task of the organism to avert that experience.

Psychoanalysis, under the sway of ego psychology and our concern with adaptation, has taken Freud's second theory of anxiety as the basis for our continued thinking on the subject, with various workers constructing lists of the dangers that elicit anxiety. Anxiety in our patients is generally assumed to represent the ego's response to the threatened breakthrough of unacceptable impulses or an anticipated loss of an object necessary for the maintenance of inner stability. In this view, anxiety is always related to psychological content.

Recent neurobiologic findings, however, suggest other interesting possibilities. The discovery of benzodiazepines in 1956 and of benzodiazepine binding sites in the brain in 1977 has led to a series of investigations concerning the biology of anxiety. I mention only a few of the interesting findings.

One line of research includes the following findings.

1. The locus ceruleus seems to be a regulatory center for neuroexcitatory activity and may serve as a regulatory center for the anxiety level of the organism.

2. Benzodiazepines potentiate the activity of those inhibitory neurons that are responsive to γ-aminobutyric acid (GABA). The inhibitory neurons are

specially concentrated in the locus ceruleus, and the activation of these neurons diminishes anxiety.

Another line of research includes the following findings (Crowe et al. 1981).

1. There is increasing evidence that panic attacks differ from generalized anxiety in other than simply quantitative ways. Klein and coworkers have suggested that in certain people panic attacks are a primary event that secondarily leads to learned anticipatory anxiety and phobic behavior.

2. There is also increasing evidence that panic anxiety is responsive to antidepressant medication.

3. There are not yet confirmed data that many school-phobic children are responsive to antidepressant medication.

On the basis of these kinds of data, one could postulate that there are several different groups of people who are chronically anxious, often phobic, perhaps with intermittent panic attacks, who have developed their anxious personality structure secondary to a largely contentless biologic dysregulation. Although psychological triggers for anxiety may still be found, the anxiety threshold is so low in these patients that it is no longer useful to view the psychological event as etiologically significant. One group may have a hyperactive alerting system, related to a failure of GABA activity, resulting in excessive anxiety signaling and breakthrough of anxiety states. These individuals are benzodiazepine responsive. The second group may be understood as suffering a lowered threshold for separation anxiety—the postulated trigger for panic. In effect, this is a return to a version of Freud's early anxiety theory: the trigger for anxiety is a biologic event, as in "actual neurosis," but now the trigger is separation, not dammed-up libido. The newer theory postulates that panic is an evolutionarily constructed response to separation, but the mechanism may miscarry and fire independently of appropriate environmental triggers. That neurons mediating separation responses and the creation of panic both seem responsive to tricyclic antidepressants suggests, of course, the psychologically known links of separation and depression. In these two groups of individuals, the presence of anxiety is not an indication of a primary disorder of conflict or self or object relations; these are secondary to the disorganizing effects of anxiety. Furthermore, the biologic dysregulation is not only a developmental event but an ongoing one. These persons are currently physiologically maladapted for maintenance of homeostasis in average expectable environments. Klein claims that individuals with panic disorder who are treated with imipramine cease to have panic attacks but then require psychotherapy to undo the learned anticipatory anxiety and phobic behaviors that were developed as magical efforts to cope with unpredictable panic.

This theory suggests that the psychoanalyst is now confronted with a diagnostic decision in his anxious patient. What portions of the anxiety are, in their origins, relatively nonpsychological, and what portions are the clues to psychic conflicts that are the originators of the anxiety? The neurobiologic theory does not suggest that all anxiety is a nonmental content but rather that a distinction must be made between psychological coping and adaptive efforts to regulate miscarried brain functions which create anxiety with no or little environmental input and psychological coping and adaptive efforts to regulate disturbances of the intrapsychic world that lead to anxiety and are environment sensitive. Clearly, we have not yet arrived at the point where we can easily make that distinction, but there is good reason to attempt it. In instances in which an underlying biologic malfunction is suspected, there is powerful warrant to attempt a biologic intervention that may then facilitate psychological interventions. Let me give an example.

## Clinical Vignette

A woman entered treatment describing a history since midadolescence of intermittent depression, timidity in relations with men, and very high rejection sensitivity. Any relationship with a man was colored from the start by her expectation that the man would probably leave her. The prospect of desertion precipitated such anxiety and rage that she was then prone to behave in ways that brought about the rejection she allegedly feared. The patient recalled as a small child always being extremely upset when her parents went out in the evening, requiring hours before she could calm down. She was mildly school phobic. The patient entered analysis and worked through the consequences of a relationship with a profoundly narcissistic mother who, it became clear, was also chronically depressed. A sister of the mother had been hospitalized with an uncertain diagnosis of schizophrenia. In early latency, the patient had turned from the mother toward the father, whose favorite she was, but the father seemed to go through a profound personality change, presumably a depression, when the patient was about ten years old. The patient remembers her father becoming extremely withdrawn, going to work, coming home, and watching television by himself. The patient and father began to have tremendous battles when the patient began to date, as the father regularly disapproved of the patient's boyfriends, most of whom were chosen to elicit that disapproval. The father died when the patient was sixteen years old, during a period when they were angry at and not speaking to each other, and the patient felt continuing guilt and rage that she had never had the opportunity to make peace with her father.

From the very beginning of the analysis, the transference was characterized by severe anxiety reactions at every disruption of the tie to me.

Weekend breaks were extremely difficult, canceled appointments were a crisis, and vacations seemed a major trauma. As the analysis progressed, the patient became generally calmer, was able to pursue her work successfully, began to develop a much higher level of self-esteem, and had somewhat better relationships with men. Despite these improvements, she episodically reverted to the symptoms with which she had entered treatment: a mixed depressive-anxious state with feelings of shame and worthlessness, terrified that she would be rejected by her boyfriend, a female friend, a work supervisor, me, or anyone else. The termination phase of the treatment was difficult but seemed to be successfully negotiated.

Two years after termination the patient called me, just before the beginning of my summer vacation. She was already on vacation and was in a state of mixed depression and panic, the kind of feeling with which she had entered analysis. There were no apparent external precipitants other than the preconscious reminder of my vacation time, and she felt extremely discouraged over this uncontrollable state. While her description of her feelings was extremely familiar, this time it occurred to me that she might be describing a recurrent biologic dysregulation and that a search for further psychological content might not be productive. That thought had also occurred to her. Despite much trepidation, she agreed to a trial of imipramine. She responded well to the medication, despite side effects, and stated that she felt relieved and reorganized and had the sense that an outside intrusion into her life, the severe anxiety, had been alleviated. On medication, although she was not free of anxiety, she had a feeling that she was in some way more in control of herself than she had ever been.

The case is suggestive. This woman later decided to return for further analysis to deal with aspects of her conflictual life that had not been successfully analyzed while anxiety and mood dysregulation were, perhaps independently, dominating her ongoing psychological life.

Current research indicates, with varying degrees of certainty, multiple levels—cellular, neural network, and experiential—for the organization and regulation of anxiety and for the development and alteration of pathologic anxiety. The elegant research of Kandel and associates (1979) has elucidated the actual neurochemistry of some forms of learning in the snail, including what may be considered aspects of anticipatory and chronic anxiety. The interaction of the environment and the adaptive responses of the organism can now be partially understood in terms of basic cellular neurobiology. The readiness with which an analyst attempts to affect the patient's self or his locus ceruleus through a new relationship or medication has philosophical and ethical connotations, and in the current absence of specific indications for either or both treatments, the treatment choice will reflect individual bias. We are alert to the issue of efficacy. If we can demonstrate that physiologic interventions are more efficient ways to achieve a portion, at least, of the effect we seek—relief of pain and opportunities for new growth—as physicians, we welcome the most effective treatment.

The question may be asked, "Are psychoanalysts interested in changing the patient's life or changing the symptom?" Analysts used to find it easy to answer this question. We believed that symptoms were surface manifestations of deep disturbance, as in the rest of medicine, and that the symptom was not the target of our ministrations. In fact, we thought that too easy symptom removal would confront the patient with the task of constructing a new symptom to provide defenses against underlying threatening wishes. This idea of symptom substitution has not been borne out by recent work. Experience with behavior therapy, focal psychotherapies, and pharmacotherapies seems to demonstrate that, contrary to expectation, symptom removal, in many although not all instances, may lead to enhanced self-esteem and possibilities for new experiences and renewed characterologic growth. Most analysts have long realized that excesses of dysphoric affect inhibit the effectiveness of psychoanalysis by fixating the patient on the affective state and limiting the patient's cognitive associational capacity. For the patient whom I have described, I believe, retrospectively, that pharmacologic assistance earlier might have permitted a much clearer focus on her content-related psychodynamic problems and would also have made it more difficult for her to use her symptoms masochistically as proof that she was an innocent victim of endless emotional pain.

I would like to draw another implication from the brief clinical vignette I gave. Most analytic treatment carries with it a strong implication that it is a major analytic task of the patient to accept responsibility for his actions. In the psychoanalytic view, this responsibility is nearly total. We are even responsible for incorrectly or exaggeratedly holding ourselves responsible. It is our job to change our harsh superegos, and it is our job to do battle with unacceptable impulses. However, it now seems likely that there are patients with depressive, anxious, and dysphoric states for whom the usual psychodynamic view of responsibility seems inappropriate and who should not be held accountable for their difficulty in accepting separation from dependency objects, or at least they should not be held fully accountable. There is a group of chronically depressed and anxious patients—perhaps they are part of a depression spectrum disorder, as Akiskal (1983) suggests—whose mood regulation is vastly changed by antidepressant medication. The entry of these new molecules into their metabolism alters, tending to normalize, the way they see the world, the way they do battle with their superegos, the way they respond to object separation. It may be that we have been coconspirators with these patients in their need to construct a rational-seeming world in which they hold themselves unconsciously responsible for events. Narcissistic needs may lead these patients to claim control over uncontrollable behaviors rather than to admit to the utter helplessness of being at the mercy of moods that sweep over them without apparent rhyme or reason. An attempt at dynamic understanding in these situations may not only not be genuinely explanatory, it may be a cruel misunderstanding of the patient's effort to rationalize his life experience and may result in strengthening masochistic defenses.

## RESEARCH IN SEXUALITY

Psychoanalysts have long been torn by arguments over the appropriate attitude toward homosexuality and other gender-deviant behaviors. Neurobiology will not settle the argument, but advances in neurobiologic understanding of gender role add intriguing new insights to our outlook on homosexuality. There is evidence from research with mice that there are two independent brain systems for sexual behavior—one for male behaviors and one for female behaviors, the activity of each depending on genetic, prenatal, environmental, and hormonal influences. It seems that females may be masculinized, defeminized, or both, and, conversely, males may be demasculinized, feminized, or both. Hofer reported that

> females whose uterine position was between two males show slight modification of their genitals in the male direction, are more aggressive, do more urinary marking of their cages (a male trait), and are less attractive to males than their litter mates with uterine positions between two females. The implication is that the proximity to males in utero and some sharing of their placental circulation resulted in their being exposed to somewhat more testosterone during the prenatal period. However, it was found that these masculinized females were not defeminized. They were no different in their response to estrogen and they were as capable of all female reproductive functions, including maternal behavior and the raising of young, as their female litter mates who had been together in the uterus. Thus, with different amounts and timing of exposure to testosterone in male animals, behavior may be feminized without being demasculinized. (1981, p. 273)

Hofer concluded that "a number of sex related behaviors may depend to a certain extent on the presence of testosterone in early development, that both genetic males and genetic females possess the potential for both masculine and feminine behavior traits, and that traits for the opposite sex may be increased or decreased without necessarily impairing the behaviors related to the genetic sex" (1981, p. 273). In other words, depending on the amount of testosterone present in the environment, we can produce effeminate males, fully capable of male sexual function but with female behavioral traits, or we can produce demasculinized males, incapable of male sexual behavior later on even in the presence of testosterone; the converse can be done to females. The fetal mouse brain is exquisitely sensitive to the organizing effect of hormones.

Psychoanalysts tend to assume that the presence of effeminate characteristics indicates the presence of a feminine identification and is a result of that identification. The data of neurobiology indicate that there may be more than one source for effeminate behaviors and that effeminate behaviors may not connect with identifications except in complex secondary ways and may be totally distinct from homosexual tendencies. Moreover, a recent, unconfirmed study by Zuger (1984) suggested that early effeminate behavior in male children is congenital and is the best single indicator of later homosexuality.

Another study, in a human population, was done of a group of genetic males with an enzyme defect that did not permit them to convert available testosterone in utero into an effective genital-masculinizing substance (Imperato-McGinley et al. 1979). Although their brains were exposed to normal intrauterine androgen, they were born with female-appearing genitalia, were given female sex assignment, and were brought up as girls. As these phenotypic females entered puberty, they began to produce their own testosterone and at that time developed normal male genitalia. What makes this group especially interesting is that these individuals seemed to have little difficulty in changing their gender identity and gender role at puberty; of the eighteen studied, fifteen married and showed no evidence of undue stress or distortion of their male role. This result is contrary to the studies of Money and our current wisdom, which conclude that core gender identity is firmly fixed by eighteen months and very little affected by later changes of external genitalia. In this group of patients, it is as if the fetally hormonally masculinized brain maintained masculine neuronal networks that made later masculine role behavior easily available, overriding the usual psychological influences. Very early, intrauterine patterning of the CNS seems powerfully determining for later sexual behaviors. In yet another experiment,

> male rats born to mothers stressed during their last trimester of pregnancy by periodic restraint and bright light failed to develop normal male sexual behavior

in the presence of receptive females and assumed female sexual positions when approached by normal experienced males. They were thus demasculinized and feminized as a result of their mother's experience during pregnancy. Treatment of the affected animals with testosterone did not fully correct the deficiencies in male sexual behavior and only served to exaggerate the inappropriate female-type behavior. This means that the alteration was in the *neural systems mediating the behavior,* not in the amount of male sex hormones produced in childhood. Individual animals showed different patterns that were consistent for them. Some were asexual, responding neither to normal females or normal males. Some were bisexual, some only responded with female behavior to males, and some were indistinguishable from normal heterosexual males. (Hofer 1981, p. 180)

These experiments indicate rather conclusively that prenatal experience patterns the brain, at least in mice, and may do so to such a degree that later experience does not significantly alter the early neural patterning. It is a large leap from animal studies to humans, even though there are suggestive data in humans supporting similar conclusions. It seems reasonable, in the light of the studies I have cited combined with earlier psychoanalytic studies, to suggest that there are several pathways to the same end behavior—for example, effeminate behavior in males or perhaps even obligatory homosexuality. The influence either of specific molecules on the brain in utero or of special forms of learning through identification may lead to altered, that is, effeminate, behavior. At this time we have no way of determining the preponderance of biochemical or interactional etiology (both considered biologic) in any individual, nor do we yet know whether it matters in terms of later plasticity. Is the chemically determined effeminate male any more or less likely to give up his effeminacy, if that were desired, than the psychologically determined one? What are the limits of the plasticity of the adult brain? We do not know. Without an answer, it at least behooves the psychoanalyst to be aware that he should proceed with caution. A conviction that all homosexuality is part of a normal range of variability or a conviction that all homosexuality is psychopathologic is unwarranted at this time.

There are now many experiments in human and animal infants that demonstrate the lasting effects of very early life experiences and the powerful shaping of later behaviors by even single early traumas or particular behaviors of the mother. In some instances, a fair amount is known about the chemical regulators of these brain changes. At this borderline of neurobiology and psychoanalysis, we are quite in the dark concerning the question of later plasticity of both neural networks and behaviors. Are some treatment failures and endless analyses a result of the too rigidly prewired brain? It is a potentially convenient excuse, but it is possible that some of these cases represent such neural prepatterning. Again, we need more knowledge before we can usefully address the question; in the meantime, it might be wise to keep the possibility in the back of our minds. One other example illustrates an experience that is becoming increasingly common in the psychoanalytic community.

## Clinical Vignette

I recently saw in consultation a thirty-six-year-old male scientist who came to see me for referral to a new analyst because for external reasons he had to interrupt his previous treatment. He gave a classic description of himself as someone with a narcissistic personality disorder: grandiose, self-inflated, full of unfulfilled promise and promises although innately well endowed and perhaps even potentially brilliant—a brilliance that showed in flashes but never in steady achievement. He was married and had three children; he had married a passive, frightened woman and was himself emotionally detached, remote, and distant. He had entered treatment because he recognized his pattern of making a superb first impression and then disappointing his admirers and himself. He had passed the stage of boy wonder in his early thirties and had begun to worry that he would burn out.

He had been in treatment for a few months when he experienced his first clear manic episode, which lasted several months. During the next year he had his first major depression and clearly began a bipolar course. His analyst refused to consider medication, so the patient medicated himself with lithium obtained from a friend, with his analyst's knowledge. His own description of the result was, "The lithium stopped the crazy swings during which I couldn't do any analytic work and was in great danger of either wrecking my life with my financial schemes during my manic periods or killing myself during my depressions. On lithium, I knew I had a severe character problem and needed analysis." The treatment had been enormously helpful, and he was eager to resume.

Possibly, the stress of analysis and the specific address to this patient's characterologic defenses played a role in the appearance of his bipolar disorder. It also seems possible that he would have been untreatable, and would perhaps not have survived, if medication had not been available for the disorder of affect. I cannot think of a significant analytic advantage gained by withholding the medication, and although many transference issues were not resolved at the time he came to me for consultation, there seemed to be no great impediment to his continuing a genuine analysis while taking medication. It was my view that the medication should be properly supervised by a physician, thus probably assuring him better care and interfering with a bit of the narcissistic grandiosity of his conviction that he could do everything himself. This combination of neurobiologic advance and psychoanalytic effort seems at least additive and perhaps even synergistic. Analysts will have to learn how to do this better than we have in the past, developing appropriate criteria for combined treatments.

## DISCUSSION

We should not be surprised if advances in neurobiology continue a centuries-old process of confining the realm of mind and psychiatry. It was not very long ago that diseases such as tuberculosis, parkinsonism, tertiary syphilis, and neurodermatitis were considered psychiatric diseases. More recently, syndromes such as Gilles de la Tourette, rheumatoid arthritis, ulcerative colitis, essential hypertension, dysmenorrhea, premenstrual syndrome, and temporal lobe and petit mal epilepsy were considered by some to be psychological in origin and suitable subjects for psychoanalysis, at least in part because the disease course was so obviously event responsive. Current work in personality disorders indicates that some of the behaviors of obsessive-compulsive, explosive, depressive-masochistic, or borderline patients may reflect genetically determined biologic abnormalities that are in part pharmacologically modifiable. Psychoanalysts should welcome any scientific knowledge that removes from our primary care illnesses which we cannot successfully treat by the methods of our profession because the etiology lies elsewhere or that facilitates our analytic treatment by assisting us with intractable symptoms. We should also not be excessively modest about the contributions we can make to the care of these patients. Psychoanalysis is a powerful instrument for research and treatment, but not if it is applied to the wrong patient population.

It is most unlikely that there will be any direct bridges from neurobiology to the unconscious or to consciousness. Neurobiology explains at a different level than psychology, and knowledge of the brain will not fundamentally alter our mode of inquiry about the mind. What modern neurobiology does is to make it increasingly apparent that knowledge of the brain can help us to refine our knowledge of the mind and, in some instances, by its effects on our theory at its boundaries, it will set different limits to what we consider to be the mind. As Kohut (1980) pointed out, the realms of material observation and experimentation and intrapsychic observation and experimentation are discontinuous. Introspection and extrospection are different processes.

Again, what is to be sought is congruence and limit setting on both sides. Psychoanalytic knowledge of unconscious operations poses interesting problems for the biologists and provides important hints for experimental work. The flow goes both ways.

Psychoanalysis requires a theory of development that will help explain the phenomena important to us: the world of internal representations and meanings, the world of attachment and object relations, the world of sexual differentiation, the world of fantasy and wish, the world of intrapsychic conflict, and the modes of learning and the biologic substrate that make these worlds possible. We also need far better data, experiments, and theories for understanding the effective agents in the complex undertaking of analysis; neurobiology can help us to understand which of our concepts are unlikely and which are congruent with biologic experimentation. We should be extremely uncomfortable with any theory that is incongruent with neurobiologic discovery. Eric Kandel (1983) put the matter succinctly. He said, "The emergence of an empirical neuropsychology of cognition based on cellular neurobiology can produce a renaissance of scientific psychoanalysis. This form of psychoanalysis may be founded on theoretical hypotheses that are more modest than those applied previously but that are more testable because they will be closer to experimental inquiry." I think Freud would have been pleased by this prospect.

## References

Akiskal, H. S. 1983. Dysthymic disorder: Psychopathology of proposed chronic depressive subtypes. *American Journal of Psychiatry* 140:11–20.

Crowe, R.; Pauls, D.; Kerber, R.; et al. 1981. Panic and mitral valve prolapse. In *Anxiety: New research and changing concepts,* ed. D. F. Klein and J. Rabkin. New York: Raven Press.

Freud, S. 1905. Three essays on the theory of sexuality. In *Standard Edition,* 7:179. London: Hogarth Press.

————. 1912. The dynamics of transference. In *Standard Edition,* 12:99. London: Hogarth Press.

Hofer, M. A. 1981. *The roots of human behavior.* San Francisco: W. H. Freeman.

Imperato-McGinley, J.; Peterson, R. E.; Gautier, T.; et al. 1979. Androgens and the evolution of male gender identity among male pseudohermaphrodites with 5-2-reductose deficiency. *New England Journal of Medicine* 300:1233–37.

Kandel, E. R. 1979. Psychotherapy and the single synapse: The impact of psychiatric thought on neurobiologic research. *New England Journal of Medicine* 30:1028–37.

———. 1983. From metapsychology to molecular biology: Explorations into the nature of anxiety. *American Journal of Psychiatry* 140:1277–93.

Kohut, H. 1980. Introspection, empathy, and psychoanalysis: An examination of the relationship between mode of observation and theory. In *The search for the self,* ed. P. Ornstein, 1:205–32. New York: International Univ. Press.

Zuger, B. 1984. Early effeminate behavior in boys: Outcome and significance for homosexuality. *Journal of Nervous Mental Disorders* 172:90–97.

# Contributors

*Arnold M. Cooper, M.D.,* Professor of Psychiatry, Cornell University Medical College; Training and Supervising Analyst, Columbia University Center for Psychoanalytic Training and Research.

*Aaron Karush, M.D.,* Professor Emeritus of Clinical Psychiatry, Columbia University College of Physicians and Surgeons; Training and Supervising Analyst, Columbia University Center for Psychoanalytic Training and Research.

*Otto F. Kernberg, M.D.,* Professor of Psychiatry, Cornell University Medical College; Training and Supervising Analyst, Columbia University Center for Psychoanalytic Training and Research.

*Steven Marcus, Ph.D.,* George Delacorte Professor in the Humanities, Professor of English and Comparative Literature, Columbia University.

*Helen C. Meyers, M.D.,* Clinical Professor of Psychiatry, Columbia University College of Physicians and Surgeons; Training and Supervising Analyst, Columbia University Center for Psychoanalytic Training and Research.

*Robert Michels, M.D.,* Barklie McKee Henry Professor, Cornell University Medical College; Training and Supervising Analyst, Columbia University Center for Psychoanalytic Training and Research.

*Lionel Ovesey, M.D.,* Clinical Professor Emeritus of Psychiatry, Columbia University College of Physicians and Surgeons; Training and Supervising Analyst, Columbia University Center for Psychoanalytic Training and Research.

*Ethel Spector Person, M.D.,* Director and Training and Supervising Analyst, Columbia University Center for Psychoanalytic Training and Research; Professor of Clinical Psychiatry, Columbia University College of Physicians and Surgeons.

*Joseph Sandler, M.D.,* Freud Memorial Professor of Psychoanalysis in the University of London; Training and Supervising Analyst, British Psychoanalytical Society.

*Roy Schafer, Ph.D.,* Training and Supervising Analyst, Columbia University Center for Psychoanalytic Training and Research.

*Daniel N. Stern, M.D.,* Professor of Psychology at the University of Geneva; Lecturer in Psychiatry, Columbia University Center for Psychoanalytic Training and Research.

*Milton Viederman, M.D.,* Professor of Clinical Psychiatry, Cornell University Medical College; Training and Supervising Analyst, Columbia University Center for Psychoanalytic Training and Research; Director, Consultation-Liaison Service, New York Hospital.

# Index